1 A SOUTH SHROPSHIRE LANDSCAPE FROM THE BROWN CLEE:
Looking over Corvedale and Wenlock Edge to the Wrekin

THE PILGRIMS' LIBRARY

THE ENGLISH COUNTRYSIDE

A SURVEY OF ITS CHIEF FEATURES

With an Introduction by
H. J. Massingham

Contributions by
H. E. Bates, Harry Batsford, Adrian Bell,
E. F. Bozman, Geoffrey Clark, J. Fairfax-
Blakeborough, Charles Fry, H. J. Massingham,
C. Henry Warren

and 113 Illustrations
from Photographs

★ ★

LONDON
B. T. BATSFORD LTD.
15 NORTH AUDLEY STREET, W.1

First Published, May 1939

MADE AND PRINTED IN GREAT BRITAIN
FOR THE PUBLISHERS, B. T. BATSFORD LTD., LONDON
BY JARROLD AND SONS LTD., NORWICH

CONTENTS

ACKNOWLEDGMENT

THE publishers would like to acknowledge their obligation to the photographers who have supplied the illustrations to this book, namely: Mr. Charles E. Brown, for figs. 16, 38 and 64; Mr. Eric D. Cheshire, for figs. 47, 48, 52, 53 and 55; Mr. J. Dixon-Scott, F.R.P.S., for figs. 8, 11, 12, 18, 21, 22, 30, 31, 33, 34, 37, 39, 40, 50, 51, 59, 60, 66, 71, 73, 76, 81, 83, 84, 88, 90, 91, 92, 96, 100, 103, 104, 105, 111 and 112; Messrs. Dorien Leigh, Ltd., for figs. 26, 61, 79, 85 and 106; Messrs. Eagle Photos, Ltd., for figs. 6, 9, 10 and 69; Mr. Herbert Felton, F.R.P.S., for figs. 19, 29, 41, 49, 63, 82, 89 and 99; Mr. Leonard Gayton, for fig. 57; Mr. F. A. Girling, for fig. 24; Mr. A. E. Hick, for figs. 17, 97, 98 and 108; Mr. H. D. Keilor, for figs. 2, 77, 93, 109 and 110; Mrs. Sylvia Lewes, for figs. 68, 80 and 101; Messrs. Musto, for figs. 7 and 20; Miss Joan Parry, for figs. 3, 42 and 43; Messrs. Philipson, for figs. 67 and 113; Mr. Sydney Pitcher, for figs. 13 and 25; Miss Frances Pitt, for Fig. 1, the Dufaycolor frontispiece; Mr. John H. Stone, for figs. 4, 15 and 27; Mr. F. R. P. Stringer, for fig. 107; Mr. J. P. Taylor, for figs. 74 and 78; Mr. Will F. Taylor, for figs. 5, 14, 23, 28, 32, 35, 36, 44, 45, 46, 54, 56, 58, 62, 70, 75, 86, 87, 94, 95 and 102; Messrs. Topical Press Agency, Ltd., for fig. 72; and Miss M. Wight, for fig. 65.

INTRODUCTION

THERE is a dualism in this book, none the worse for that, perhaps, in a civilisation that has buried difference, not strife but difference. What is more, the two parties in it are opposed in spirit while professing the same loyalties, and that, again, is healthily contrary to the age whose contentious forces serve the same idols in calling themselves by different names. There are shadings-off, properly enough, between the one party and the other, nor is there any depth of division in aim: the real cleavage is one of varying vision. Since the office of introducing a book of these contrasting elements has fallen upon me without my being in any way responsible for the choice of themes and of their respective authors, I feel myself at liberty to attach myself to one group or the other and to waive the tiresome acrobatics of trying to hold a balance between them. Once, I went with the majority which here offers a descriptive and topographical account of certain characters of the English landscape from the point of view of the detached, appreciative, aesthetic connoisseur. Now I belong to the minority which considers the English rural scene as made with hands and, therefore, that the canvas is incomplete unless the painter be taken with the picture.

This Bates-Bell-Fry minority (Mr. Warren would naturally have been of it if he had not taken an absorbing ride on the good nag, Memory) adjudicates Hodge as the greatest landscape-painter in the history of our native art. Virtually he remade our island Nature and he took just under four thousand years—from 2000 B.C. to about A.D. 1830—to finish the job. Remade, of course, not made, since it must be allowed that his fairy godmother gave him a pair of superlative presents, geology with one hand and climate with the other. These inexpressive modern terms body forth no imaginative image of that signal generosity. The changeability of the weather within the bounds of the climate and the diversity of the rock-formations within the bounds of the four seas account for the unique quality observable in the English landscape—its multiformity within, I might say, the palm of the hand. In remoulding England, that is to say, the countryman was granted a whole continent of varieties within the spatial limits of a single country—infinite riches in a little room—and the fruit and virtue of his achievement were simply this, that, with the true humility of the artist who subdues his hand to what he works in, he was faithful to those variations ordained by the primeval rock. He became his theme; he got rid of the encumbrances that were in the way of its due and right expression. He remade England by fitting himself into its manifold parts, so that in the long run it can hardly be decided whether he made the country or the country made him. What is certain is that they cannot be kept apart.

Mr. Bates has, I think, made the generic term, Hodge, somewhat ambiguous. I doubt, he says, "if the poor have ever beautified the English landscape. It is the rich and the prosperous who have left on it the hall-mark of beauty," and a sentence or two farther on, "In the same way, the Enclosure Acts, benefiting the rich, bestowed on us the most beautiful common inheritance, next to grass, that the English possess"—namely, the hedge. He then proceeds with his customary power, zest and eloquence to describe—the pre-Enclosure hedge. It is a common delusion of country writers that England under the open-field system of "shots" or "lands" or "selions" was as striped and naked against a background of scrub and heavy woodland as a zebra's back. Yet the miles and miles of mixed hedgerow that Mr. Bates particularises, all of these pre-dated the Enclosure. The post-Enclosure hedge was invariably straight instead of winding and of quicks in uniform lines instead of those fifteen varieties of growth which burgeon before our eyes in the lyrical urge of Mr. Bates's magic quill. Where imported growths assert themselves in the quick hedges of the Enclosures, the winds and the birds, in other words downright neglect, were responsible for them. In praising the husbandry of the hedge, Mr. Bates has given all the best tunes to his adversary. Now I have nothing against the park and the manor, though in my view the Palladian house, which was the direct result of the Enclosures, is an urban rather than a rural architecture. Its severely classical proportions lack the plasticity which distinguishes the manor of Gothic origin, an origin never lost in basic structure but tinkered with (just like the earlier churches) by succeeding styles and fashions in such a way as to create a composite whole in exquisite harmony with the variables of the landscape itself. The Queen Anne or Georgian country seat is never *local* (apart from the fact that it was rarely built of local materials) in the sense that its predecessors were, and the quintessential beauty of our landscape is its regional variety proliferating like the branches of a tree from a common root.

Mr. Bates again seems to me to display some hastiness of statement when the ultimate consequences of the Enclosures are called to mind, namely, the uprooting of the peasantry (in which I include, of course, the yeoman freeholders) from the land which it had made. There have been intermediate stages, but there is no doubt at all that the crumbling of the countryside into a decay as pitiful, as heartrending as we see to-day, must be referred back along a chain of economic causation to the Enclosures. But, even if this be questioned, and I do not think it is questionable, how loose are our general terms that wool, for instance, was the making of the Cotswold craftmanship that has made the Cotswolds twice themselves! Who raised the wool but the shepherds, and who the manors and cottages and barns but the masons? What we really mean is that certain conditions fostered the security and favoured the creative labours of the Cotswold craftsmen, but it is quite clear that showers of prosperity poured upon a sterile soil will not set it blossoming. The horse must be there to draw the cart, however lavish the expenditure of grease. There is no automatic coupling between wealth and workmanship.

At first sight, it might appear that the claim for Hodge the husbandman as the painter of the English landscape—and be it remembered that if God made the hills, it was Hodge's sheep that turfed them, Hodge's burial mounds and stone circles that focused their grandeur and Hodge's stone walls that ribbed and articulated them—were somewhat compromised by Mr. Bell's richly toned etching of the Fens. Mr. Bell describes a purely man-made landscape whose intensive cultivation is intermixed with mechanical device that extends into the country the methods of urbanised mass-production. Cultivation there is a business rather than a craft, and business and craftsmanship are to my mind fundamentally incompatible. It was the importation of the commercial idea into the countryside of the Tudor graziers in the sixteenth century that submitted the crafts and so the country and so the landscape to a process of slow strangulation. The fruits of that grafting set our teeth on edge to-day.

There are two very good reasons why a *living* countryside can never be mechanised except at the expense in the end both of the landscape and the life. Apart from the contradiction in terms between life and mechanism, an industrialised countryside no longer depends upon itself but upon a financial system whose node is the city. If it breaks down, the country reverts and ceases to be the

4

2   BLOSSOMING ORCHARDS, NEWINGTON, KENT

3 A CHILTERN BEECHWOOD

landscape patiently modelled by millenia of husbandry.
Secondly, a man-modified Nature (which is what English
country is) has been built upon growing things, that is to
say, upon bread and cheese, on the basis, that is to say, of
utility. Now utility is the be-all if it is not the end-all of
craftsmanship and craftsmanship can never be properly
understood unless it be realised that its beauty comes last
because its utility comes first. When the masons were
building Ely Cathedral (which is to the Fens in terms of
landscape what the sun is to the sky), they were considering problems of structure, or how best to praise
God in terms of stone which should interpret what they
knew of the laws of Nature and the universe. Nature,
too, considers utility in terms of life and that is why the
craftsman can be seen all through the ages to fit so
marvellously into Nature, until he makes a countryside
that is a third entity fusing the qualities of them both.

It actually is possible to epitomise the history (as Mr.
Fry has done so judiciously) and interpret the significance
of the English countryside in six words—axe, crook,
plough, scythe, chisel and billhook with their antique
prototypes. What made that countryside, in other words,
were a multitude of satellite crafts revolving within the
orbit of one supreme craft, the craft of agriculture. They
made the country, but they also made the countryman,
and therefore the two are twain. The corollary follows
that, if the countryman be killed, so will the country and
incidentally its landscape, and that is the reason why,
speaking for myself, I am distressfully sceptical about
"scientific agriculture," the mechanisation of farming
and the other nostrums allied to this purely urban idea.
They are palliatives that lack the finest knowledge of all,
the intuitive and inherited knowledge of the craftsman.
Is the child of the Industrial Revolution, whose massacre
of the crafts may be read in Lord Ernle's *English Farming
Past and Present*, the doctor to medicine the country and

the countryman to that sweet health they owed yesterday? This saviour of the Machine Age looks uncommonly like a wolf in sheep's clothing. What saving the countryside boils down to is the restoration of the peasantry. If the simple (but not too simple) proposition be granted that Hodge the craftsman created the England the older among us knew as children, first as a member of the self-acting and self-sufficient, the local and traditional village community, and later as the helot of a landed aristocracy, it is clear that the National Trust and well-wishing societies of kindred aims can attack the symptoms but not the seat of the disease.

It seems to me equally clear that the purely aesthetic attitude is not enough, and that its weak spot is the peril of the picturesque. It fails to consider, that is to say, that in all craftsmanship utility precedes beauty, the flower of the union between fitness and purpose. The English countryside is the unique flower of craftsmanship, manifested in the soil and above the soil and adapted to the specific needs of particular regions. The response to the geology of a multiform kingdom was flawless. It is fading as we watch: a twilight of uniformity diffused from the big towns draws the "gradual dusky veil" over those well-known and richly modelled features. The darkness both blotches and blurs them; the first we call urbanisation and the other neglect, and it is from our own neglect of linking the utility with the beauty that appreciation of the beauty alone becomes a cause of stumbling. There is no such danger apparent among the contributors to this volume because they are knowledgeable men. But the unnatural rupture between the country and the town has become so acute in our own time and the power so completely transferred to the town that the country really is regarded by the enormous majority as a picturesque playground. I remember not so long ago standing before a piece of country that might

6

well have been called a temple for that arch and pretty goddess to receive offerings from her lovers. Actually it was a ruin: the stone walls aped a line of jagged cliffs, the barns gaped, the thatch on the roofs was a nursery garden, the field-gates would not shut and the hedges were straggling across the weedy fields. Hodge had left it a widow.

Urbanisation and neglect are in fact different expressions of the same thing, and the remedy for them both can only be the reanimation of that regional country life which came to its ripest in the period immediately preceding the Black Death and reached the highest curve of the spiral once again just before the Civil War. The games, the feasts, the processions, the co-operative farming of the villagers, the folk-lore, the plough-tackle, these were as integral a part of the English landscape as the hills, the streams, the woods, the birds and the wild flowers. The well-being of the husbandman cannot be separated from the well-being of the land: they stand or fall together. Many hard things have been said about the commoners of the old village community, and to those who share the conventional view I would recommend the reading of Professor C. S. Orwin's *The Open Fields*, an account, published last year, of the only survivor of the Enclosures and the Industrial Age—the village of Laxton in Nottinghamshire. Those open-field villagers, though deprived of half their privileges, curtailed in their land and a mere museum piece, are still healthy and vigorous and operate a system more democratic, so their faithful recorder declares, than any this country has ever known.

The mirage of progress has so distorted our view of history that we fail to perceive how often it repeats itself, not pedantically to the letter but rather in the manner of a theme-song. Husbandry, local distinctions, co-partnership between earth and man, a chain of communities

7

fitting the particular into a right relation with the universal, are solidities among the quaking grounds of social system. The English countryside can only remain in being, landscape and all, on the condition that these indispensables to it be revalued and rebuilt.

H. J. MASSINGHAM

REDDINGS
    LONG CRENDON
        BUCKS

4 THE WAY TO THE FARM

5 THE CORN HARVEST IN SURREY

Charles Fry

THE EVOLUTION
OF THE COUNTRYSIDE

I

THE two factors that have contributed most to the character of our countryside are the English temperament and the English climate. Naturally it is the underlying formations, and the treatment to which they have been subjected by different agencies of nature, that provide the foundations of every landscape; but the fact remains that, here in England, it would be difficult, set down haphazard from an aeroplane, to tell if one had landed on the limestone slopes of North Oxfordshire or in the clay vale of Berkshire, among the grasslands of Leicestershire or the fields and hedges of the Home Counties. The average scene, at its best, is so congruous and familiar to most English people that they can seldom bring themselves to conceive it in terms of geology. In fact, they are apt to take it altogether too much for granted, forgetting the centuries of development that have brought it to its maturity, or preferring to concentrate instead on the dwindling beauties of their few tracts of real wild or highland. But the truly English

9

picture—the picture that would come to the minds of most exiles overseas—is that of the mild rise and fall of a countryside of field, hedge and coppice, of villages and farms; a picture of which a Dorset poet has left the almost perfect rendering:

> Sweet Be'mi'ster that bist a-bound
> By green an' woody hills all round,
> Wi' hedges reachen up between
> A thousan' vields o' summer green,
> Where elems' lofty heads do drow
> Their sheädes vor hay-meakers below,
> An' wild hedge-flow'rs do charm the souls
> O' maïdens in their evenèn strolls. . . .

It is with the evolution of just such a landscape that this chapter is chiefly concerned.

Nevertheless, if we are to trace the process to its origins, it will be difficult to avoid at least a beginning in geology. Here the record is chequered and infinitely protracted; in the course of perhaps a thousand million years the portion of the earth's crust that is England has been shaped and sculptured by the prolonged effect of mediums working steadily and without respite, alternating with briefer convulsions of intense violence. It has undergone many vicissitudes of shape, size and formation. At first it probably extended far to the north-west of its present dimensions as part of the lost continent of Atlantis, though for the greater part of its geological history it has remained the north-west corner of the European continent, at first linked to the mainland by flat valleys where the North Sea now intervenes, with the Thames and Wash as Rhine tributaries. For long a chalk land-bridge remained to France, the migration path of many animals and races of men. Only in human, and almost in historic, times was this passage cut through by the sea and our country made an island, with results not only influencing human development in England but the whole course of European history.

Thus, from the earliest ages there has been an England, but, until it took its present shape in fairly recent geological times, it would have been an England strange in form and appearance to those now familiar with its structure. It is a pity that geology does not normally enter into the education of the average Englishman, who is frequently as ignorant of the formation of his own country as of its geography. No really adequate account is possible here; but attention can at least be drawn to the importance and fascination of a record which, covering a comparatively small area, comprises all the great formations except the Miocene, overlapping one another, it may be noticed, with a general downward tilt from west to east. Sediments of vast thickness were deposited during untold ages in a primeval sea; these, with the igneous rocks resulting from early volcanic upheavals, were hardened, uplifted, folded, and worn down by long periods of erosion to form islands in the seas of succeeding epochs—Jurassic, Chalk and Wealden —which have deposited the great areas of later soil to the South and East. Thus it is that in Stretton Dale in South Shropshire the pre-Cambrian Long Mynd, to the west, shows in its slates and sandstones the ripple-marks of a very ancient sea, while to the east rise the broken ridges of Caradoc, with its attendants, the Lawley and Ragleth, equally of pre-Cambrian date but consisting of volcanic ashes and lavas. Some of the isolated monticules of West Midland England are inconceivably old, such as the Wrekin, Shropshire's typical hill, which was eroded and worn down long before the Alps and the Himalayas were upthrust, and the Malverns, of pre-Cambrian gneiss, both of which probably stood out for millions of years as bold islands above far later, though still ancient, seas. Even the Miocene era, if the

formation itself is unrepresented in England, has left its
mark in the crumbling and folding of the chalk in the
South-east, with an area of most intense activity in the
tangled Dorset coastline.

Here, then, the oldest rocks of the earth's crust appear:
sedimentary, as in the Long Mynd and Stretton Dale;
igneous, as in the adjacent Caradoc and in Charnwood
Forest, Leicestershire, where they bear the marks of the
sandstorms of tropical deserts. English landscapes have
sweltered in the moist heat of giant fern forests, which
now form the coal measures responsible for our industrial
development, while great areas also show the scouring
of solid ice-caps. Long-vanished volcanoes have left the
trace of their active existence in sheets of lava and dikes
of igneous rock, farflung over many miles of countryside.
As for the fauna, we know that fabulous creatures have
wandered over familiar districts and swum in English
seas: six-foot water scorpions, great fish-lizards, flying
pterodactyls, dinosaurs, and the fierce carnivores which
preyed upon them, down long ages to the mammoth
and sabre-toothed tiger-cat that were the contemporaries
of primitive man.

Nevertheless, the influence of geology on English
scenery is now comparatively slight. If the rock formation provides the bones of the landscape, we have to
reckon, apart from the secular influence of climate, with
the gradual work of man in draining, clearing, cultivating, planting, and finally imposing the hedge-pattern that
is the peculiar beauty of our countryside. The geological
stamp now seldom impresses itself except in the extremes:
the oldest, hardest and hilliest rocks, or those flat alluvial
expanses that are the last additions to the country.

Such, then, were some of the forces that set their seal
to the structure of our landscape. But the England of
the Old Stone Age, that is to say of that distant epoch
whose nearer limit can probably be fixed at about

10000 B.C., can have shared few recognisable characteristics even with the England of the Roman invasions. There were the downs and hills, of course, to wrinkle the face of the vast tundras of grass which covered most of the lower country, broken by tracts of wild heath and swamp; but early man had as yet little need for the isolation of the ridges, for he was a nomadic hunter, to whom even the rudiments of agriculture were unknown, gaining his subsistence by following the herds of bison, reindeer, and wild horses that cropped the plains, and living on their meat. It was an empty, treeless England that as yet heard little but the sough of the wind and the thudding of hoof-beats, followed now and then by the quick, nervous footfalls of the hunter.

By the close of this age, a gradual increase in the warmth and moisture of the climate had begun to clothe most of the lower country with dense, often impenetrable forest. The nomadic hunter of the Old Stone Age had gradually succumbed to the dwindling of the herds; his successor of the New Stone Age, Neolithic Man, was of a superior intelligence which had absorbed the conception of husbandry, and could by this means support himself in one place, in contrast with the fortuitous nomadism of his predecessor. Nevertheless, since his implements were crude, his field of operations was strictly limited. The clearing of the richer, heavier forestlands was beyond his powers; nor, with the tools at his disposal, would he have been capable of cultivating them. Quite naturally he established himself upon the upland ridges—the chalk downs of Surrey, Sussex and Kent, of Berkshire, Dorset and Wiltshire, together with the Cotswolds, the Mendips, the Blackdowns, and other ridges of the West—where the light surface soil could easily be tilled by hand with the mattock. Here, in Lord Ernle's words,[1] "the least labour told the most, and . . .

[1] *The Land and its People.*

13

the transition from the nomadic life of pastoral hordes to more settled agricultural communities was the easiest. Fertile valleys, tangled with forest growth, remained uncleared when dry and comparatively treeless uplands were occupied and cultivated. . . . The uplands were grazed by flocks and herds, while the steep sides, or the pockets of soil below the rise, were scratched up for scanty patches of corn. Nor did the Downs serve agricultural purposes only. They were the sites of mysterious megalithic monuments. They were camps and battle-grounds and burying-places. They were also natural highways. In districts along the lines of the Downs it was a common tradition that, on quiet nights, could still be heard the tramp of armed hosts and the creak of their heavy chariots as they passed from camp to camp along the ancient tracks."

Some traces of the Neolithic village of about 2000 B.C. remain, such as those on Windmill Hill near Avebury and on Whitehawk Hill near Brighton; while even the great entrenchments of Maiden Castle, Dorchester, are probably a Celtic elaboration of a Neolithic scheme. Surrounded by a ditch and earthen rampart topped with a stockade, through which entrance was made by a causeway, lay a rough circle of thatched huts, with small cultivated strips adjoining which were hoed with mattocks somewhat similar to the primitive *caschrom* still occasionally to be found in use in the Scottish Highlands. Here, little protected from the winds, Neolithic man raised his crops and tended his few pigs and cattle and sheep; and perhaps from his chalk stronghold looked out sometimes a little fearfully over the dark tangles of the forest that spread away over miles of Wealden distance on the one hand, or to the grey gleam of the Channel through a fold of the Downs on the other. It is possible that a thin stream of his blood still flows in our veins; in any case, it is in his lonely little

6 THE RIDGEWAY: A PREHISTORIC TRACK OVER THE BERKSHIRE DOWNS

7 SCOTCH FIRS ON A BERKSHIRE COMMON

communities of the ridges that we can recognise the earliest ancestors of our present villages.

The successive waves of colonisation of the Bronze and Iron Age Celts (800–500 B.C.), and their superior implements and methods, did much to amplify this narrow, struggling existence. The Neolithic hut circles might be enlarged to the scale of the mighty earthwork *enceintes* of Maiden Castle, a fortress-township which was probably not only the headquarters of a military chieftain, but also a market for the produce of the thatched villages, with their squarish arable fields, which clustered round. To its wooden gates the farmers and their flocks might crowd for safety in war; here also in peace might arrive the trading caravans which wended their slow courses along the trackways, laden with lead from South Wales and the Mendips, gold and tin from Cornwall and Devon, amber and jet from Yorkshire, and other materials for the crafts of the court artificers. Such men were obviously by no means the woad-smeared savages of Caesar's dispatches and the Victorian history-books; nevertheless, they were content to remain to a large extent ridge-dwellers like their predecessors. Though, during the centuries that preceded Roman colonisation, they had tended gradually to extend their cultivation from the hill-sides down into the valleys, the major tracts of forest, fen and heath remained to all intents and purposes untamed—dark, dangerous wildernesses, spreading over some two-thirds of the land, and probably regarded with a dread that is echoed in the supernatural fantasy of Arthurian legend.

It is remarkable that little was done by the Romans to reclaim these wastes for agriculture, even in the southern and eastern parts of the country upon which they really imposed their rule. For beyond the line of the Fosse Way, which passes through Cirencester and Lincoln, the land was little more than garrisoned—and often lightly—

by a system of fortresses linked by military roads. Peaceful settlement was reserved principally for the South and East, where the majority of the Roman cities, London included, arose, and where the great track system of prehistoric times was largely utilised in the network of military highways. In the era of dissolution and invasion which followed the recall of the legions (A.D. 407), while the Britons were pushed ever farther towards the west, and their lands appropriated by Picts, Scots, Jutes and Saxons, many Roman sites, as was the case with Silchester, were abandoned from superstitious causes; elsewhere, buildings were demolished for their materials or, later, to repave the crumbling road-surfaces. By the consolidation of Anglo-Saxon conquest in the seventh century, few vestiges of Roman imperialism can have remained save in ruined buildings and an incomparable system of roads. Vast tracts of the country retained their pure primeval character, and on lower ground the throttling growth of the forests threatened all but the most substantial clearings.

In an England now generally hedge-chequered and cultivated well up to the 1,200-foot mark, it is difficult to realise the loneliness and foreboding that these great wildernesses must have inspired. Perhaps one might feel some sense of it lost in a winter twilight on the bare, tussocked moors of the Scottish Borders, over whose bleak distances, though they were once traversed by the Northumbrian Watling Street, it is now possible to wander some twenty-two miles without encountering even a minor road. Dartmoor, in winter, can be a forbidding place, as can be many of the moorland summits of the Pennines or of the Welsh Border. But probably never again in England will its inhabitants find themselves "lost in the forest." Arden is gone, and Sherwood, and the great *Silva Anderida* that once enveloped the Sussex and Kentish Weald, save for the comparative fragment of Ashdown, within whose depths, by some stretch of the imagination, some of the old fears might be revived. Much remains of the New Forest, but it has been tamed and perhaps rather suburbanised, while Dean is scarred by its industrial patches, and in Epping, that last fragment of the huge tangle that once covered South-eastern Essex, despite its mighty trees and deep undergrowth, one is almost within earshot of the roar of London.

Similarly with the Fens. It would be hard to recognise in those flat vistas of intensively cultivated fields, stretching to a faraway horizon etched with tiny trees, that lost land of waterlogged morasses, infested with wild life of every kind, that for centuries baffled all major efforts at reclamation. Save for the one small tract of Wicken Sedge Fen near Cambridge, preserved in its primeval state as a nature sanctuary, all has now been drained and tamed and tidied into one of our richest agricultural provinces. But with the Heaths it is a different matter—those haggard expanses of "heathy, furzy, briary wilderness," the *Bruaria* of Domesday, beautiful and sullen by turns—whose shallow, sandy soil has always repelled the cultivator. They still abound about the country, and though some have shrunk to mere village commons, others, such as brackeny, pine-clumped Breckland, with its sudden pools, can still tell us something of the ancient loneliness. So it is with the heathlands of Dorset, whose landscape was described by Hardy, under the collective name of Egdon, in the first pages of *The Return of the Native*:

"The untameable, Ishmaelitish thing that Egdon now was it always had been. Civilisation was its enemy; and ever since the beginning of vegetation its soil had worn the same antique brown dress, the natural and invariable garment of the particular

17

formation. . . . The great inviolate place had an ancient permanence which the sea cannot claim. Who can say of a particular sea that it is old? Distilled by the sun, kneaded by the moon, it is renewed in a year, in a day, or in an hour. The sea changed, the rivers, the villages, and the people changed, yet Egdon remained. Those surfaces were neither so steep as to be destructible by weather, nor so flat as to be the victims of floods and deposits. With the exception of an aged highway, and a still more aged barrow—themselves almost crystallised to natural products by long continuance—even the trifling irregularities were not caused by pickaxe, plough, or spade, but remained as the very finger-touches of the last geological change."

The immutability of such places can give us food for much thought. They have endured in their ancient state entirely by the cause of their sterility; but with the richer ploughlands and pastures we rarely envisage the effects of some breakdown in human institutions, some sudden defection from organised agriculture, which would leave them at last untended to go the way of nature. The first results of such a change can be realised from any abandoned railway cutting or old slag-heap. Later effects may be judged from such a case as the great landslide from the upper cliff at Rousdon west of Lyme Regis, where in little more than a hundred years a jungle has grown up that would do justice to an Asiatic climate. But it is seldom nowadays that one can examine more than a few square miles of England in its "original" state. Our countryside, the "man-made" countryside that we know to-day, has been wrenched from nature foot by foot, and preserved by the everyday toil of the ages. Nevertheless, even two centuries of neglect might well find it reverted to its character of Anglo-Saxon days.

8 A SURVIVAL OF THE ORIGINAL FENS AT WICKEN, CAMBRIDGESHIRE

9 A BIRCH GROVE IN THE FOREST OF DEAN, GLOUCESTERSHIRE

II

These Forests as I say, the daughters of the *Weald*
(That in their heavy breasts had long their griefs conceal'd)
Foreseeing their decay each hour so fast came on,
Under the axe's stroke, fetch'd many a grievous groan,
Whereas the anvil's weight, and hammer's dreadful sound,
Even rent the hollow woods, and shook the queachy ground.

Drayton wrote these lines in Elizabeth's reign, when
the process of denudation was far advanced. But to trace
it to its source, we must pick up the story where we left
it, in an England exhausted by war and invasion, now
settling down quietly to husbandry once more under its
Anglo-Saxon masters.

It was a period that added immeasurably to the sites
of habitation. For the first time on such a scale began
a widespread settlement of the forests, the heavy soil of
which, since the introduction of the Saxon eight-ox
plough, could be turned to much arable profit. Perhaps
the follower of a theyn would be given permission to
hack out a clearing and there build a log-house, which
would be surrounded by the shacks of servants and
dependants. Soon the settlement would be enclosed by
a wooden stockade, which gave it the status of a *tun*, a
word which, in the suffix *ton*, testifies to the Saxon origin
of innumerable English villages, and provides, of course,
the derivation of our "town." An average settlement of
this sort might contain some twenty or thirty family
groups, each gaining a living from the cultivation of the
open fields which spread around, patchworked like
modern allotment strips, and the pasturing of their cattle
on the small meadows adjoining. Slowly the forests
would be beaten back to provide further agricultural
land for these lonely little communities of the backwoods,
which, of necessity, were almost entirely self-supporting,
since for protection's sake they were usually established

far off the beaten track and away from the Roman roads, which were still capable of military exploitation. By contrast, it is interesting to recollect that the majority of our pre-industrial towns originally marked the intersection of a road and a river.

Saxon settlements were probably seldom, in the first place, organised on feudal. lines; but as the danger of Danish raids increased, there can be little doubt that, particularly in southern districts, the smaller man tended increasingly to bind himself to the more powerful one by ties of service, in return for the military protection that was becoming essential for his safety. Thus, the ground was often well prepared for the rigid, but on the whole temperate and workable, feudalism imposed by the Conqueror as the basis of his rule. As Domesday well shows, not one in ten of the pre-Conquest manors remained in Saxon ownership at the time of its compilation, while Norman soldiers were now widely rewarded for their services by permission to carve out estates in the wilder and more backward parts of the realm, hitherto under little control, such as the North, the far South-west, and the Marches of the Welsh Border. The result was to reduce to servitude innumerable Englishmen who had been free, and to decimate the class of freeholders which had previously flourished, particularly in the Danelaw; though at the same time many squatters and backwoodsmen remained exempt by their inconspicuousness, to form the nucleus of a later class of peasant freeholders which maintained an existence throughout the Middle Ages.

The political aspects of feudalism are beyond the province of this chapter, but its agricultural application, which, in attenuated form, survived in places until the eighteenth century and even after, is wholly relevant. Its unit was the manor, the lordship of which might be vested in the King, the Church, a noble possessed of many others, or even an individual living on his own land. Briefly, it was organised as a village farm, of whose arable land a part was retained by the lord as his demesne and the rest allocated among the villeins, theoretically in equal holdings. At first the demesne lands were scattered among the multiplicity of ploughed strips that comprised the three great fields, which were farmed co-operatively in yearly rotation, the first usually sown with wheat or rye, the second with barley and the third left fallow; later, it was more likely to form a compact unit around the manor-house—the origin of many a later "home farm." In return for his "customary" duties on the demesne, the villein was allowed to consume the produce of his own virgate, or holding, which was also distributed in long thin strips among the fields with an eye to ensuring the equality of each man's portion. In addition, he had his rights to the meadows and common pasture, the latter generally adjoined by a "waste," or fragment of the natural wilderness, which provided the village with "fern or heather for litter and thatching, hurdle-wood, and tree-loppings for winter browsing, furze and turves for fuel, acorns and mast for swine, as well as large timber for fencing implements or building."

In the distance, the site of such a settlement might be marked by a tuft of trees breaking the monotony of the flat fields around. Spreading, perhaps, along the banks of a stream would lie the meadows, which were divided up annually by lot among the villagers and put up for hay. From St. Gregory's Day to Midsummer Day each man's portion would be fenced off with hurdles, but after the hay-harvest these would be removed, and the meadows would become a common pasture for livestock. Beyond them stretched the arable fields already described, their criss-cross strips separated by unploughed ridges, or balks, which formed a maze of bush-grown pathways, many of which have given us the direction of our village lanes. From seed-time to harvest the strips were held in individual ownership, but after the harvest, and until the round of cultivation began again, they were laid open to the livestock, which roamed them under the care of the common herdsman, shepherd or swineherd, thus providing the only form of manuring known for centuries to come. The heavy communal ploughs, at first entirely of wood, were dragged by teams of oxen.

While the fields and meadows thus provided grazing at certain seasons, there was always, in addition, a tract of rough, overgrown land that was entirely given over to pasture, usually fringed by the "waste" already described, in which the community shared rights of usage. This pasture, with its adjacent waste, was the origin of our village common, which, for reasons to be set forth, seldom survives as more than a sad little fragment of its former wild extent—that is, if it survives at all. During the Middle Ages, and for long after, these lands were guarded jealously from the intrusion of those outside the village partnership; cattle were driven off them, cottages pulled down, and trespassers, if not actually "prosecuted," were liable to rough handling. This is not surprising, since, within the rigid framework of co-operative agriculture, they provided the one element of personal benefit for the individual. Thus, large tracts of England, apart from the immensities of heath, fen and forest, wold and fell, still unreclaimed, were jealously preserved from the plough in a half-primeval state, to supply a rough pasturage seldom more than sufficient to maintain the cattle alive through the winter, or such simple necessities of village life as fuel and timber.

At first the life of these small communities was very hard and primitive. Their houses were seldom more than hovels of wattle-and-daub or mud, arranged in a rough cluster or along a straggling street, each, however, having its green little garden, fenced or hedged, for the

growth of home produce. The most conspicuous buildings, and certainly the only ones built of stone, would
be the church and the manor-house, the former still
probably no larger than a modern chapel, the latter a
rough little hall or keep almost overwhelmed by its barns
and outbuildings. By day the village would be practically deserted save for a few women, children and old
people, and the beasts and fowls which made free of the
thresholds and fouled the ways between the houses. The
men, and many of the women as well, would be scattered
at work over the bleak, open fields, while in the distance
a few cattle in the charge of a boy might be seen cropping
the common, with perhaps a small flock of sheep watched
over by a shepherd.

Such were the lineal ancestors that provided the sites,
many of the field-names and even some fraction of the
fabrics of our comfortable villages; lonely little settlements that now formed regular patches of clearing in a
countryside shaggy and wild beyond anything we know
to-day. For though much had already been done in the
way of reclamation, an immense work still remained.
This is made obvious, as Dr. Coulton reminds us,[1] "in
some of the enormous parishes in the North and in the
Fenland. On the Yorkshire moors, at first, there were
villages only at the very edge. Then, as in the cases of
Blackburn and Whalley, the hinterland of the moor was
gradually exploited, and the priest found himself parson
no longer of a handful of parishioners, but of several
hamlets also, with their attendant chapels. So again at
Doddington, on the edge of the Cambridgeshire Fens.
That parish, by gradual draining, became so large and
rich that within the last century the tithes of the rectory
were worth £10,000 a year. Everywhere, then, the
population was thinly scattered in the Middle Ages, and
yet in one way less scattered than it is now. There were

[1] *The Medieval Village.*

next to no outlying farms. Nearly all the habitations were grouped in villages."

Though the common-field system remained the basis of agricultural practice for several centuries to follow, by the dawn of the Tudor period other factors had contributed to change the character of the village, and, in some measure also, the character of the landscape. The gradual disintegration of the feudal system during the century that followed the Black Death, the rise of the yeoman and tenant farmer, and the emergence of a new class of landless, or almost landless, labourer, working for a wage, had done much to undermine the structure of manorial economy; yet still, notwithstanding migrations and disturbances, the greater part of the land was cultivated on the co-operative method, largely by the same families whose livelihoods had for generations depended upon its givings. At the same time, with the rising tide of wool prosperity, large tracts of hitherto empty country—down, wold and plain—had been appropriated as sheepwalks to enrich the graziers and staplers of such districts as the Cotswolds and High Suffolk, while elsewhere the effects of the boom were plainly evident in the decay of villages where the demesne lands, or the consolidated holdings of enriched tenants or copyholders, had been put down to grass, with a consequent loss of employment to the agricultural labourer. Such evils, set forth with equal bitterness in the prose of Sir Thomas More or the doggerel of popular poets, had to some extent been mitigated by the reign of Elizabeth; yet if we may picture the same village and its surroundings of that age —a village neither over-prosperous nor over-depressed —it will be obvious at once that something like a social revolution has taken place.

Above the same tuft of trees that marked the site of the medieval settlement a tower or spire might now rise, clean-cut and glistening with fresh limewash. Some of

24

10 AFTER THE HAY HARVEST ON THE MARLBOROUGH DOWNS

11 THE HEDGER AT WORK IN WARWICKSHIRE

12   PLOUGHING IN SURREY

the older hovels might remain, but the bulk of the village would more likely consist of compact, two-storied houses, tiled or thatched, built of oak beams and white plaster, some with glass in the windows and some with brick chimneys. The manor-house would almost certainly have been rebuilt or added to since our last visit; possibly it would still be occupied by a local landowner, or possibly it would have degenerated into a farm-house or cottage row, while an Elizabethan mansion, vast and picturesque, would be building in the distance amid a deer-park thinned out of the wilderness. The pasture would still be there, fringed by the waste, but now browsed by more and fatter livestock, and there would still be the meadows beside the stream. But the three great fields, now more thinly sprinkled with workers, would have dwindled somewhat in the intervening period, and at their edges we should find a fringe of small hedged fields containing cattle or sheep, such as now occupied the demesne lands around the manor-house. In the village itself—a more solid and tidier affair these days—we might find a new mill and a new inn; the smith would be busy at his forge, and from certain more pretentious houses might come the clack of looms, to remind us that weaving had been established in the neighbourhood. But were we to climb to the top of the church tower, we should look out over a countryside of which more than the half was still wilderness—heath, rough woodland, moor or fen— despite the two or three towers of neighbour churches now visible in the distance. Though much of this waste country was gradually being reclaimed, much more remained unused and practically unpopulated except by a thin sprinkling of "heathers" and squatters, whose presence would be made known by an occasional wisp of smoke rising above a tumbledown cabin.

Nevertheless, since late-medieval times the forests had been steadily shrinking to the demand for more agricultural land and more fuel. Now, in the old sense, they were forests no longer, and though Shakespeare might write nostalgically of Arden, we may assume that by his day its woodlands had dwindled to a remnant of their old vastness. Now, too, as Drayton's lines show, iron-working was making tremendous inroads into the Wealden timber, while up and down the country the necessity for better housing required an unceasing supply of oak beams for the vernacular timber-framing. It was a process which the call for ships during the Dutch wars of the next century brought to its conclusion; and it is an interesting thought that, chiefly through the agency of Samuel Pepys and his successors at the Admiralty, England, by the dawn of the eighteenth century, had been very largely denuded of its heavier timber, save for a thin sprinkling of coppice in most districts and the splendid plantations of its great houses.

Almost until the nineteenth century, much of the waste land remained unused because it was subject to flooding. We may think here of the great alluvial stretches of such districts as the Vale of Pickering and the Vale of York, once useless but now rich farming countries, and more particularly of the Fenland south of the Wash, where the lower reaches of the Witham, Welland, Nene, Ouse and their tributaries converged in a marshy wilderness of sedge, intersected by sluggish streams and shallow lakes, with here and there an island of firmer soil tufted with willow and alder. Practically the whole of this area was liable to winter flooding, but from earliest times it had supported a sprinkling of inhabitants who understood its vagaries and could find a living by snaring, fishing and fowling. It is true that some embanking and draining had been done south-west of Lynn even before the coming of the Romans, which the latter were able to enlarge into the old sea-embankment whose importance is still reflected in the place-names thereabouts, such as

*Wal*pole, *Wal*soken and *Wal*ton. This work was some-times continued locally, but on a small scale, by the successors of the bands of ascetic monks who had settled in Saxon times on patches of firm ground in the peat, some of whose monasteries, such as Ely, Crowland and Peterborough, developed into rich foundations of the Middle Ages; the channel still sometimes known as Morton's Leam, for instance, commemorates the rule of that cardinal at Ely. But it was not until the seventeenth century that anything approaching a comprehensive scheme was inaugurated by the Earls of Bedford, em-ploying a Dutch engineer, Sir Cornelius Vermuyden, who constructed the long straight cuts of the Bedford River to short-circuit the winding Ouse, thereby draining some 100,000 rich acres of what is now known as the Bedford Level. This scheme, however, was allowed to lapse, and it was not until the last century that it was in fact completed, and also in some measure superseded, by the successive works of Smeaton, Rennie and Telford, whose drainage windmills, scattered at intervals about the levels, must have introduced a picturesque note into the bare, sky-filled vistas. Now, of course, they have been replaced by steam pumping-houses, as the sedgy morasses have been replaced by flat expanses of arable cultivation; and the whole district, despite an occasional flood scare, has settled down securely to enjoy the profits of some of the richest and most intensive farming in England.

The Fens, of course, from their extent, formed an exceptional instance; but it is strange to realise that a district so large and potentially profitable could have remained neglected and practically derelict until the seventeenth century. The heaths, as has been seen, often provided another problem. Large tracts of them were held in common trust by the village farms, in the organisa-tion of which they supplied an essential factor. They were the perquisites of the villagers, and as such were jealously guarded—as a very few remain jealously guarded to this day. Much of the remainder were gradually absorbed and enclosed, but a few have always resisted human appropriation. Egdon, Breckland and their fellows remain austere survivals of the older landscape of an England of which, as has recently been said, the true glory nowadays is "its meadow-green and its ripening corn and the deep shade of its woods; the thatched roof and the quiet stream." But then, as Hardy has written, "it is a question if the exclusive reign of this orthodox beauty is not approaching its last quarter. The new Vale of Tempe may be a gaunt waste in Thule: human souls may find themselves in closer and closer harmony with external things wearing a sombreness distasteful to our race when it was young."

However this may be, it seems certain that from these sterile places a lively "sense of the past" can best re-create some semblance of the English "wilderness," at a time when the areas of cultivation mostly alternated with equal areas of waste, much as they do in parts of North America to this day.

III

Probably the countryside was never more beautiful than during the 'thirties of the last century—a time of the utmost agricultural depression. For though, as Lord Ernle has pointed out, "the years 1814–36 were the blackest period in the history of the agricultural worker," the face of the land—as at other black periods, not discounting our own—can have given small indication of the desperate struggle for existence that was being maintained within so many of its venerable cottages—little buildings whose quaint dilapidation was beginning to intrigue epicures in the contemporary taste of the

Picturesque. Its soft meadows and rich-soiled plough-lands were the admiration of visitors from abroad, as was the chequerwork of hedges which had been thrown over them like a mesh, enveloping all but the wildest and hilliest places. These latter had now achieved a rural loveliness that has suffered a considerable degeneration since the invention of the internal combustion engine. The wildernesses and wastes of the England of Celia Fiennes were giving way to the vistas of a Wordsworth or a Turner, the comfortable landscapes of a Constable or a De Wynt. True, there were unspeakable patches of growing extent where the "dark satanic mills" were turning with increasing momentum, but to the gentleman secure in his country-house library, with its view over his beloved plantations, or to the middle-class citizen enjoying the suburban fruits of his gilt-edged securities, they remained well outside the orbit of the everyday conscience. England, such people considered with good enough justification, was a beautiful and peaceful land, a worthy background to their own unhurried activities. There was discontent about the countryside, it was true, but if an outbreak of rick-burning was dealt with firmly by a few hangings and transportations, the trouble would pass, and the people would settle down once more to the old bucolic subservience, touching their forelocks or bobbing their curtsies in return for the crumbs of philanthropy that were never wanting from the rich man's table.

But despite this comfortable attitude, things were far from well with the countryside, as any perusal of contemporary records will show. The trouble had started in the eighteenth century, and had resulted in an almost universal revolution in agricultural practice during the reign of George III—a revolution that has so direct a bearing on the appearance of the landscape to-day that it must necessarily be dealt with in some detail. For it had become increasingly obvious, as that century passed its first quarter, that something had to be done about the land if the land was to be preserved for agriculture at all. The great areas of the open arable fields, of which about a third were left fallow each year, were rapidly approaching exhaustion through centuries of over-cropping, while of the remaining country, as has been seen, a large part was occupied by commons, moors and heaths, and much more was unreclaimed owing to flooding. Meanwhile, a more scientific outlook was being stimulated by the experiments of certain landowners and agriculturalists, such as Jethro Tull, who invented the wheat drill, Lord Townshend, who reintroduced marling on light lands and experimented in the rotation of crops, and Coke of Holkham, who brought similar experiments to a very profitable conclusion on the poor, sandy soil of his Norfolk estate. But, for obvious reasons, such innovations were only practicable on enclosed land. When carried out over hitherto unused country they had met with little opposition; but as the century drew on, other property owners, such as those of the Midlands, whose lands were still largely cultivated co-operatively by the villagers, became alarmed and exasperated by the rapid rise in values of enclosed country of less intrinsic worth than their own. Enclosure thus became the order of the day, and during the third quarter of the century developed by breakneck stages. With a Parliament composed almost exclusively of landowners, there was obviously no serious difficulty in putting theory into practice, and this was effected by rushing innumerable private Bills through Parliament in two remarkable spasms of energy, one between 1770 and 1780 and the other between 1800 and 1820. There was no means of appeal for the smaller man save by a Bill in Chancery, and by the latter date it is safe to assume that practically the whole of England up to the 1,000-foot level was patterned out with hedges and walls, save for those few intractable patches which had always resisted appropriation.

There can be little doubt that there was ample justification for the enclosure of the common fields; had this, in fact, not been effected, it is doubtful whether England could have continued to feed its rapidly increasing population. But there is equally little doubt that the enclosure of the commons and wastes dealt a blow to the village community from which it has never really recovered. Throughout the seventeenth and eighteenth centuries, this community had generally comprised not only a sprinkling of self-supporting small freeholders (the total for England was about 160,000 at the beginning of the eighteenth century), but also many part-time labourers and handicraftsmen who retained holdings in the fields, or at least rights of pasture and common that enabled them to keep a beast or two to augment their livelihoods. The effects of enclosure were automatically to wipe out these classes and to transfer agriculture from a partially co-operative to a wholly private-profit basis. To quote Lord Ernle once again,[1] "farming ceased to be a subsistence and became a trade. The united effect . . . was to sweep away many small freeholders, tenant farmers and commoners who had lived by the cultivation or use of land in combination with the practice of domestic handicrafts. Their places were taken by the large corn-growing, meat-producing farms which met the needs and fashions of the day. The organisation of the village, in which wealth and poverty, employers and employed, were almost imperceptibly graded into one another, was broken up. With the destruction of the primitive framework went the traditions of the peasant, his inherited ideals, his ancestral customs, his habitual solutions of the problems of existence."

Thus by 1830 the countryside, though considerably

[1] *The Land and its People.*

less industrialised than to-day, had assumed much of its present appearance, and its population had resolved itself into its three present categories of landlord, farmer and hired labourer. And it was the latter who felt the first pinch. Under the stress of war and industrial expansion the country had become little more than "a factory of bread and meat for the towns"—a factory profitable enough to all while the Napoleonic wars lasted, but ill-equipped to face the rigours of a post-war slump. After Waterloo wages fell to pre-war levels, but even at the lowered rates unemployment increased by leaps and bounds. The rural worker, perhaps the most highly skilled and conscientious in our whole industrial system, was reduced in many districts to conditions that will hardly bear comparison with those of the "depressed areas" to-day, and to a servile reliance on the demands of his employer from which even now he has barely escaped.

The fact, then, is clear, that if enclosure, and the agricultural reorganisation it entailed, created much of the loveliness of our countryside, it also destroyed its traditional ways of life and the character of its community, which was the cell from which so many of our democratic institutions have emerged. It is significant that the tradition of village craftsmanship, though it lingered on in backward districts, was virtually extinguished at about the time of Waterloo. The technique of timber-framing, which had remained for centuries the rural vernacular for building, reaching its production peak between 1550 and 1630, lapsed when the supply of homegrown oak ceased in the eighteenth century, and though brick at this time began to make its first considerable appearance about the countryside, at first mostly in farms and more substantial houses, its quiet elegance smacked rather of the town than of the country. At about this time, too, stone began almost universally to

13   THE HEDGE CHEQUERWORK OF THE COTSWOLD FOOTHILLS

14 PARK-LIKE COUNTRY AT WOTTON, SURREY

replace other materials in districts where it was quarried, as in the whole Pennine region of the North. Hitherto its use had been restricted to more important buildings, with notable exceptions in a few favoured districts such as the Cotswolds, rich beyond the average from the boom in wool. These new materials were at first woven harmoniously into the texture of the countryside; it is only from about 1850 on that the discordance begins, with results that can be despairingly adjudged in every English district to-day.

With agriculture reorganised on capitalistic lines, the successive booms and depressions of the last hundred years have not rendered the life of the country population an easy one. The dismemberment of the rural community has laid it open to the attacks of outsiders and parasites of every kind, from the politician down to the ribbon builder. At the present moment landlords, farmers and labourers are alike feeling the effects of depression, a depression so severe that it must seem to many that the only possible remedy can lie in some form of land nationalisation. One of our greatest industries lies stricken, and as a result, one of our greatest heritages of beauty is in danger. It would be well for those who sentimentalise on the dwindling beauties of the countryside to devote more study to the practical aspects of the case, and to take up cudgels on behalf of that betrayed and neglected member of the population, the countryman. And it would be well, also, if they would realise something of the fight that has already been put up to preserve not only the status of English agriculture, but also the dignity and integrity of the rural scene.

For the latter effort we owe much to the landowner and to the farmer. Though at times, from an agrarian point of view, the former may appear the villain of the piece, there can be no doubt that from an aesthetic one he has made an immense contribution to the landscape.

From Elizabethan times until the nineteenth century, the area of England embraced by purely pleasure grounds showed a consistent increase. At first such lands were maintained chiefly for sporting purposes; but as we come to the eighteenth century, the cult of formal planting takes a remarkable hold on the somewhat stilted imagination of the country gentleman of the day, as any examination of the "country seat" engravings of Kip, Badeslade and others will show. Mansion vied with mansion in the extent and ingenuity of its surrounding groves and avenues, its distant thickets and woodland masses. In the engravings of Kip and his contemporaries, these serried plantations are shown in their youthful state; their maturity was disciplined into more rigid conformity by the "landscape" school of William Kent, "Capability" Brown and others, in which the architectural taste of the day demanded an obelisk to every vista, a temple to offset every grove. The later eighteenth century, under the broader influence of mentors such as Humphrey Repton, saw a considerable relaxation of this formality. The classical landscape of a Hubert Robert gave way to the comfortable fortuitousness of a scene by Joseph Farington, and the country gentleman found new enjoyment in surroundings which, in his opinion, emulated, and even excelled, the effects of nature. In fact, Sir Uvedale Price could write in 1794:

> "There is no country, I believe (if we except China), where the art of laying out grounds is so much cultivated as it now is in England. Formerly the embellishments of a place were confined to the garden, or a small space near the mansion; while the park, with all its timber and thickets, was left in a state of wealthy neglect; but now these embellishments extend over a whole district; and . . . give a new and peculiar character to the general state of the country."

"Park-like scenery" has become a byword in speaking of the English landscape, and its creation dates from the close of the eighteenth century. The wealth of the ruling and commercial classes in the years that followed added immeasurably to the extent of England's ornamental lands. Confidence in the future had already for long allowed a man to plant for posterity; now the movement continued unabated, though it is regrettable that nine-teenth-century eclecticism saw fit to introduce into its plantations some foreign elements much at variance with the natural character of the landscape. Nevertheless, it may still be said with reason that the well-kept park of one of our country houses is one of the most satisfying things of its kind that exists. It is sad nowadays to see them dwindling and shrinking, or to watch the felling of their splendid timber to make way for the utilitarian little rows of some new building development.

As a result of enclosure, the landlord's solicitude for his park was generally extended to the agricultural lands of his estate. In this he had the solid backing of the farmer, and both took pride in maintaining the pastoral character of their meadows, the beauty of their hedgerow timber and the inviolability of their patches of copse and thicket. Both classes were sportsmen to a man, and it is often undoubtedly to their delight in hunting and shoot-ing that must be attributed the impeccable preservation of our hedges and woods. But the farmer was always more than a sportsman; grumble as he well might in times of depression, and grudging as he might be to admit the fact, he regarded himself, as he regards himself still, as the trustee to the nation of the soil, the guardian of its traditional fertility. However bad the times, it is seldom that the soil has been overworked, or for that matter, until quite recently, neglected—for it is sad nowadays, going about the country, to observe the extent of land falling out of cultivation even in an agricultural country with the traditions of North Norfolk. Nevertheless, it is the writer's contention that, should England one day become once again a corn-growing country, the shrinkage of the hedges demanded by modern methods of production would be a slow process, and it would be long before the countryside would begin in any sense to resemble those wide, bare expanses of arable to be found in the wheat regions of the United States and Canada.

However this may be, the fact remains that, at the time of writing, England is steadily diminishing the amount of its arable and putting whole new districts into permanent pasture, so that it seems that for many years to come the countryside is likely to increase its areas of green. And it is this fresh, brilliant greenness, after all, that is half the charm of our landscape. If the sum total of the influence of climate on English scenery is hard to assess, this one major fact remains as obvious as it is permanent. Generations of foreign visitors have recorded their surprised pleasure at finding an island of which the predominant tone is green *all the year round*. This, of course, is the direct result of a damp, rainy climate, the chief winds of which come moisture-laden from the south-west; and it can, *and does*, rain on any day in the year. The grass is thus nearly always thick and luxuriant, and almost without exception keeps its colour through all the four seasons. Whether this permanent greenness, practically or aesthetically, is worth the price of so many overcast and cloudy days, such comparatively slight sunshine and such frequent rain, is another matter. But it has become so much a matter of course to English people that they often fail to realise its uniqueness until they visit other lands. Parts of Virginia are not unlike an ampler and wilder West Country, and still bear some stamp of the English countryside, but by autumn the rolling distances are a seared brown. Only after summers of exceptional dryness, such as those of 1934 and 1935, do the long slopes of our chalk downs or limestone uplands wear a grey-brown upper coat of dried grass-stalks, patched with the pallor of an occasional field of stubble.

This permanent effect of *climate* is distinguishable, of course, from the more transient effects of *weather*, that add another charm to the landscape. One may think of the shifting patterns woven by the cloud-shadows across the hill-sides or over hedge-chequered vales; of the still clarity of the horizon before rain; of the iridescence of the early morning haze. One may remember the light, rare sunshine of a February morning, or the frosty splendour of an autumn sunset; the ripe beauty of the countryside in full summer, redolent of the art of John Constable; the first primroses along the lane-banks, or the brief shimmer of bluebells in the beech-woods. These recollections, and many like them, are the property of all English people in these days of easy access to a countryside which, in spite of much recent spoliation, remains a possession of which any nation might be proud. Nevertheless, our pride will have to take practical expression, and quickly at that, if the beauty that still surrounds us is to be preserved, not as a dead but as a living thing.

H. E. Bates

THE
HEDGE CHEQUERWORK

I WAS born on that large East Midland plain that takes in Northamptonshire and its nine adjoining counties, Buckinghamshire, Oxfordshire, Warwickshire, Bedfordshire, Lincolnshire, Huntingdonshire, Leicestershire, Cambridgeshire and the smallest and perhaps the best of them all, the dillin pig of the litter, Rutland. As it also takes in Essex and Hertford, and parts of Yorkshire and Nottingham and Worcester and most of Norfolk and Suffolk, it must be reckoned the largest plain in England. If you reckon it in terms of impressive landscape features it is probably also the dullest plain in England. Its hills, until you come to the boundaries of the Chilterns in the south, the Cotswolds in the south-west and the real hills of Nottinghamshire and Derbyshire in the north, are not much more than bumps made by generations of gnats on the green skin of the land. It contains no natural lakes until you reach the Broads almost on the sea-coast to the eastward; it contains the remnants of half a dozen forests, but in countries other than England they would

15   THE EVENING HAY LOAD

16 HEDGEROW ELMS IN DEVON

17 WINTER IN A HERTFORDSHIRE LANE

probably be reckoned as copses. Its only true and permanent natural features are its rivers, and it is in reality five river plains—six if you include the Humber—in one: the Ouse, the Nene, the Welland and the Trent flowing out to the east, the Avon down to the west. Judged by the standards of Devon and Somerset, the Yorkshire hills and dales and the magnificence of Cumberland and Westmorland and the hills of Gloucester and Derby which make its boundaries, it has nothing to offer. When I compare it with Kent and Sussex, in which most of my life is now spent, I see it as a country without richness and without any great variety of scene and colour. In my mind's eye I see it as the greenest piece of England, which it most probably is, and for some reason the most orderly. It lacks that enchanting disorder of deep-bellied hills, thick woods, sly lanes, rich coloured villages and luxuriant hop-gardens which is the south country. It is a pattern of sobriety. Against the southern plain, the great weald running from the North Downs to the South, with which I propose to compare it, it is like the homely girl compared with the beauty, the plain oak trouser-polished chair-seat compared with the mahogany Chippendale, the suet-pudding compared with the trifle. Yet, as I hope to show, this plain homely pudding pattern of elm and grass and hedges is the basis on which the entire English countryside is built. It is the very thing which makes the English country what it is: something different from any other country in the world.

For more than twenty years I felt myself to have been unlucky in having been brought up in such country. I spent a childhood unconsciously entranced by it, magnifying dribbling little brooks to the brave beauty of torrents, tiny nightingale copses to the deep luxuriance of woods. I grew up to know the ash and the elm and the willow better than any other tree because they were the staple trees of the landscape, and to know hardly any other

5*

type of field than pasture and the massive ploughed parallels of steel clay that would later be roots and corn. I knew no other hedgerow except the rule-straight line of laid hawthorn or the high cow-rubbed umbrella-shaped variation of it that is, as W. H. Hudson once pointed out, one of the greater glories of the English landscape. But it was only natural as time went on that I should grow tired of a landscape in which a beech-tree was a rarity, in which alder or sweet-chestnut were never seen, and in which fields and copses were giving way more and more to raw Edwardian villas, rows of workers' cottages and an occasional factory. At twenty I disliked the Midlands; at twenty-five I hated them; at thirty, having left them, I began to understand them. I began to see how fortunate I had been to have been brought up on that diet of clay pudding which is as fundamental to English scenery as Yorkshire pudding is to English dietary.

I feel that I was fortunate for this reason. A man brought up in Devonshire or the dales of Yorkshire or the Westmorland lake country is often found never to have any real taste in other scenery. He has been brought up too well; he has never known what it is to be poor. Whereas a man brought up on a flat plain diet, as I myself was, has a taste capable of being educated in any kind of scenery. For him Exmoor and Dovedale and Windermere are pure caviare; the North Downs and the Malvern Hills and the Cotswolds are piled dishes of fruit. Poverty has given him perspective. Again, fine scenery makes a man proud and jealous. To a Westmorland man there is nothing like his native hills and waters; to a Devonian there is nothing like Devonshire; and all the world knows what a Yorkshireman thinks of Yorkshire. These men are as proud and jealous of their native muckles as high-coloured cocks. In the final estimate of grandeur there is nothing in the world that can beat their own. They can never say, and never would if they could, "This reminds me of Derwentwater" or, more unthinkable still, "this is as good as Yorkshire." But the man brought up on the plain pudding country is decently humble, knowing there are places much better than his own; he knows too that there are places just like his own. The only time I went to Cheshire I saw the Midland countryside repeated exactly in the Cheshire plain, and I got from it a sense of friendliness and comfort. As I drive through the flattest parts of Somerset I see a countryside of willow and osier, elm and grassland that in its unexotic ordinariness might be any part of a dozen homely counties. The same goes for the eastern parts of Yorkshire, though every Yorkshireman will probably call it an insult, for much of Worcestershire and Berkshire and in fact for odd unexpected bits of every county in England. It should never be forgotten that most of the English countryside as we see it to-day is man-made; and that the part most completely shaped by man is this plain, fundamental chequerwork of flat field and hedgerow. And in one sense this is the only part which matters. It is the thing which nourishes the community, without which England would be poverty-stricken. It is essentially utilitarian; yet it provides exactly those pictures of which Englishmen in foreign countries are supposedly reminded at homesick moments, and which foreigners take away with them and cannot get over: the tranquil, orderly, park-like greenness, hedges of hawthorn in bloom, cattle grazing in deep meadows, sheep folded in pastures as short and green as lawns. In America, for example, they have a million square miles of countryside which will knock even Yorkshire into a cocked hat; in the State of Minnesota alone they claim ten thousand lakes; and in New Hampshire you may drive for hundreds of miles through country as rich and glorious as Devon and Somerset and the English county from which the state gets its name. But the country they cannot repeat and for which all Englishmen are deeply and honestly envied is the country about which I am writing. This, to them, is the real England.

It would be a mistake, I think, to agree that it is the real England: to the exclusion, that is, of all other parts. In praising England it is a fatal thing to extol one bit over another. For another remarkable thing about English scenery is its capacity for variation in a small space. If you travel across the plain of Lombardy from Milan to Venice you see exactly the same flat, dike-crossed, willow-spiked countryside for something like five hours. It is not possible to do such a thing in England for five minutes. To speak of Northampton-shire as if it were an elongated shape of pasture decorated into shapes of hawthorn hedges for the whole of its area would be absurd. From its north-eastern end, where its hawthorn hedges are giving way at last to low stone walls and an accompanying feeling of space and sturdy dignity, down to its south-western end, where the walls are beginning again and the land is rising like bare folds of dough towards the Cotswolds, it can produce a dozen tricks of change, though the fundamentals remain the same. This is true of all its neighbours, of all their neighbours in turn. They each have the same infinite capacity not only for variation in beauty, but also in ugliness. There is a twenty-mile strip of Northampton-shire, five miles wide, running from the Bedfordshire border to Leicestershire, where it is possible to see how badly man-made landscape withstands the final attack of man and machine. The towns, once villages of golden and russet ironstone, crowned by the most magnificent church-spires in England, are like gawky, raw-limbed boys that have outgrown their first long trousers. They are neither one thing nor another, neither town nor village, neither new nor old. Red brick has broken out

18 PLOUGHING IN UPLAND, NORTHAMPTONSHIRE

19 THE WINDMILL, EGGINGTON, BEDFORDSHIRE

like a rash among the sheep-coloured and russet walls and houses of local stone, with which nobody builds any longer. The factories are harsh red scabs on the slopes of the river valleys. They do not belong there. They have made a plain, homely country into depressing half-rural, half-urban slums of industry.

The moment you step off this strip of industrial development you begin to see the East Midland plain at its best. No writing on the English countryside is complete without a reference to the architecture, and here, from Higham Ferrers on the Nene up through Oundle and Stamford and over the border into the toy hilly-hollows of Rutland, it is the architecture rather than the land which enchants. It stands as naturally on the landscape, the soft grey limestone interspersed with odd corners and patterns of gold-brown ironstone, as a flock of sheep in which there is a sprinkling of brown. This stone is exactly right for the soft undulation and calm colours of the land. It is a superb instance of nature providing on the spot exactly the right medium for man's activities; and it seems to me beyond doubt that if man had gone on using this limestone, decorating it with deeper tone-patterns of iron, this piece of the Midland plain running out of Northamptonshire into the whole of Rutland would have been as architecturally famous, perhaps more famous, than the Cotswolds themselves. But much of what was done, and done largely up to the eighteenth century, still remains. The square at Higham Ferrers, the whole of Oundle, almost the whole of Stamford are all completely entrancing. But if Stamford stands with Cirencester as a perfect example of the English stone-built town at its best the villages for twenty miles round are as absolutely satisfying and sound and beautiful as the names themselves: Rockingham, overlooking the entirely green Welland plain, Uppingham, Fotheringhay, with a superb church standing like

43

a small lost cathedral over the graves of kings, Elton, Deene, Colly Weston, which gives the stone tiles that are one of the best features of the whole district, Kingscliffe, Weldon, giving the famous creamy stone, Lilford, with a mansion and a stone humpbacked bridge over the Nene that is not equalled anywhere in England, Caldecott, Oakham, the silly, one-eyed, one-policeman, charming county town of Rutland, and last and probably best of all, Apethorpe. For every thousand eulogies of what are to me the much overrated villages of Devon you will not see a single mention of Apethorpe. Yet Apethorpe is the last word in villages planned and governed and preserved by and according to the standards of the great house. If all examples of rural dictatorship could produce results like Apethorpe then I would vote for a wholesale return to the principles of the Victorian squirearchy. This village does not contain a single house out of keeping with the enormous pale stone mansion standing behind its stout defences of woodland. It is the perfect thing. It has little of the picture-page picturesqueness of villages which seem to have been made exclusively for photographers and tourists; it is simply something that has been made honestly and reverently, out of the God-provided stone of the district, primarily for use, secondarily but triumphantly for beauty. Its soft handful of straight-cut stone is a magnificent example of what the English system of squire dictatorship could do at its best. It is not bettered anywhere in England.

I have not mentioned this stone architecture, remarkable and lovely though it is, simply for the purpose of dilating on something beautiful. I would like to go on talking of it, in its humblest and sturdiest in the stone walls which replace the hedges, at its most splendid in the mansions: Kirby Hall, Deene, Burghley House, Lilford, Castle Ashby, Drayton House, Lyveden New Building, Apethorpe, and the famous spired churches.

But this is only one bit of the green pudding country, a thumb-nail fraction of all England. The purpose of mentioning it is really to go on and compare it with something else. For it is obvious that the land, this kind of land more than any other, is nothing without the architecture, and it seems to me that the architecture of the pudding country is often far more remarkable than that of more impressive districts. It is as though the inhabitants of a plain and ordinary countryside felt a lack of any specially striking beauty in the landscape and built impressively or decoratively in order to make up for it. In the almost too rich countryside of Devonshire, for example, the greater part of the architecture will not bear talking about; it has the uninspired carelessness of a self-satisfied people. Whereas on the really flat, and to some people depressing, plain of Huntingdonshire and Cambridgeshire the architecture, though humble, shows many signs of being in the hands of a dissatisfied and urgently restless people. The people of the warm, damp honey-valleys of Devonshire carry on no struggle with nature; life is extremely and perhaps dangerously soft. But the people of the Fens and the outer Fen districts keep up a constant struggle; they are continually at war with sea-winds, an unhealthy countryside and incursions of flood and sea. The whole ground under their feet is artificially guarded against disaster. Such a people might easily be excused for taking no interest in what their houses looked like. Yet a continual struggle against adversity and the oppressive fact of living on a drab and totally flat surface has heightened both their need for colour and their determination to secure it. Thus the cottage architecture of the extreme eastern section of the Midland plain, over a wide area of Bedfordshire, Huntingdonshire and Cambridgeshire, is almost exotically colour-washed. Cream and white are not enough for these people; they must have yellow and orange, beery shades of brown, deepest terra-cotta, crushed strawberry pink, the blue of blue-bags, an occasional fling in flamboyant red, a wash of startling emerald. In such a village as Kimbolton, a model of well-preserved rural quietness, a village in a thousand, the short, beautifully kept main street might be the home of a collection of irresponsible house-painters. It glows with orange and white and brown and green and black, one of the most extraordinary and lovely streets in England. And it is worth noting that England is not the only country in which such a desire for colour is shown by plain dwellers: the landscape of Holland is full of houses similarly coloured, so in less degree is the plain of Lombardy, and so, as a glance at the pictures of Van Gogh will show, are the plains of Southern France.

But arguments about the country have a way of not completing themselves. The flat county of Hertfordshire, the southern end of the plain, ought to oblige me by producing a remarkable architecture in stone or paint embellishments. But it doesn't. It produces something quite sober. Perhaps, rolling gently down to London like an enormous park, it is quite beautiful enough in itself. I never drive through it without a sense of extreme restfulness. All across it the hedge and elm and grass chequerwork is seen at its best, simple, undesigned, and yet somehow designed for permanence. There is nothing except the new arterial roads to disturb its placid continuance from Essex to the Chilterns. It does not suffer from the sudden upheaval which a river of any size gives to a piece of land; it is reputed to be one of the coldest places in England, but I have never seen any proof of it. The essence of its character is its green, friendly tranquillity. No foreigner, anxious to confirm any ideas that England is a sort of enlarged park, would need to go any farther out of London than this. It is the English hedgerow countryside at its undisturbed and dignified best.

South of the Thames all the countryside, plain and hill, weald and woodland, undergoes vast changes. There are northerners who call it too beautiful; we have visitors who cannot keep awake in the strong, soft air coming up from Romney Marsh and the Weald, and who, on waking, eat vastly. The south country is undoubtedly rich and good; its springs are earlier, its autumns push their full fat bellies into the face of winter and knock it almost into the lap of spring. Its variations of landscape in a short space are enormous. They have filled books. But only the Weald, I think, has any place here.

The Weald, once entirely forest, is only partly a plain. But where it is a plain it shares with the Fens the inverted distinction of being one of the unhealthiest spots in England. The thin, sallow Kentish faces indicate the consumptive price paid for the privilege of being born and reared in some of England's most beautiful villages. The land is extremely low; in winter the fat clay is a pudding of stodge that pulls the guts out of a man; in summer it turns into a land of concrete. It floods easily; it is a common sight to see hop-gardens standing like the graveyards of derelict ships. If you inquire about houses in the Weald the house-agent feels forced to remind you, in apology, "of course its down on the Weald." There is a feeling of oppression that the black rich land of the Fens never gives; the Fens have a mysterious, uplifting air of width and a sort of spacious desolation. They impress; the Weald depresses. Yet the Weald enjoys an immense reputation for beauty.

This beauty again springs almost entirely from the pattern drawn by man on the original flat canvas of the land. Here, as in the whole length of the limestone ridge from Somerset to Rutland, the natural materials for building could not have been better. The forest provided the wood, the land the bricks. The result is one of the most glorious combinations of architectural material that England can show: the multi-coloured, winey-blue Wealden bricks and the massive age-blanched timbers that show up in the house-fronts like the skeletons of wooden ships. The Weald is full of such houses, and even of villages comprised almost entirely of such houses: Smarden, Biddenden, Benenden, Frittenden, Rolvenden, Goudhurst, Sissinghurst, Cranbrook, Appledore. They are perfect examples, Biddenden and Benenden almost too perfect, of the English show village. They light up the land with their patterns of dark timber and white plaster as effectively as the colour-washed houses light up the Midland plain. Yet they belong to a world that continually seems to me entirely different. It is the creation of a world of yeomen farmers. Its chief architectural glories are its huge honest farm-houses, with their sky triangles of oasts. The great country mansion, seen at its most perfect in Midland houses like Drayton and Burghley and Kirby Hall, has scarcely any place here; the sublime, heavenly spired churches of the Northamptonshire lowlands are cathedrals in comparison with the squat, square-towered churches of the Kent and Sussex plain. After a lifetime of craning my neck at spires I can hardly lower myself to look at these humble little places. Mr. G. M. Young in an essay on the English country house has remarked that the Domesday landscape "reached its high point of pride and beauty in the middle of the nineteenth century; and its mid-point everywhere in the country house." This is right; but it is worth noting that of the illustrations which adorn his essay only one is of a house in the south country, and there is no doubt that the entire scheme of domestic and ecclesiastical architecture is less impressive here than in the Midlands, the north and the near west. I will not attempt any explanation of that fact here, though the Weald of a hundred years ago, seen through

48

20 THE FIELDS OF THE HOME COUNTIES: NEAR KIMPTON, HERTFORDSHIRE

21 AN OXFORDSHIRE LANE

the eyes of Cobbett, must supply part of the answer. In winter this morass of land, impassable even for judges on circuit, its roads axle-deep in mud, was nothing but an enormous chilly pudding of sour and unhealthy clay. At the same time the plain of Northamptonshire and Rutland had reached the height of its fashion as a country retreat. One glance at Stamford, with buildings as noble as many in Bath and its six remaining churches, all that are left of twice as many, is enough to show how elegant and complete that fashion was. The Weald can produce nothing like it. It is a world composed of farmers as opposed to landed gentry, a world uninfluenced by an aristocracy which, however false and corrupt and despicable in other respects, knew the secret of building the most magnificent houses that England has ever seen.

But though the two plains are so entirely different in many ways and each poorer for lacking something which the other possesses abundantly—oast-houses and stone mansions are only two examples of it—they are alike in one thing. They are built and bound together by the same fundamental pattern: the pattern of hedge and tree and pasture. It is true that in the south country the hedges have entirely changed in character, that elm and ash have also given way to a predominance of oak and beech, and that the pastures seem less wide and rolling, but the sum of both is worked out over the same common denominator. And of all three it is the hedge, I think, which is most truly English. Other countries can produce fields, a wealth of trees beside which our own appear often very ordinary. But no other country can produce anything which, like stitchery, binds together the varying pattern of the landscape in such a way that the pattern is made infinitely more beautiful.

If this seems extravagant, try to consider the English landscape without the hedge. It would not be the English landscape. The abolition of the common field system no doubt robbed the poor, a century or so ago, of many dearly held privileges; but in the quick hedge it bestowed a common glory on all of us. Though it goes against all my principles to say so, it was not the first time that a score for the great landowners was also a means of beautifying the English landscape. In fact I doubt if the poor have ever beautified the English landscape. It is the rich and prosperous who have left on it the hall-marks of beauty: the great parks, the woods, the magnificent country mansions, the castles, the New Forest, the beautiful southern farm-houses, towns like Bath and Stamford, villages like Long Melford and Burford. In the same way the Enclosure Acts, benefiting the rich, bestowed on us the most beautiful common inheritance, next to grass, that the English possess. Without the hedge we should all be poorer. I was brought up in a district notable for its lack of trees, but which should have been famous, as I now know, for its magnificent hedges. Without those hedges, huge lines of hawthorn umbrellas, making shade for cattle, that countryside would have been unbearably dull. Nothing else could have made it so beautiful in May-time, when the cream of the hawthorn bloom rose on the four sides of every field, making the air over-faint with scent. Nothing else could have created so happily the first rich drowsy feeling of summer.

In the South I have become acquainted with an entirely different hedge. In the Midlands the commonest hedge is undoubtedly the plain straight-set quick. Time has embroidered it with wild rose and blackberry, occasional ash-seedlings, bits of maple, but the quick remains indomitable. In the south, hedges are far more varied; quick is merely one colour, and no longer the common colour, in the pattern. If I walk out of my house I come straightway on a hedge which reads like a catalogue of shrubs: holly, dwarf oak, elder, maple, willow, wild-cherry, spindle, hazel, wild-rose, sallow, honeysuckle, blackberry, wild-clematis, blackthorn and always binding it together, hawthorn. Along other lanes I shall see other variations: ash, sweet chestnut, viburnum, dogwood, crab-apple, alder. There is scarcely any end to the variations of the South-country hedge. This means that it is a thing of constant fascination throughout the twelve months of the year; in winter the comforting polished clumps of holly and their scarlet berries and the toy wooden balls of oak apples, in very early spring the catkins of hazel and sallow, the mouse-ear leaves of honeysuckle and elder, in spring the catkins of alder, the white stars of blackthorn, the emerald bread-and-cheese of hawthorn itself; in late spring the little odd trembling bouquets of wild cherry on coppery new leaves, the hawthorn bloom, in summer the glory of wild rose and elderbloom and honeysuckle; in autumn black and scarlet berries, nuts, the slit cerise-and-orange spindle seeds, old man's beard, acorns, the first bare wine-dipped dogwood branches, the shining, comforting holly again.

But this is not all. This is only what the hedge is. It takes no account of what lives in or under it, or what flowers it shelters. In the Midlands we never expected a hedge to yield more than a patch of violets, a run of celandines, some pinky wild geraniums, late summer riots of willow-herb in damp places. In the South every roadside hedge is a spring glory of primrose and bluebell, white anemones and violets, clouds of lady-smocks and campion; a summer tangle of foxglove and meadowsweet, wild canterbury bell and bay willow-herb, a hunting-place for wild strawberries. The hedge, beginning as a simple device for the division of the land, has become the haven sheltering every sort of flower and weed that pasturing and the plough drive out. Taken for twelve months of the year, in fact, the Southern hedgerow is the most constant of all sources of satisfaction in the landscape. Yet even it, I think, reaches its glory at the flowering season of its commonest flower. When the kex is in bloom the hedge is etherealised. The light dense cloud of creamy flower lace, smothering the hedge itself, lifts it from earth. I can't remember any writer ever pausing to pay proper tribute to the kex, humblest of all flowers, rabbit-feed when young, make-believe lace in the games of little girls when in blossom, superb material for the whistles and pea-shooters of small boys at the height of summer. It is one of the things, like the hedge itself, which we take for granted. Yet I never see it now without marvelling at its effect of lace-light foam. It is something whipped airily out of the milk of spring.

But flowers are only a moderate part of the life of a hedge. Its position as a sanctuary for small birds and animals is unique, and the records of English small bird life would be poorer if it were not for the hedge. This is not the place to begin a disquisition on bird life, but the springs of most of us would be poorer if there had never been such a thing as a bird's nest in a hedge. The moment of crushing up against the hedge, the thorns pricking the body, the groping forward with one hand, the last stretch of fingers to the nest, the moment of touching eggs, the cold shock of touching raw, featherless young birds: these are all things which the hedgerow, more than anything else, has allowed us to experience infinitely. I see my own children, even at the age of four or five, reach out for this experience of nest-hunting in hedges more eagerly than for any other experience in the countryside, and I find it satisfying to think that in adult life it will be the hedge that provides them with one of the richest of childhood memories.

The Southern countryside produces one other type of hedge that is not seen elsewhere. It is the colossal,

22 PASTURES NEAR THE LITTLE CHURCH OF BERNERS RODING, ESSEX

23 THE FIELD PATTERN OF THE VALE OF AYLESBURY FROM THE CHILTERNS

specially trained and pruned hedge of hop-gardens, composed generally of thorn and trained to reach the height of, and make a screen for, the hops themselves. These enormous slices of hedges reach a height of ten, fifteen, or even twenty feet. They are unique to the hop-growing countryside, form the only example of a hedge trained to protect a specific crop. In fact there is now a cult of hedge-cutting, in Midland districts especially, which virtually means the removal of the hedge from arable land. Hedges are hacked so low in order, apparently, to give crops more air and light, that they have ceased to be any protection against wind and cattle at all. A well-laid hedge, like a well-cut ditch, is rapidly becoming a rarity in the countryside—to the complete detriment, as I see it, of the nature and character of the land. Well and properly laid, a hedge is just as beautiful as when in full growth, a supremely satisfying thing to mind and eye. Good hedges and good drainage are, in fact, two of the fundamental necessities of a good agricultural system, yet both, drainage especially, are now often painfully neglected. Before the War the two jobs, like thatching, bred real craftsmen, men of special ability, true to a tradition. The land is poorer for the loss of these men, who were a natural part of a prosperous system.

For, as I see it, the real beauty of the English countryside depends almost entirely on the vigour and prosperity of the agricultural system behind it. This is obviously not true of places of particular natural beauty like Dartmoor or the moors and mountains of Cumberland, Yorkshire, Wales, Derbyshire and so on; but it is undeniably true, and most true, of the type of country with which this essay is specifically dealing. The pudding countryside, unspectacular, quiet, homely, derives its beauty almost solely from the care and order with which it is governed and worked. Like a garden, which begins to be hideous as soon as neglected, it depends almost exclusively on the activities of man for its charm. Grass can be properly green only when properly grazed or cut; arable becomes a wilderness of thistle and dock as soon as plough and seed are withheld from it. If ever the English agricultural system should collapse—and at fairly regular intervals there are signs of its doing so, though it never does—the humble green pudding countryside would be the first to suffer and go into decay with it. We make a great struggle, and rightly so, to preserve acres of downland and moor and woodland and forest from the dangers of so-called progress. We rightly estimate that it would be a catastrophe if the English countryside were bit by bit robbed of such natural features. But if the day ever comes when the English farmer can no longer afford to grow oats and barley, wheat and potatoes, to lay fields for hay, to graze cattle and herd sheep, then we shall be faced with a still deeper catastrophe and the loss of a kind of beauty which we take as naturally for granted as the air we breathe.

Perhaps we take it too much for granted? Consider the English landscape without moor and fell, downland and mountain, and then try to consider it without this plain, pasture-and-arable pudding which is a common part, almost, of its every county. Consider it without fields of wheat, pink-bellied oats, grey-mauve sweet stretches of beans in flower, yellow splashes of mustard, white seas of barley, fields of white peas, blue flax, hops, lucerne, roots, sanfoin, potatoes in flower; all the established crops of the English landscape. Consider it finally without grass and hedgerow, the common and constant elements which bind the whole pattern together. Consider for a single moment an English landscape deprived of these simple and accepted things. And then ask yourself how easily you could give them up.

24 GRAZING FIELDS NEAR SNITTERBY, LINCOLNSHIRE

25 THE WYE AT SYMONDS YAT, HEREFORDSHIRE

C. Henry Warren

VALLEYS
AND ORCHARDS

MOST Englishmen, if only because of the natural formation of their island, are essentially more at home in
the lowlands than on the heights. The popular idea of
an English village is of one in a valley, where it can be
overlooked from the hills, clustered about its ancient
church; and similarly, the general conception of a farm
in this country is of a more or less commodious homestead in a valley, sheltered by ample trees, with broad
fields like open hands stretched out to receive the sun,
and a river flowing not far away. There is always a river
not far away, in England; and although, judged by
Continental standards, our rivers may for the most part
be small and even insignificant; they are perhaps the
more intimately known for that. Certainly they are not
the kind about which national songs are composed, as in
the case of the Rhine or the Danube or the Volga; but
at least they are the kind in which a boy can bathe and
in which (even to-day) a farm-hand can tickle an occasional trout. They permit of such homely occupations
as the gathering of water-cress or the growing of

7   55

osiers for basket-weaving; and although the mill-wheels they once turned are silent now and weed-clogged, men still lean over the weirs on summer evenings and watch the swallows floss the clear water under the bridges. Such rivers, insignificant as they may be, influence the lives of those who live near them in the most subtle and sensuous manner.

For some time I lived in a cottage on the western edge of the Cotswolds. In front of my garden a meadow—itself a garden of cowslips in spring and a haunt of bee-orchises that fell with the swaths of grass in summer—dipped down to the Severn Valley. Standing at my door, I could see across the lowland orchards and pastures to the Malverns on the one hand and to the Welsh mountains on the other. Those far, blue ridges might be hidden by mist or cloud from time to time; but seldom was there a day when I could not clearly follow the course of the river down to its wide, muddy estuary. Year in, year out, the Severn was part of my view: it was even part of my very consciousness. By day I could see where it curved through the trees in great muscular loops, like a gigantic silver snake; and by night, though I could no longer see it, I knew where it kept its sinuous course, from the cluster of lights that was Gloucester to the brief girdle of lights that was Sharpness. I saw it hold the summer sun like burning glass, while the brow of our hill was cooled with quiet breezes. I saw it lashed with driven rain (I could even hear it sometimes) while our own roof remained dry. And in flood-time I saw it swell and overflow into a whole galaxy of little lakes that looked for all the world like a painted clay model of Erie, Ontario, Michigan and all.

Often we would go down from the hills and discover the valley at closer quarters. These few steep miles carried us into another world altogether. The keen expanse of open sky was exchanged for glimpses and patches of it seen through the orchard trees. The close-bitten turf of the high wolds, herb-scented beneath the feet and starry with a thousand tiny flowers, gave place to grass of an intenser green, a juicier blade. As for those dry-stone walls that are the pride of the hill-men, they were nowhere to be seen: instead, the pastures and orchards of the valley were enclosed in tousled and seemingly untidy hedges, often concealing narrow, sunken lanes. The lark was no longer lord of the skies; but we heard the mewing of the sea-gull; and sometimes we would be rewarded with the sight of a kingfisher, meteorically brightening the meadows, or of a heron, statuesquely posing on one leg against a background of reeds. Even the smell of the air was different—always there was the scent of the river. For sheep, nimbus'd against the sun, there were cattle standing knee-deep in muddy ponds, swishing at the flies with futile flicks of the tail. The occupations of the natives changed, and the farmers practised a different branch of husbandry. But perhaps the most startling contrast of all was in the architecture. Occasionally we would pass a grey, lime-stone cottage whose drip-stones and decorated porch reminded us of the inimitable style we had left behind on the hills; but somehow it looked out of place and as likely as not its craftsmanship was none too sure. The majority of the cottages now were of timber and plaster and thatch, and there was nothing out of place or unsure in these. Their black-and-white patterns seemed to harmonise with the tree-shadows all around them, and something of the curve and flow of the river itself was in the deep-eaves of their thatch.

At other times, the valley, as it were, would come up to us. One morning some lads on bicycles would arrive at the cottage, carrying baskets of elvers. They would whip off the wet cloths and show us a wriggling mass of silvery worms, minute and opaque. These, we learned, would make a most delectable dish if fried with bacon-fat and mixed with beaten eggs. Cookery apart, how-ever, the arrival of the elvers was a reminder that the Severn bore was "on show"; and so, when the best time and place had been decided upon, after consulting the local newspaper, once more the journey had to be made down into the valley. For to live by Severn and miss the bore is like living in East Anglia and missing the corn-harvest. At Longney the Severn curves sharply: we therefore took our stand on the bank there, well away from the river, and waited. Punctually to the scheduled minute the bore arrived, announcing itself with the roar of an oncoming train. Taking the bend, it flung spray and foam high into the air, and then swept onwards again, sinister and remorseless—and a little disappoint-ing. That day the full tide rose to a height of thirty feet; but the bore itself, on which boats seemed to ride with the greatest of ease, was only about three feet high. When at length the tide receded, the lanes and roads adjoining the river were covered with slush, and talk was all of record bores in the past, when the level reaches down by Arlingham were flooded and rabbits were trapped by the hundred. The men propped their long, pear-shaped elver-nets against the cottage walls and waited till evening should bring the second and (at least for onlookers) more spectacular bore, since then the darkened scene would glimmer with the lights of many lanterns bobbing above the water to entice a heavy catch.

The bore, however, was not the only spectacle that lured us hill-folk down to the valley. Each year, about the second or third week in April, Nature staged a scene of peculiar and indeed almost absurdly theatrical beauty. If whistling boys with baskets of elvers strapped to their bicycles had been our reminder in March that we must go down to Longney to see the bore, now it was a less

26   THE SEVERN VALLEY FROM THE COTSWOLDS

17. ORCHARD COUNTRY NEAR THURSBURY, GLOUCESTERSHIRE

likeable ambassador that called us. Smashed yellow petals littered the roads out of Herefordshire into Gloucester, and we knew thereby that the daffodils were out in the meadows by Newent and Dymock. No matter how many people made that annual pilgrimage—and on a favourable Sunday they would number several hundreds —the quantity of daffodils never seemed appreciably to diminish. In fact it was difficult to avoid treading on them. To gather an armful it was not necessary to stray more than a few yards from the original starting-place. They filled the meadows and overflowed into the ditches by the roadside. Impertinently they penetrated into cottage-gardens and they gleamed like shafts of sunshine in the depths of the woods. The best time to see them was on a week-day, if possible, because then they had the meadows to themselves and provided an unusual setting for the routine activities of the inhabitants of that singular valley. But on a Sunday they became a traffic in living gold. Motor-cars emptied their occupants all along the lanes; bicycles were flung down by the roadside or propped against gate and hedge; whilst for those who did not choose to do their own picking, there were country children posted every few yards along the neighbouring highways with limp bunches held out for sale at a few pence a time.

Thus, from my Cotswold cottage, I seemed to enjoy something of the best of two worlds: I lived on the hill, I looked over the valley. There were times, perhaps, when I may have wished the position were reversed. There were those days in winter, for instance, when the meadows round the cottage were white with snow, whilst the meadows down in the valley still kept their usual green. A clear contour set us apart from the rest of our fellows. Or there were those other days in spring, when it was the hill that was green and the valley that was white—but not the white of snow. But no, I am sure I never wished for such a reversal for long. It pandered to our pride to be walking in the snow when the mundane valley still kept its preen: the men and women down there, we felt, would certainly be lifting up their eyes to the hills on such a morning. And as for orchards in bloom, are they not best seen from above? I know that the proper place to stand, according to the guide-books, when the orchards of the Vale of Evesham are white as summer clouds is on the top of Bredon Hill: similarly, I suppose I saw more of Severn's orchards in bloom from my green look-out in the hills than if I had lived in their midst. They say it is the spectator who sees most.

On the other hand, it seems to me that the spectator would have little enough cause to boast about his advantage if he himself had never been a participant—never, in this case, lived in a valley. Aesthetic appreciation is inferior to actual participation: to see a thing is not as good as to live it. Those flowering orchards down in the Severn Valley, for instance, would have been no more to me than a pretty picture (they might as well have been an airman's view of the clouds—which indeed is what they somewhat resembled) if I had not, at some time or other, myself enjoyed the actual, sensuous *experience* of orchards in bloom. It was well for me, therefore, that I had been born and bred amid orchards; nor did it matter that these orchards were in Kent and not in Gloucestershire. And of all the orchards with which I was so familiar in my youth, one, for some reason which I am at a loss to discover, dominates all the others in my memory to-day. It is a cherry-orchard.

What is it you see when, remote from home, you shut your eyes and say the word: "England"? The answer will probably depend upon where you were born, or, at any rate, where you happened to live during the most impressionable years of your life. For me, the picture that invariably springs to mind is of this cherry-orchard in Kent. I see it now as a cherry-orchard *in excelsis*; but even at that time it must have had the general reputation of being something quite out of the ordinary. And yet I remember its trees were so old and so knobbly that it seems to me now as if only a very optimistic (or impecunious) farmer would have bothered with them any longer. Mr. Champion, however, was neither impecunious nor unwisely optimistic; but he allowed those gnarled and shabby trees to stand; and every spring he was rewarded with what I can only call a miracle. This miracle attracted the villagers as another kind of miracle will attract pilgrims to a shrine. A rutty lane was the orchard's only approach, and on a certain Sunday evening in May, there would be more traffic along that lane than in all the other days of the year put together. Slowly, as befitted the day and the clothes we wore, we went to see the cherry-trees in bloom. Every now and then we would pause in the lane, for no reason that a child could discover, or irritatingly hold up the journey by gathering in little knots as we came upon friends and neighbours, chattering and laughing as if this and not the cherry-blossom were the reason for our walk.

Then at last we arrived at Mr. Champion's orchard. Other orchards in plenty had been passed on the way—and duly admired, or criticised—but this was the orchard we had come to see. For a while, as we stood looking at the blinding mass of bloom, words failed us: little clicks of the tongue, and oh's and ah's, were apparently the only vocabulary we could find whereby to express our amazement. For amazed we certainly were. It did not matter that last year (and as many years before that as anybody could remember) the orchard had looked much the same, and would, in all probability, look much the same again next year: the miracle never failed to stir us to the same intensity of wonder. At length, oh's and ah's would give place to a more precise approval; or, to be more exact, the women would lapse into domestic chatter again while the men drew nearer the trees and appraised them with all the countryman's critical concern for crops that are the mainstay of his life.

Of course, I knew that orchard at other seasons of the year: in autumn, for instance, when each tree vied with the spindle-berry bushes for variety and delicacy of colour, and we came shuffling along under the walnut-tree avenue that ran through the middle of it, picking up the wet, bruised nuts that had been bashed off the trees; in winter, too, when the lichened twigs and branches were snapped off by the winds and women came with prams and push-carts that creaked and were ever on the verge of complete dissolution, to gather kindling; and in summer, when the pickers shook their ladders into secure positions against the trees and buried themselves among the rustling leaves, till only the occasional sound of their voices betrayed where they were busy filling their baskets with the ripened fruit. But it was in spring, when the trees were in bloom and we all took our Sunday walk to admire them, that the orchard became for me a vivid, sensuous experience. I stood in among the trees, and the brightness of the clustered flowers was almost explosive in its intensity. I heard the lambs crying out against a background of insistent bee-harmony. And all the while I could smell the honeyed scent of the cherry-blossom as the wind stirred among the cooling leaves. Truly I can say Mr. Champion's cherry-orchard got into my blood. There will never be another cherry-orchard, or orchard of any kind, to compare with it. That is why, I suppose, there always seems to me something lacking to-day when I see an orchard where there is no grass underneath the trees, no lambs playing, no ewes calling.

And that is also why, I suppose, whenever I left my

28   A SHROPSHIRE LANE IN SPRING

29   KENTISH CHERRY ORCHARDS

30   AN APPLE ORCHARD NEAR CORYTON, DEVON

31   AN APPLE ORCHARD NEAR BRADFORD, SOMERSET

Cotswold look-out to go down into the valley to relish again the living experience of orchards in bloom, I mostly preferred to cross over the Severn and make my way into Herefordshire; for Mr. Champion's orchard, like most of the orchards in the Medway Valley, was close to hop-gardens—and there are hop-gardens cheek by jowl with the orchards of Herefordshire. I liked to see the white kilns of the oast-houses pointing a straight finger above the trees and to pass on the road lorries loaded with great balls of tarred twine ready for tying the hops. Those kilns called to mind the happy days before most hop-drying was done by electricity—memories of the mysterious dark interiors of oast-houses at night, lit only by the light of hurricane-lamps, with men in red woollen caps moving about among the rustling, pungent heaps of hops and other dim, Rembrandt-esque figures stoking the furnaces down below. And those lorry-loads of yarn called to mind one of the hop-garden activities which familiarity could never make less attractive to a boy—the wiring and stringing of the hop-poles by men who nonchalantly strode down the muddy alleys on stilts. Children do not seem to like playing with stilts nowadays, but I know that to look over the tops of walls and hedges from the precarious height of a pair of stilts was considered with us the peak of enjoyment (and no mean achievement, either) and it may well have been that at least some of our enthusiasm was due to a familiarity with the sight of farm-hands walking about on stilts in the hop-gardens.

There was one rural activity, however, which, though common enough in Herefordshire, was unknown to us in Kent. Not until I moved west did I begin to savour any of the pleasures of the cider and perry "industry." Herefordshire and Monmouth, Somerset and Devon, these are the great centres of this ancient activity. To see it still being practised with some at least of its primitive poetry, the search should be confined to the smaller farms: otherwise to-day it is mostly a matter of trim apple-trees in martial rows, up-to-date factories, and all the paraphernalia of an accurately organised trade. This latter method has its obvious advantages and I am far from decrying the judicious introduction of science into the ancient practices of husbandry; nevertheless, there is a certain poetry about the processes of a wooden cider-mill, with farm-hands turning the cumbersome winches and the clear juice oozing out of the "cheeses," that is inevitably lacking from the routine of a rigorously organised factory. When mists began to trail thin, lawny scarves about the valley orchards, and scarlet blotches stain the branches of the pear-trees, there is something prodigal and very close to the spirit of autumn in the sight of rosy, bruised apples lying in careless pyramids on the grass, waiting to be carted down the lane to the nearest mill. I know of one valley village in the West Country where the cider-press is housed in an old barn in the village street; and throughout the shortening days carts come rumbling in from the outlying farms and small holdings, loaded with apples and pears, and even the garden windfalls are brought along by women and children in any old bucket or basket. If the farmer should happen to be too busy by day on some other job, he can be seen working on the winch at night, while a couple of guttering candles fling long shadows over the walls. The smell of the fermenting fruit fills the village street—a happy reminder of the cups that will cheer the haymakers in the valley-meadows next June.

The men of Devon and Somerset drink cider as the men of the eastern counties drink beer or as the Latins drink wine; and it is characteristic that those little oaken barrels which, until glass bottles ushered in a skimpier age, were taken by the men into the fields, should be called cider-kegs in the west and harvest-bottles in the

east. Corn-harvesting is hot and heavy work in comparison with fruit-picking, or indeed with any work in
the orchards or meadows; and beer is the drink for
thirsty men. An East Anglian harvest-bottle held as
much as nine and ten pints, and this was in addition to
the quantities of small beer provided by the farmer.
They drank well, and worked well, in those days—and
do not seem to have been unduly tired at the end of a
heavy day. "I'm not so very old myself," as one farm-
hand said to me recently, praising the quality of beer in
earlier times; "but I can remember when, after a long
day's work with the scythes, the men would come home
at night singing." As for the harvest-bottles themselves,
and the cider-kegs, work of craftsmen whose pride in
their job was matched by the esteem with which they
were held in the life of the village community, they are
now mainly relegated to the dreary status of museum-
pieces.

Hops for beer and apples for cider—but there were
valleys beyond the hills that enclosed my Cotswold view
where neither of these activities played any substantial
part. In a sense it may be said that all the great rivers of
the West radiated inland from the area enclosed within
the extreme limits of that view; and the Wye to the west,
the Avon to the north, and the Thames to the east, no
less than the Severn, each contributed its share to the
enlargement of my river-sense. Particularly was this true
of the Wye—surely the loveliest river in England. From
Chepstow up to Tintern, the dull castellated rocks tower
above the winding water and still carry near the summit
the intermittently decipherable remains of Offa's Dyke.
But such grandiosity, though beloved of coach-tours,
especially when autumn "tints" add to the general entice-
ment, is not after all very typical of this country's river
scenery; and I for one prefer the Wye in its less spectacular reaches. There is, for instance, an incomparable

stretch of the river between Monmouth and Ross. The broken walls of Tintern Abbey, undeniably appealing, particularly when seen from the opposite hill of St. Anne's or when blocked against the setting sun, have been left behind; and just before entering Monmouth, where the main road to Ross crosses over the river you take the path through the water-meadows to Symonds Yat. To have walked that river-path in early spring, when the willows glisten with their rising sap and a pale fire of primroses runs along the banks under the hedges, is to have enjoyed some of England's lowland scenery at its best. On one side of the river is the railway and on the other the main road to Ross, but neither is busy or near enough to be a nuisance. Occasionally a swan drifts by with the tide, indolently regal, or a silent angler fishes in mid-stream. If it is solitude you like on such a walk, you will not find yourself disturbed at this time of the year by the happy crowds that later converge on Symonds Yat from the towns of the Midlands like a hosting of the starlings. Even the ferry that should carry you across the river may have to be shouted for; or, if you are lucky, and one of the infrequent trains is due, you may find youself being oared across by a railway-porter ferrying himself to work in his own boat.

Ruined castles and historic remains are as integral to the valleys of the Welsh Marches as vineyards to the upper reaches of the Rhine; and so it will not surprise you, when you have climbed the Rock and descended between roadside banks of celandines and white violets to where the Wye makes one of its most imposing detours, to find an angelus turret incongrously sur-mounting a group of farm-buildings. Crossing the fields for a closer investigation, you discover a chapel con-verted into a barn, with untidy slats nailed over the unglazed windows, pigs snuffling in their straw at one end of it, and a smoking midden heaped against its main

32 THE RIVER WYE NEAR BRIDGE SOLLARS, HEREFORDSHIRE

33   A WEST DEVON VALLEY NEAR LIDDATON

entrance. Well, farming is presumably more important, even in this country, than the preservation of ancient monuments; and if this crumbling chapel should disturb you, there is balm not far away at Goodrich Castle, where an efficient Office of Works is endeavouring to secure from further decay one of the most formidable keeps that ever rose out of rock-hewn moat for the protection of its chance-appointed owner.

Herefordshire, in common with the neighbouring counties of Shropshire and Worcestershire, excels in those black-and-white houses which were one of the strongest contrasts when we left the Cotswolds to go down to the Severn Valley; and although the Valley of the Wye is not perhaps the most favourable region for seeing them, there is one stretch of country towards the Radnorshire border where they are not only plentiful but often of a particularly startling magpie variety. "Glory be to God for dappled things," sang Gerard Manley Hopkins; but his catalogue of "pied beauty" omitted the timber and plaster architecture of those western counties which he knew so well. Weobley and Pembridge, whose close array of black-beamed, white-plastered houses is almost blinding when seen on a hot summer's day, are well away from the Wye; but there are isolated and none the less lovely examples to be found almost anywhere in the countryside round about Eardisley. John Abel, whose neglected tomb, decorated with scarcely decipherable representations of adze and compass and other builders' implements, stands in the flowery churchyard of Sarnesfield, erected several of the largest and best of these marvellously ornate Tudor houses; but it was James Brydges who, in 1589, erected what is perhaps one of the most attractive of them all. It is true that "The Ley," like that chapel-barn down by Goodrich Castle, has dwindled to a less stately usage than its builder and original owner intended. The decorated manor-house of yesterday has become the somewhat dilapidated farm-house of to-day; and its tenant-farmer, being much more concerned with the problems of ill-favoured agriculture than with the aesthetic appreciation of old and historic buildings, cannot for the life of him understand why anybody should bother to come out of their way to see his house. Its splendid exterior carving, its elaborate pargetting, its ample, mullioned windows and plentiful display of bleached oak all tell of a rural, domestic prodigality long since forgotten. Nevertheless, I cannot help thinking "The Ley" might easily have come to a sadder pass than it has: better the present homely usage, surely, with lace curtains in the windows and cabbages in the front garden, children's voices in the scantily furnished rooms and the lowing of cattle in the yard, than a prim relic preserved for the chatter of parrot-like guides?

Mostly these half-timbered houses are roofed with tiles: all the same, thatch is the characteristic roofing of the lowland West Country. Nothing could suit better with the valley contours; but although thatch is chiefly admired by the urban visitor for its picturesqueness, it is its utility that appeals to those who live under its shelter. Thatch is cool in summer and warm in winter. For all its advantages, however, it is to be feared that thatching is to-day a slowly dying craft. Most crafts are handed down from father to son, but nowadays the sons are all going into the towns. This is the present state of thatching no less than of the other country crafts. But there is another factor operating in the decay of this useful and ornamental work, namely, the inferior quality of the straw now obtainable. I dare say something of the thatchers' complaints is due to that ingrained prejudice which (not always unwisely) old country craftsmen and farm-hands still persist in showing when confronted with modern methods. I have in mind an old thatcher

who put the case to me a little while back. As he laid
the little bundles of straw (yealms) in place, combing
them and pinning them down with spraddles of hazel
and elm, he complained to me of the quality of the straw
he was compelled to use nowadays. "It's the binders,"
he said; "they don't cut the straw close like the scythes
did and they snap and crack it about till it's next to no
use at all. Straw was a lot longer then. Yes, and what's
more, it wasn't as brittle as the stuff I have to use now.
Them chemical manures are all to blame for that." The
justness of his second criticism is doubtful but there is
plenty of sense in his first. Although thatching is a
dying craft, there are still plenty of good thatchers in the
valleys to whom a neatly laid roof, decorated according
to his simple fancy on ridge and gable, is a source of
quiet pride to himself and of lasting pleasure to the
observer. Most villagers when they die have their
memorials in the fields and lanes where they worked
rather than in the churchyards where they are buried,
and a thatcher's memorial (since a good thatch will last
the best part of a lifetime) endures longer than most.
"That was one of old Nat Weller's thatches," will be said
long after he is dead; "he was one of the best thatchers
for miles around."

And so the Severn, occupying the forefront of the
view from my Cotswold cottage, was necessarily the
river that monopolised my immediate attention, with the
Wye, the Thames and the Avon beyond. Now it is one
of the surprising features about our English valleys that,
although one may be separated from the other by no
more than a moderate ridge of hills and both may enjoy
identical climates, each has a distinct character of its
own. The Avon, which joins the Severn at the altogether attractive little town of Tewkesbury, is a case in
point. "The silver Avon" is a favourite description of
this river; and if you would see how applicable, for once,

69

such a generalising adjective can be, you should climb to the top of Bredon Hill and look down from its western slope on to the villages south of Pershore, each threaded like a bead on a silver string. Bredon Hill stands islanded in the great Vale of Evesham, and in spring the plum- and damson-trees foam beneath you like a threshed sea. That is the popular time for visiting this handy vantage-point; but the view is almost equally dramatic, though in quite a different way, if you climb the hill one late afternoon during a severe bout of delayed frosts. Anxious farmers, to whom these few days, or, rather, nights, may mean the whole difference between profit and loss, have lighted smoke-pots and "smudge-fires" and bonfires down the open tracks of their orchards in the hope of warding off the disastrous frosts. Sparks and wayward flames flicker in the dusk, and the valley seems to be smouldering and about to burst into flame.

For the student, too, no less than for the observer, there is a unique attraction in the Vale of Evesham, since it seems as if here at last is one solution to the modern problem of a decaying farm-industry. Almost every kind of market-garden produce thrives in these fields beyond Tewkesbury, from onions to lettuces, from celery to brussels sprouts—and particularly brussels sprouts. On the very coldest winter mornings, when the east wind cuts like a knife, men and women with improvised aprons of sacking tied over their coats may be seen stripping the frozen sprouts from the stalks, while others bundle them into bags made of netting and load the waiting lorries. Mainly the Vale is worked on a competent system of small holdings that range from five to as much as fifty acres apiece. The families that run the holdings are largely self-sufficient. Only at fruit-picking time, and pea-picking, is this admirable community intruded upon by an influx of strangers from the surrounding towns and villages. Then the fields that have been so quiet all the rest of the year are filled with the chatter of women and the cries of children—much as in September the silent hop-gardens of Kent are suddenly filled with Cockney voices happy in their new-found freedom, calling to one another down the long alleys and teaching the country pickers the latest songs from town. In the Vale, however, only a comparatively few camp on the spot, the others being taken to and from their homes in buses and lorries.

Such, then, are some of the characteristics of landscapes and occupation in the valleys; but I have left till the end perhaps the most outstanding characteristic of all. To the foreigner's eye our English hedges are one of the most wasteful aspects of our prodigal methods of husbandry. Think, our foreign critics say, of all the cultivable land you thereby waste! Wasteful our hedges may be; but it is no less true that England would lose one of her loveliest features if they were done away with. And, after all, as Robert Frost says, "something must be left to God." From those spring days when they are decorated with the green rosettes of the hawthorn ("bread-and-cheese," as the children call them) and offer a convenient nesting-place to countless birds; through the summer days when they are laced with the bloom of wild parsley and jack-in-the-hedge and the starry stich-wort; on to those autumn days when they flame with hedge-maple and smoke with the silky seeds of Traveller's Joy—the English hedgerows are a wastefulness we should do ill to amend. To realise how essential they are to our most typical landscape, it is only necessary to travel from one side of the country to the other, from west to east, where the fields of arable are divided from one another by bare baulks, and hedges as the West Countryman knows them are almost non-existent.

9

Long may the valley farmer allow his land the largess of its hedgerows; and where there are hedgerows there will always be the familiar sight of the aproned hedger with his bill-hook and axe. Brother to the dry-stone waller up on the wolds is this hedger down by the river, but in what a different world he lives and works! Whereas the dry-stone waller will probably have to work for days on end with only the larks in the wide skies above him for company, the hedger in the lowland lanes will have every passer-by for company. Not that he will necessarily cease work whenever somebody stops to pass the time of day with him; all the while he is talking, his eye will be expertly assessing the hedge upon which he is engaged, choosing which branches to cut for stakes, or how best to fill up the gaps. An axe for chopping the stouter branches and a bill-hook for hacking away the brushwood, and perhaps a hooked stick for clearing away the undergrowth—these are his simple tools. With his gloved hands he layers the chosen boughs, all but severing them at their base, with only just enough wood left for the sap to flow through, then securing them to the upright stakes and neatly "feathering" the top. It looks a simple enough job; but for all that a hedger will have as much pride in his hedges (and be as critical of his neighbour's) as a thatcher is of his own and his rival's thatches—and both are eminently characteristic of our valley and orchard landscape.

34 A CORNISH COMBE: CRACKINGTON

THE FOOT OF THE SOUTH DOWNS NEAR FIRLE, SUSSEX

H. J. Massingham

THE DOWNS

I

WHEN Gilbert White compared the Downs with "a chain of majestic mountains," he was recollecting the country about Ringmer and Lewes, and his figure would not have been anything like so applicable to any other downland region of England except that narrow limb between Butser and Bow Hill, the gate into Hampshire, and Beachy Head. These are the legitimate South Downs, the over-written and exploited range that should be considered not as the archetype of downland country but simply as the extremity of the southern extension of the chalk-mass that occupies three-fifths of Wiltshire. The distinguishing characteristics of the South Downs are markedly distinct from those of Wessex. Their elevation is on the whole lower and their appearance less wild; they are more uniform, and their eastern and western portions are fairly evenly divided at Chanctonbury where the way towards the Seven Sisters is nearly all bare and towards Butser nearly all wooded. The roads and rivers—Lavant, Arun, Adur, Ouse and Cuckmere—

73

all slice through the Downs from north to south. Gilbert White's "chain" is thus a precise description of the physiography of the South Downs. Actually only two of the roads, both of them very ancient, run parallel with the natural flow of the range east and west, the one a green ribbon on the crest, the other, Underhill Lane, at its feet. The consequence is that the South Downs are not a rampart like the Berkshire Downs nor a magnified boss like the Wiltshire Downs, nor a dancing complex of ridges of easy amplitude like the Marlborough Downs, but rather a line of "uplandish" and elongated islands whose structural forms are best appreciated in the eastern region.

These are at their most beautiful and sculpturesque between Mount Caburn and the sea—dome, buttress, col, bay, promontory, combe, spur, shoulder and curving slope offering variations of outline and contour within a broadly simplified scheme whose purity is in no way compromised by their interplay. Blackcap Down above Plumpton, with its saddle of beeches and plume of pines, thus becomes a pivot for the eye from sweeps of many miles; the shapelessness of Ditchling Beacon is conspicuous from the serene and effortless mouldings of the Downs in its neighbourhood, while the configuration of the group—Firle, Windover, Wilmington—acquires an enhanced value from the flatness of the Cuckmere Valley to which they are anchored. Here is the quintessence of the Sussex downland. Here the Downs reach the grand style, but as a whole they are more to be regarded for their grace than for their grandeur in comparison with nobler but less classical shapes elsewhere.

The way to see them is from the foot of the northern scarp, not from the despoiled littoral strip on the south where the gradients are too long-drawn-out for strength of line and sharpness of impression. Nearly all the

artists miss the precision and confidence of this northern
waved barrier by smudging it and creating a woolly
effect in the attempt to achieve softness. They allow
the texture of the grassy surface, the light-winged play
of shadows over it and the curvilinear structure to
obscure its etched clarity. In the wooded area, the chief
treasure is the yew-forest of Kingly Bottom as seen
half-way down the slope of Bow Hill. I know of no
other part of Sussex, even Windover Hill, where the
sense of antiquity is so penetratingly distilled both from
the memorials of ancient man on the bald crown and the
tenebrous aisles of the rusty trees below. Here is true
wildness, austere and august, but not estranging.

The downland villages, those that have survived the
nutcrackers of Brighton and London, have happy local
mannerisms in the squat towers and shingled spires of
the churches, the tile-hanging, weather-boarding and
abundant use of half-timbering in combination with
flint and brick in the cottages and the charm of dollish-
ness. This is shared by the flora that, especially in
orchises, becomes scantier every year, though the blue
rampion still holds out. Apart from the monkeyishness
of tourists, this is largely due to the decline of sheep-
farming in recent years. That in its turn has rung the
knell of crook-making at Pyecombe, Falmer and Kings-
ton, and in generosity of line between barrel and "guide"
the Sussex crook was pre-eminent. The decline of hurdle-
making is a direct result of the diminished flocks of
Southdowns, and the succulence of Southdown mutton
was the work of the herbage as much as the virtue of the
sheep, but this velvety turf is reverting into ranker
growths. Though the ox-teams have gone, a few
wooden "turn-wrest" ploughs are still used in ploughing
the chalk of the foothills. Professional hand-weaving
is more flourishing in Sussex than in any other county.
The trug-basket of Hurstmonceaux, on the other hand,

is more properly a Wealden industry, as are coopering, rope-making and tanning from oak-bark, all of which have gone. Locksmiths, wheelwrights and underwood workers are also mostly of the Weald. The greatest down-land industry of all, the flint factory, in the number of which Sussex easily surpassed all other counties put to-gether, has been a "bygone" these fifteen hundred years.

If the Giant of Wilmington paid a visit to the Giant Helith, of Cerne Abbas, he would find himself in a New Found Land that at the same time kept on reminding him of his former home. The chalk of Dorset is more varied, more extensive, altogether wilder and grander, but, taken as a whole, less purely cretaceous than that of Sussex. Cranborne Chase, a border country between three counties, though mainly Dorset, is a rolling chalk plateau like that of Salisbury Plain but much com-promised by the greensand of the New Forest and the clays of Blackmore Vale. Borrowing all round, it yet remains one of the most individual tracts of country in England. It is heath, forest and down all in one and in unequal measure, very solitary, packed with memorials of the ancient dead including the Mizmaze on Braemore Down, primeval and less friendly to man than the dolphin backs of the long, thin Sussex line. It is more secretive than the open face of Salisbury Plain, more like Egdon Heath, and is a wilderness like it, not because its changing features bear any resemblance to the uniform wastes of Egdon, but because it belongs to the dead. The villages are mostly hidden in the border valleys and show decidedly less variety in the use of materials and ingenuity in combining them than the Wiltshire villages to the east. The way to see The Chase is either from Winkelbury above flinty Berwick St. John, where its junction with Salisbury Plain can be followed by the eye, and from Gussage Cow Down over against dark-mantled Pentridge. The long summit is a palimpsest

36 FIRLE BEACON IN THE SUSSEX DOWNS

37 TELSCOMBE VILLAGE, IN A HOLLOW OF THE SUSSEX DOWNS

and from its broad back scrawled over by our fore-fathers all this dark land can be surveyed, stained with darker woodland and lightened with seams and patches of soft green where the bare chalk has held its own.

The Stour is virtually the southern boundary of The Chase, but the high chalk sweeps the farther bank in a series of headlands crowned with green citadels, while the gateway to the range that is the midrib of Dorset from east to west, are the mighty portals of Hod and Hambledon. Westward the change is from plateau to lofty ridge, not melodious with flowing lines as in North Wiltshire but broken in continuity, shaggy with vegetation, more abrupt in contour than is the true habit of the chalk, irregular in course and growing more and more restless in expression. Nevertheless, this difficult line of downs from Shaftesbury, once Paladore, to Beaminster excels in sudden magnificences not to be rivalled anywhere else among the chalk ramparts of England. The glorious half-moon of smooth green heights south and south-east of Shaston, Monks Down, Win Green, Melbury Bubb, Fontmell Down, Sutton Hill and Hambledon, are downland at its loftiest inspiration, its noblest composition of forms, its ultimate of majesty. The same epic characters manifest themselves in the gliding lines of the "protuberances," as Gilbert White would say, flanking the upland hamlet of Ibberton, Woolland Hill and Bell Hill, with the sharp punctuation of Bulbarrow, covered in Tertiary scrub, to the south.

Then by way of Cerne Abbas, Sydling St. Nicholas, the sweet of the downland villages of Dorset, and Maiden Newton, the Downs make their great sickle curve that embraces Dorchester. The imperious height of Eggardun is the keystone, and looks across to Pilsdon Pen that opens the tumbled highlands crossing the Devon border beyond Beaminster "that bist abound wi' green an' woody hills all round." Now the downland returns upon itself, recovers its classic proportions and forms part of the cliff-line that along its eastern extremity of Ballard Down by Swanage runs parallel with the Purbeck range. The purity and unencumbered spaciousness of this southern littoral, offset by the powerful contrasts of other rock-formations sharing the end of the land with it, make this paramount among all the high adventures of the chalk.

The more individual rural industries of Dorset—reed-drawing for the lovely craft of Dorset thatch, and the making of Blue Vinny cheese—lie just off the chalk, namely, in the neighbourhood of Bridport, where rick-thatching also has local peculiarity.

Though The Chase overlaps into Hampshire and extensive outcrops of chalk heave out of the Tertiary crust slabbed or smeared over the rest of the county, its northern and southern ranges are long arms pushed out from the central mass of Wiltshire. Both reach east to the sea, the one as the North Downs from Farnham to Dover, the other as the South Downs from Butser. These are the forearms; the upper arms as far as the shoulders of Salisbury Plain are the only important Downs of Hampshire. All over downland, this particular conformation of a central core throwing out spurs in various directions is repeated in little. Bow Hill on the Hampshire–Sussex border may be called an epitome of the entire chalk physiography between Eggardun and Dover, Eastbourne and The Wash. The northern ridge of Hampshire is only articulate to the eye as far as Basingstoke where it founders under clay and greensand until it picks up again as the causeway of the Hog's Back and broadens out between Box Hill and Epsom. Beyond Epsom to the sea, the North Downs are cloaked with woodland because of the layer of clay-with-flints superimposed upon them. Consequently, chalk as a building material plays a lesser and

38 THE LINE OF THE PURBECK DOWNS FROM CORFE CASTLE, DORSET

29 WINTER IN THE WILTSHIRE DOWNS

timber and brick a greater part in the architecture of
Kentish villages than among the open downs of Hampshire, Wiltshire and Sussex; and even along the "Saxon
shore," where flint walls occur frequently enough,
Kentish cob and rag (a local sandstone) share equally
with the proper materials of the chalk.

This northern limb extended across three counties
hardly ever reaches grandeur except for a few miles east
from where it joins the Wiltshire trunk. Here on Chute
Common, at Inkpen and at Ladle Hill, the grand primeval
chalk bursts out naked from the furry mantle of the
Hampshire woodlands, once continuous with the
Wealden forests of Anderida Silva to the east. These
high dramatic moments (I refuse to consider Inkpen as
Berkshire's in spite of modern cartographic busybodies)
have an especial value and fervour from the extreme
beauty not only of the Downs but of the woodlands,
tender in spring, polychromatic in autumn, through
which the great ridge plunges like Leviathan. From the
Roman road of Chute Causeway, poised over the steep
green gully of Hippenscombe and Haydon Hill, the eye
maps out all the South from the Chilterns to the Isle of
Wight (eighty miles) and from Butser to The Chase.
At the same time the chalky lanes between Tangley,
Chute, Tidcombe and Buttermere reveal the most
intimate downland in England. Leaving out of account
the splendours of the Dorset chalk, I regard this country,
happily neglected and quite unspoiled, as the chief
loveliness of English chalk. All this country, so finely
varied but orderly in structure, and the woven carpet of
the Kennet Valley below it, was up to a few years ago a
centre for the wooding crafts. Nearly all of them have
vanished and the holdings of the woodmen have reverted
to wilderness. Flint architecture, especially in the barns,
is well represented at Faccombe, Buttermere, Vernham
Dean, Linkenholt, Litchfield and elsewhere.

10

Though not quite on the border of Salisbury Plain, the commanding, beech-capped mount of Quarley, on whose slopes juniper, the one indigenous tree of the chalk, grows in dark profusion, is the real jumping-off point for the adventure of Hampshire's southern range. The swinging highlands from Old Sarum to Ladle Hill and from Cranbourne Chase to the packing of the hills round the Sussex border are visible from it. Danebury, the cirque of hills round Stockbridge, where the Test winds like an old pastoral tale, and a complex of ancient ways and guiding groves of yew are the prelude to the old Belgic township on St. Catherine's Hill above Winchester. Farther east, the Downs tend to be expressionless until they begin to sweep in a half-moon round the once "Happy Valley" of the Meon that is rapidly being denatured. Quarley and Butser, that end-stops this grand crescent, are the gateposts at each end of this southern ridge. Yet strictly speaking, Hampshire is nearly as cretaceous as Wiltshire.

Wiltshire, being the core, butt, node or navel of all the chalk in England, shall have but cursory handling here, since the theme is too large to be treated except in shorthand or at large. There are two Wiltshire Down-lands, Salisbury Plain south of and the Marlborough Downs north of Pewsey Vale, the cloven path between a stormy and a spread, quiet sea. The Plain humps as at Bratton, Yarnbury, Battlesbury and Sidbury; it erupts into the pustules of the military encampments; it is deeply scored by the five river valleys whose waters meet at Salisbury; it is tufted by the Great Ridge and Grovelly Woods that sprout from the Tertiary daubs over the chalk, and it streams out into fjords like the south-western spurs (particularly the watershed between the Nadder and Ebble Rivers) to White Sheet Hill, Winkel-bury and the five Deverhills. But essentially it is a calm, green, gently heaving ocean once bristling with a

million sails of pasturing sheep. Most of the turf is now
bankrupt where it is not developed, because the sheep
have all but gone.

The northern Downs are totally different. They, too,
are a sight for Cortez, but here the land is scooped out
into long swells with shallow sliding troughs and folds
between them. The queer thing is that Avebury is still
the capital of North Wiltshire as Stonehenge is of South.
The villages mostly hide; visible modern works make
ugly faces and only this pair, the first of man's thoughts
on the surface of the chalk, rest seaworthily upon the
surge of verdant miles. From Barbury to Avebury along
the Great Ridgeway and from Avebury to the Calne
woodlands, the rolling ridges swing their way, lonely as
the clouds, rounding into bluffs like Martinsell, Sugar
Hill and Walker's Hill, buttressed by flying tongues of
turf, dipping and careening in endless intricacy of slope
and crest.

On the Wiltshire Downs, thatch has been extensively
used from the era of pit-dwellings and Celtic villages up
to the other day. "Clunch" (or the harder, deeper
blocks of chalk) has almost as long a pedigree from the
ramparts of Celtic townships to cottage walls that still
survive. Sarsen stone, left by the palaeozoic seas on the
surface of the Downs, has made not only temples,
dolmens and the corridors of long barrows but came in
handy for village architecture 1,500 years later, not to
mention the walls of churches like Winterbourne
Bassett and Berwick Bassett. Wiltshiremen also made
use of brick (from the clay smears), pudding stone and
rounded nodules and angled nuggets of flint, and this
medley of materials was finely combined and patterned
on many a Wiltshire home when local life was a reality.

Berkshire chalk covers a long but not very broad
stretch of country eastward from Richard Jefferies's Lid-
dington Hill as far as Windsor. But only the sculptured

block between Ashbury and Streatley, where the
Great Ridgeway from Avebury joins the Icknield Way
from the Chilterns' foothills, is of pre-eminent value as
landscape. This great solid carved in the round is
hardly distinguishable from the Marlborough Downs
close to the border between them, and yet the Berkshire
Downs, like those of every other county where downland runs, have their own distinctive idiom. In structure,
they are the simplest and most massive of all; their line
is the levellest (in spite of Uffington Hill) and the cleanest
in downland; their concavities are on the whole shallower
than elsewhere, and they possess only one river-valley,
the Vale of Lambourn, much less deep than those of
Salisbury Plain, while upland villages are very few.
The villages congregate on the much lower plateau
south of the Thames basin, an arable country and under
the lofty scarp near the Wiltshire border. These last are
of special interest because, while calling upon the customary downland materials, particularly sarsen, they
show definite influence from the Cotswolds across White
Horse Vale. The tableland group between Blewbury
and the Sinodun Hills are much more lavish in the use
of flint than is Ashbury and its satellites.

The right ways to see the Berkshire Downs are to
travel the Great Ridgeway (probably Early Bronze Age
in origin) as far as Streatley on their crest and the Port
Way (probably Celtic in origin) right under their knees.
As in Sussex, the southern slopes are too gradual for
bold effects. From the Ridgeway, the heavenly bodies
seem nearer to earth than in the spreading Vale. From
the Port Way, the sight is caught by the sheer magnitude
of the ridge, its aloofness, the delicate plasticity of its
moulding and subtlety of texture. The gods once strode
it. Between Lambourn and the Ridgeway is a natural
amphitheatre, a sacred place of the ancient dead, and still
sacred if for the lines of its beauty alone.

40   PLOUGHLANDS ON SALISBURY PLAIN

41 SUMMER AT WINTER HILL IN THE BERKSHIRE DOWNS

Across the Thames at Streatley, the Chilterns take up the running in a slight bend to the north-east, assuming their own individual dress and form about Ewelme. Here again downland reveals a geographical variation in deference to the spirit of locality. The Chilterns have their dialect too, expressed not only by a prodigality of beech-woods but by gathering up in miniature the special features of chalk landscape. Combe, headland, arc, spur, fold, scarp-line, common, juniper-studded slope are all here but reduced in scale. These childlike characteristics are best appreciated in the extreme south-west of the range. It is a toy stage of essential downland. Some of the villages are admirable—Turville, for instance, only a hamlet but with no one house like another, and drawing upon nearly all the downland materials in its tiny compass. It becomes a composite unity from the position and weight of the squat flint church-tower, whose heaviness is relieved by the display of whitened eighteenth-century Gothic windows in the cottages. The Norman two-gabled tower of Fingest is unique. On this Lilliput, it is hard to believe that the Chilterns are in parts thirty miles broad.

Beyond Dunstable, a piece of true downland scarp, the range becomes a low plateau from Hitchin and Baldock to Newmarket. Striping East Anglia, the chalk is an indeterminate col washed on either side by the boulder clays of the Ice Age, and halts at the West Norfolk Heights at Hunstanton on the Wash. Of the starfish whose body is Wiltshire this is the longest limb of all. It picks up again still farther north as the Lincolnshire Wolds, still a neck of low elevation, and finally reaches Flamborough Head across the Humber. But from Dunstable onwards its downland style is fitful and much adulterated.

The more surprising, therefore, is it to find East Anglia richer in flint architecture even than Wiltshire. The "flush-work" or geometrical flint patterning or chequer-work between freestone panels on the towers and plinths of church after church between Norwich and the sea, and in some of the public buildings of Norwich itself, is an exquisite local aptitude of the fifteenth century that has no parallel elsewhere. Nowhere, not even along the Kentish seaboard, are the flints squared with such perfection of native art.

II

There is only one specifically downland handicraft that to-day survives the wreck of craftsmanship at the Industrial Revolution and its slow foundering ever since. Hurdling is not a prerogative of the chalk, though once much practised on it, and the one turner left in Berkshire lives on Bucklebury Common, some miles off the Downs. But chair-leg "bodging" is an authentic industry of the Chilterns, and to the best of my knowledge is traditionally pursued nowhere else in all downland except among the highland beech-woods in the south-western corner of the range. I therefore propose to devote the second part of this chapter to a description of this highly skilled and individual craft.

Bodging is on its last legs: none of the present masters have apprentices, so that when the present little company of bodgers, all of them old or oldish men, have passed to the country churchyard, there will be none to take their places. Machinery is, of course, one reason for the decline, the production, that is to say, of chair-legs of inferior quality and design at a superior speed in the making. A machine-made chair-leg is at once betrayed by the stiffness of its appearance, shallow mouldings and lack of invention in the turnery. The scandalous rates of pay are a yet more potent cause for the imminent extinction of a craft that, persisting in the traditional designs, turns just as good chair-legs nowadays as are

42　THE WORMSLEY VALLEY IN THE CHILTERNS

43　A CHILTERN FARM NEAR WEST WYCOMBE

44 SHEEPSCOMBE, NEAR POYNINGS, UNDER THE SUSSEX DOWNS

coveted in seventeenth- and eighteenth-century examples of gate-leg and other tables. A bodger working ten hours a day for six days on end can only make thirty shillings a week, and it is evident that the only reasons why the bodgers that still tread the lathe on the hills do not desert to the High Wycombe factories, where they could easily secure more highly paid jobs, are partly the inborn conservatism of all rural crafts and partly their love for their free and satisfying work in its natural environment.

What wonder? The setting of these craftsmen's homes is as romantic as it well could be. One of them lives among the hanging cherry-orchards of Stoke Row. The bodgers that use the primitive pole-lathe are most of them itinerant and pitch their temporary "hovels" among the aisles and in the leafy seclusion of the beech-woods. Another, Samuel Rockall of Turville Heath, who uses the treadle-lathe, has a flint cottage that looks directly out upon a common of furze, bracken and stunted groups of trees. In the Chilterns, the effect of grandeur and spaciousness is gained only when mist clouds the network of the tree-tops, half shrouds and half reveals the valleys, folds and bottoms, and suggests the illimitable by means of form and vegetation rather than by distance. When the mist ramparts Turville Heath, it appears as wild as a parcel of prehistoric England, as withdrawn from civilisation as the stage of a fairy story. The entrance to it is of an as unquestionable a greatness as could be found anywhere—a towering avenue of ancient beech, sycamore, oak and lime with far-spreading branches and massive boles, most curiously wrought. Some are like baroque columns in clusters, others are richly fluted and bossed with huge carved nodes whose callosities resemble Gothic ornament in the grotesque. The buttresses that support these great trunks have their feet, or rather talons, deep in vivid moss.

A little nearer the Fingest Valley, winding down in a series of advancing and retreating folds, lives another bodger, Mr. Bartlett. His house lies back along a lane almost impassable in winter. At its opening an embanked and circular pool is overhung by a giant oak whose lower branches vein the untroubled water. A thousand trees are marshalled on the farther bank, and under them the wild snowdrops chastely announce the riot of spring. It is right that this seclusion and privacy should encompass the ancient craft, since only by lack of contact with the world has it endured and maintained its hold upon the tradition that keeps it ever fresh and new. These natural presences are the forms of that past which mothered all such crafts and still protects the immemorial woodmen from falling victim to the machine.

The one that I know best is Samuel Rockall, and I can see him now in memory's eye toiling up the steep on a veiled winter's day at the head of two wagons loaded with the timber he had just cut for his trade. In the misted landscape, his blue eyes, flushed cheeks and reddish hair were the only colours of the scene. An artist might have drawn him thus, but he would have left out his representative significance. The true craftsman controls and executes all the processes of his craft from the raw originals to the finished product, no matter how many they be. He is thus divided by a cleavage absolute from the one-man-one-bolt system of modern minutely subdivided industry. That is why the rural master-man remains by the law of his being close to nature. He is not merely surrounded by nature; he not only takes his tools and materials from nature, but he repeats the ordered unfoldings of nature from the seed to the flower, from the grain to the ear, from alpha to omega. This is the secret of good craftsmanship and the condition of its blossoming, that the man shall take the fruits of the earth from the hands of nature, and with his

own hands transform them into the final form he destines
for them, to be at once useful for the needs of his fellows
and pleasurable to their eyes. From mast to tree: it is
the same thing over again but on a new turn of the spiral
of creation. Samuel Rockall buys and axes his own
trees where they stand in the woodland, and so his craft
is organic. He conducts all the operations from the tree
in the forest to the chair by the fire, and like a magician
wills nature to come out of the weather into the home.

The timbers are unloaded in front of his hovel, sawn
by him into lengths and stacked in the smaller room
made by the partition. The larger room in the hovel is
so deep in shavings that the foot makes no sound, and is
so crowded with the instruments for converting logs
into legs that the eye is bewildered. Chopping-block
and splitting-block stand like islands in the ruffled lake
of shavings; shelves hold chisels of every shape and
edge; draw-knives hang on the walls; beetles, axes,
chair-legs and piles of logs lean against them, and the long
treadle-lathe occupies the whole of one end, with a little
wooden windmill by the great wheel to amuse the
children while the work is proceeding. This is one of
the toys that Rockall has made for his family when he
is not bodging, making chairs for special orders, bottling
fruit, grafting crab-apples, gardening, sharpening saws
and cobbling his children's boots. He is a living
embodiment of Blake's "Exuberance is all."

The first process in the workshop is to split up the
logs with a woodman's axe and a very heavy beetle, the
measurements being done by eye. The bodger then
moves on to the second block which stands higher for
the finer work of chopping, or rather stripping, the split
lengths ready for the draw-shave horse. He usually cuts
about forty trees in a course of fellings, and these, being
"thinnings" or timber cut to prevent overcrowding, do
more service in the preservation of the woodlands fallen

than standing. Once, as he chopped away, talking the whole time in his brisk, cheerful, birdlike manner, he told me the story of how he had obtained the chopping axe he was using, a broad, finely curved blade with edge of tempered steel and a handle short enough to be covered in the hand. He had found it buried in the woods years ago when he was felling trees, and he conjectured, by what divining powers I know not, that it had lain there for sixty or seventy years. Nevertheless, he put an edge on it again in two hours' work, for Samuel Rockall is a marked man in all the region for his prowess in putting an edge upon saw, chisel and axe. He thought he knew how this chopping axe had got hidden in the woods. In the old days, the bodgers used, as a respite from their arduous work, to set aside one day in the week for a drinking bout, since, as the master of a body of them was wont to say, "you work like hosses and drink like hasses." It was the custom, when a new-comer failed to stand the company a round, for the men to say, "Mother Shawney'll be after you," and, sure enough, Mother Shawney would for a time remove one of the novice's tools. The axe was hidden but, like the squirrel's booty, was never recovered.

The draw-shave horse is a long trestle with two crosspieces, the lower one the longer for the bodger to rest his feet. He seats himself upon it and fixes the rough chair-leg between the cross-pieces by a row of iron teeth fastened to each bar. He ties a "leather" to his chest and grasps the handles at right angles to the blade of the draw-knife, the right with the palm down and the left with the palm up. The action of the knife is upwards and sideways, so that the shavings hit the bodger's breast. The process by which the leg, shifted from one hollow between the teeth to another, is shaved and smoothed is incredibly swift and energetic, and, when half the leg is finished, he tosses the other half to him

45   THE NORTH DOWNS AT BOX HILL, SURREY

46 BLACKDOWN FROM HENLEY HILL, SUSSEX. NOTICE THE BODGER'S SHELTER IN THE FOREGROUND

in a second and is whittling off the slivers as quick as the eye can follow him. The sawing horse is a smaller trestle, between the forks of which the shaven leg is sawn according to what type of chair—and there are about a dozen variations upon the old wheel-back—and to whether it is to be leg, spindle, side- or front-stretcher. For measuring, he removes one out of the array of rectangular measuring-boards hanging on the wall.

There is still one more process to come before the consummation of turning the wood. The chisels have to be "sharped," the upright stands for holding the chair-leg to be adjusted, the right "rest" for the chisel has to be selected from those hanging by the lathe and a new "centre" fixed according to the kind of leg to be turned, all before the foot is pressed upon the treadle and the fly-wheel revolves.

The depths of the mouldings in the leg are regulated not only by the pressure of the chisel bevelled on both sides but by the pace of the treadle which stretches the whole length of the lathe. The revolutions are very rapid for the planing and shallower turning and slowed up for the deeper incisions. So like magic is the turnery —a triple ball-turning both concave and convex appearing with a suddenness that startles the eye—that the watcher is bound as by a spell. Spouts and ribbons of shavings stream off the revolving chair-leg in all manner of fantastic shapes, spiralling, twisting into coils, flying overhead and falling about the bodger's shoulders, or shooting out in little straight jets and gushes, as though the wood was not only animated but shedding one skin after another in a high state of tension. The impression is conveyed that this was the way that worlds were made, thrown off each in its spinning entirety from the Great Magician's rod. The bodger begins by marking the places to be turned and, immediately that the concentric ridges and grooves have been made in one of them, the surface is planed on either side. In this latter movement, a number of swiftly revolving rings encircle the leg, melting into one another towards one end of it or the other and these vanishing, insubstantial, madly whirling circles enhance the sense of a ferment of creation. The work as a whole is so rapid that a complete chair-leg manifests itself in about two minutes, perfectly finished and ready to take the seat of the chair. The automatic lathe, of course, revolves at an even greater speed, and by thus passing out of human control must produce the effect of mechanism upon the object turned. Where the human will is predominant throughout in the bodger's hovel, the observer becomes conscious of the subtle blending between the working out of traditional forms and the workman's independent skill and personal initiative. Each is ineffective without the co-operation of the other.

Samuel Rockall was happy to explain why he preferred the treadle- to the pole-lathe. The one advantage of the latter is that it is portable and so can accompany the wood-bodgers from one temporary hovel to another. It is similar in appearance to the treadle-lathe but is without the heavy fly-wheel whose office is served by the tapering and flexible pole of ash, willow or fir, about ten feet high, which with its butt fixed in the ground or a square opening in the shed reaches slant-wise over the top of the lathe. A slender cord is attached to the thin end and this is twisted singly round the chair-leg before it is fastened to the lathe. When set in motion, this contrivance turns the leg both ways by the winding and unwinding of the cord, and it is only on the inward turn towards the bodger that he applies his chisel to the wood. The fly-wheel, on the other hand, causes one-way revolutions so that the bodger has no need to pause in his turning. All the same, though he is thirteen years older than Samuel Rockall, who is over sixty years of age, the bodger at Stoke Row can turn a chair-leg on the pole-lathe just as expeditiously as Samuel himself. This man of metal turns the hardly credible number of three gross or four hundred and thirty-two chair-legs in a week, working fourteen hours a day with intervals for meals. Lest some orthodox trade-unionist should hap to read these words and go white with indignation, it should be gently pointed out to him that the bodgers have preferred the mastery of their time, their labour and their product to the modern desiderata of fixed hours and higher wages in a factory where the master-man is degraded to the servant who commands neither his time nor his labour nor his product. It was not only exploitation which made the demand for fixed hours of and higher wages for labour irresistible; it was the distastefulness of the work itself from which had been emptied the pleasure that independent creation alone can bring.

That this is not illusory is shown by the example of Samuel Rockall himself. He works all day long for a beggarly pittance as a return for an output of such superb workmanship that it cannot be distinguished except by the cleanness of the wood from the highly priced antique. He works so hard that his only recreation is a change of work. Notwithstanding that four persons have to live for seven days upon his thirty pieces of silver, he is one of the happiest men I have ever met, not only by temperament but because he is continually occupied upon things that are useful to others and beautiful in themselves, that are made out of the nature at his door and demand every ounce of his skill and experience. He has deliberately considered that these factors are more worth while to him than those that are prized by millions of urban workmen. Once, he found that he could not possibly make both ends meet and so took on an "improver's" job at High Wycombe behind the power-lathe. But he could only stand it for five months. He pined for the open free life, his variety of occupation and what may be termed his home-work. "I felt shut in," he said, "like a bird that's put in a cage." So he voluntarily went back to his smaller earnings, thus reversing in his own person the universal tendency of labour to flow from the country to the town. The same principle was at the back of his preference for the treadle- over the pole-lathe. Because the pole imparts a suspicion of "tremble" to the chair-leg, it is unable to accomplish such fine and varied turning as the treadle-lathe, and Samuel's ambition was to turn the finest chair-legs over all the Chilterns. So he discarded the pole for the flywheel, just as he abandoned the power-lathe of the town for the treadle-lathe of the deep, untroubled country.

Yet the shadow of a sigh stole into the brightness of his face when he showed me the grandfather clock that he and his brother had made with carving and ball-turning round the face after a Jacobean design. Beside the clock hung a bellows of better proportions than the one, a century old, beside the open fireplace. He had made this as well and chairs and toys and bobbins and many another handsome and serviceable object in oak, beech, walnut or laburnum wood, not to sell but to entertain his family and soften its economic asperities. His just perceptible sigh was not for them but that the odd moments of a lifetime had not been more frequent for him to indulge his creative bent outside the limits of bodging. Like all true masters he took great pride in his tools and had made several of them himself. Like many other old countrymen, he was a storehouse of reminiscence. Always busy, smiling, anecdotal, kindly, eager and absorbed, he seemed to point the moral that the only way to a happy life was to do and to be exactly the reverse of what our present culture or lack of it regards as desirable to that end.

Certainly the bodgers—and Samuel Rockall is not the

less representative of them because he is *primus inter pares* —are happy men. They are open, courteous in their independence, quiet and assured in the midst of their arduous labours and the rigours of their heavy, consistent output. They seem very old-fashioned because their peace is unknown to the age they live in, their content an anachronism. Like their once fellows in a thousand other crafts, they are master-men. They know their place in life, they are easy-natured, affable men because they are aloof, high up on their hills, from the stresses, strivings and self-defences of the valley. They work at incredible speed but they never hurry: they work much harder than any worker so much as knows the meaning of in modern industry, but they never complain of their long hours, even of the miserable return they get for them, because those hours are for ever varied, interesting and fruitful ones. They do not want to step into anyone else's shoes, so well-made and serviceable are their own. Modern industry menaces them and will devour their children, but their work is their castle and its domain the aisled woods within the rampart of the hills. Meeting all men on their own ground, they are secure even in the threat that is aimed at their very existence, and, when they die out, it will be with the satisfaction of having done well both by nature and by man.

Harry Batsford

HILLS AND WOLDS

THE Hills of England would seem at first sight a subject of immense extent, variety and fascination, in the pursuit of which one might find oneself ranging from the Cheviots to Cornwall, from the Lakes to Dover. But the exigencies of a thorough-paced classification have shorn us of most of the English uplands till only a small band remains. Space limits forbid the inclusion of the tangled mountain masses of Wales and Scotland, which would deserve most of a whole book to themselves. The greater part of the English higher ground—Pennines, Yorkshire moorland and Northumbrian ranges—consists rather of wide plateau-like tracts of upland cut into deep dales; hence it finds its place in the chapter on "Moors and Fells." The Lakes, the only real English mountains, are worthily dignified by a division to themselves, while the chalk hill-stretches are appropriately handed over to Mr. Massingham, so we are at a stroke bereft of all the country south-east of the line from Portland Bill to the Wash. It is at least a consolation that

47 THE RIDGELINE OF THE MALVERNS FROM HOLLYBUSH, WORCESTERSHIRE

48 DUMBLETON HILL FROM BREDON, WORCESTERSHIRE

if our company is small, it is also select, and we can aim at something more than an annotated list of ridges and summits.

Our province is a sickle-shaped curve round the Severn estuary, from Wales to Cornwall, including all the heights of the Welsh Marches, a great array; the Malverns, with the compact miniature ranges of the Mendips and Quantocks; and farther west, the heights of Devon and Cornwall.

We will take in our stride the gently rising Poldens above the Somerset fenlands, at some 250 feet surely the lowest in elevation of any independent chain of English hills. To this array are added, by way of complement and contrast, the Cotswolds, that characteristic upland lime-stone region which we have to pass on our way round.

Strictly speaking, Dartmoor, Exmoor and the Cornish Moorlands should also find a place in "Moors and Fells." But they are far removed from all the main massifs, which make up so much of northern England, and are, as it were, interjected, with marked nonconformity, into the most green and smiling country of England. Then, both Devon "Forests" are so linked up with an assortment of hill ranges, by physical nearness or geological relation-ship, that their dissociation is more than a surgical feat. Thus the Blackdowns make a separate miniature green-sand plateau, to which the Haldon ridge answers across the Exe estuary; the Brendons are an eastern extension of Exmoor, with Croydon Hill and Haddon Hill as outlying buttresses. Outliers also are the fine compact group of Bossington and Grabbist, just islanded by valley stretches; from them are visible across a dozen lower miles their cousins the Quantocks, whose features on a still smaller scale they faithfully reproduce. Hence, it is considered advisable, inevitable indeed, to treat the South-western Highlands as a whole in this chapter.

We cannot do better than begin by taking our stand
12*   95

on the Malvern Hills, which, with their line running like the Clees due north–south, mark abruptly the end of the Midland plain and the beginning of the hilly West Country that leads into Wales. Their graceful serrated line, a characteristic and unmistakable landmark, is seen on the western horizon from the north Cotswold ridge; from the Shropshire heights where we are to wander they fill in the end of the view, far off but clear to the south-east, backed by the faint level Cotswold line.

So we will follow the example of William Langland, poet visionary of *Piers Plowman*, some five and a half centuries ago:

In a summer season   when soft was the sun,
In rough cloth I robed me,   as I a shepherd were,
In habit like a hermit   in his works unholy,
And through the wide world   wonders to hear.
     I went,

But on a May morning,   on Malvern hills,
A marvel befel me   —sure from Faery it came—
I had wandered me weary,   so weary, I rested me
On a broad bank   by a merry-sounding burn;
And as I lay and leaned   and looked into the waters
I slumbered in a sleeping,   it rippled so merrily,
And I dreamed—marvellously.

But if the dreamer's physical presence was lifted high above a shaggy, scrubby, swampy Severn plain, his spirit was far from the wide-stretching rural scene, in the crowded streets of great cities, and he recked little of Masefield's

. . . croft and hop-yard, and hill and field and pond,
With Bredon Hill before me, and Malvern Hill beyond,
The hawthorn white i' the hedgerow, and all the spring attire
In the comely land of Teme and Lugg, and Clent, and Clee,
     and Wyre.

. . . covert and woodland, and ash and elm and oak,
Tewkesbury inns, and Malvern roofs, and Worcester chimney
   smoke,
The apple-trees in the orchard, the cattle in the byre,
And all the land from Ludlow town to Bredon church's spire,

for his soul was filled with the "fair field full of folk,"
high and humble, noble and debased, in all the tangled
strivings of their complex interactions. It is noteworthy
that the medieval folk do not seem to have attained that
appreciation of the outer aspect of the countryside which
we almost instinctively enjoy; they do not, as Mr.
Blunden plaintively laments, describe the country scene
by itself, just as it is suggested that rural dwellers anywhere are not landscape-conscious. Chaucer supplies
many delightful touches—the bright gladness of spring
when "the foulis sing," the tenderness of a pleasant
garden, but it is in some human connection. Langland
himself contributes such unforgettable pictures as the
wretched ploughman and the alehouse drunkard, and
both could, had it occurred to them, have pictured the
English country of their day with homely and graphic
vigour. Perhaps the landscape was for them the ordinary
everyday background holding no intrinsic beauty—its
familiarity required no record, just as it is hard to find a
contemporary description of a medieval church interior
or the roaring bustle of a fourteenth-century fair. Again,
it would be interesting to trace landscape in medieval
painting; the miniaturists have left us delightful examples
in their calendars, but here again the country is rather a
background to the human scene than a subject calling
for treatment for its own sake.

I. THE MALVERNS

So let us take a stand on the Malverns to see what they
have to proffer us in themselves, and as a preliminary to

exploration farther west. As you approach the chain from the east, the flanks stand up like a great green wall, of which large expanses in autumn show the deep bronze-red hues of turning bracken. Actually it would be an exhilarating experience to tramp the ridge along its 9–10 miles extent, from south to north, gently dipping and rising along the slightly curving crests at 1,000 to 1,500 feet. To the west the transition to the lower country is fairly gradual and masked by abundant woodlands, but on the eastern side the top is well over a thousand feet above the plain, which combines with the comparative flatness of the lower country to make up one of the most dramatic and tremendous scenes in the country. Few places so give the sense of being "high and lifted up" as the 1,444 feet of the Herefordshire Beacon. League upon league into the faint distance extends this vast expanse of the Severn and Avon vales, dotted with hamlets and copses, from which the Cotswold outliers, Bredon, Dumbleton and their fellows, stand up sharply, backed by the long line of the Wold escarpment itself. Westward, if less drastic, the prospect is more diversified, with a selection of many heights laid out, as it were, for display; there is no need to identify them, as we are about to visit them for ourselves, but the view ranges from the Dean Forest uplands to the Shropshire Clees and extends far into Wales to the Radnorshire massifs and the Black Mountains due westward. We can spare just a glance to north-east at the Clent and Lickey Hills over towards Birmingham, and in the reverse direction at the rounded dome of May Hill, with its scraggy tuft of trees. It is strange that instead of remaining lonely islands of upland, the Malverns have drawn to themselves a full swell of human tides, as they have attracted some 1,700 varieties of plants to their few square miles. The rail pierces them, main roads cross the notches or run along the flanks, and the chain of modernish settlements along

49 CORNDON HILL FROM LINLEY, SHROPSHIRE

50 EARLY SUMMER AT CLUN, SHROPSHIRE

the foot is not far off continuous, while Great Malvern clings to the slopes.

One may sigh for the days, some 120 years ago, when Great Malvern was a collection of some fifty houses. It is pleasantly and spaciously laid out with wide gardens and trees and areas of green, but the houses mostly date from the mid-nineteenth century, when the town enjoyed a boom as a spa. It is a real repository of mid-Victorian revived Gothic architecture, in every combination of stucco, coloured brick and austerity of stone, and many of the houses are of surprising size and height.

To the south-west runs parallel a sort of little cousin of the Malverns in the shape of the wooded ridge round Ledbury and Eastnor, and towards Hereford are the wooded Woolhope Hills in the form of a shepherd's crook, while the rather bare upland district round Bromyard fills the country between the north tip of the Malverns and the stretch of the Teme near Tenbury.

II. THE WELSH BORDER

A few years ago a railway guide-book characterised the stretch between Ludlow and Craven Arms with the remark: "Still travelling through an interesting farming country." Merciful Powers, the poor benighted scribe was utterly unaware that he was in the midst of the English Highlands! Certainly every topographical writer should have to undergo a compulsory course in Landscape Appreciation and pass a mild examination. Actually the Welsh Border forms perhaps the only real hill-country in England outside the Lakes, a miniature Scottish Highlands, fashioned of similar rock masses but far more green and smiling. So little is this appreciated, however, that to say you have been tramping in the Lakes occasions no remark, but if you report that you are just back from a tour in the Salop Highlands, people may look at you

queerly. From Shrewsbury to Leominster the country is
filled with smooth rounded whalebacks and long wooded
ridges, interspersed with hedge-chequered dales. It is not
a plateau region like Devon, where you must climb to
the upper level to get anywhere; the hills are more or
less distinct, and you can, if you like, run all over the place
as in West Ireland on roads below 500 feet. Naturally
there are hilly byways without end for the enterprising,
but the endless lovely views can only be enjoyed to the
full by getting to the top of the 1,500-foot ridges, and
only the weak or the sluggish will refrain from so
exhilarating a pastime. The region lends itself to any
form of exploration: motoring, walking, or rough-rider
cycling, as recommended by Mr. Thoresby Jones, along
the hundreds of ferny, flower-filled hill-lanes. Miss
Magdalene Weale scampered across hill and dale on
pony-back, and the literature of the English Country is
the richer for her tour. Anyway, the explorer is sure to
be rewarded, for in addition to the landscapes there are
fine rivers: the Severn flings itself around the whole
district in a vast sweeping arc; the Teme cuts across it,
with a little Dovedale at Hay Mill; and the Lugg can
show an equally fine gorge above Aymestrey. All
around are wide pastures, scattered woodlands and on
higher ground moorland stretches, which may present
an animated scene in early autumn with the lively crowds
of bilberry-gatherers with their baskets and tea-kettles.
And the countryside affords a changing scene all the
way from early spring, with massed primroses and bluebells and an occasional stretch of wild daffodils, to the
bronze and russet of the November oakwoods. Everywhere at all times there is a pervading atmosphere of
rural peace and a satisfying sense of deep seclusion.

It is impossible to attempt anything like a full or
systematic survey of this tangled hill country; but we get
a general idea of its lay-out by a circular sweep from a

sort of natural centre at old Stokesay Castle, by the
entrance to the great natural highway of Stretton Dale.
Immediately above us are the earthworks of Norton
Camp on a wooded outlier of Wenlock Edge, surely one
of the longest hill ridges in England, stretching for
fifteen miles in a double line without a break in that
south-west–north-east direction so characteristic of many
English hill-areas; it does not seem that any adequate
explanation of this lay-out is so far forthcoming.

In width Wenlock Edge tapers from two miles to one;
within that narrow band are packed two ranges of
different limestone—the first is continuous and fronts
the lower country with a sharp wooded escarpment;
behind it lies higher View Edge, cut into rounded humps
by the fretting of the streams at about every two miles.
The narrow hollow between holds two of the county's
most interesting houses—the medieval tower of Upper
Millichope and Wilderhope of the Smallmans, now a
youth hostel. Here Major Thomas Smallman, the
royalist hero of the well-known "Major's Leap" on
Wenlock Edge, just escaped capture by saddling his
horse and dashing off from the stables as a party of
Roundheads rode up to the front door. Westward across
the hedge-hemmed quilt of Ape Dale is the broken
upland stretch to the rear of Caradoc, the hogsback
which contrasts completely with the more massive Long
Mynd across Stretton Dale—both could not be more
ancient, both rise to within a few feet of the same height,
but the first is formed of the fire, the other of the water.
The successive whalebacks and humps of the Caradoc
chain are opposed by the series of rounded combes
locally called gutters—Ashes Hollow, the Light-Spout
Valley and the rest—into which the rushing streams have
cut the moorland flanks. An equally dramatic contrast is
afforded over by the Severn, where road and rail run in
the narrow space between the gentle shelving pastoral

Long Mountain and the sharp triple summits of the abrupt volcanic Breiddens.

The Long Mynd is separated by a high upland valley from the Stiperstones range, marked by the fantastic tor-like outcrops of quartzite along its main ridge. It makes a splendid breezy rambling-ground, and motor-cycles and even light cars push cheekily up the green Portway that marks its backbone. The range, however, has a sinister reputation in winter; there is a Deadman's Hollow and a Deadman's Lane, and the last fair of the year at Church Stretton, held on October 17th, long bore the grim title of "Deadman's Fair." The most terrifying experience recorded is that of the Rev. Donald Carr, who in January 1865 wandered in deep snow on the hills for twenty-two hours on his way from a service at Ratling-hope to his vicarage at Woolstaston on the other side of the ridge. He was hurled down snow-choked ravines, he struggled through enormous drifts, his hair was a solid mass of ice, and when he finally came upon some children they fled in fear from the "bogle." His body was a pincushion for myriads of gorse-spines, and his burst wrecks of boots are now in Shrewsbury Museum. Nevertheless he recovered to officiate for over thirty years, and the sale of the booklet on his adventure produced funds enough to provide some good modern carving at Woolstaston church.

The present writer feels a lively sympathy for Carr, since he was overtaken by a blinding snow blizzard early one February evening motoring back from Bridgnorth along the switchback narrow byway to the comfortable inn at Ditton Priors at the foot of the Brown Clee. The nightmare struggle over fourteen miles lasted for the best part of two hours, and when the blinded driver declared he could not go another yard, it was found that we were landed twenty yards from the inn. At Ditton Priors at the close of the War a Midland family on a hiking week-end found an angry crowd outside their lodging threatening to smash the windows—they had quite unjustifiably been taken for a detachment of conchies drafted to work in the Brown Clee quarries.

Next we view the great Silurian hill masses of Clun Forest, taking a large semicircular bite out of Wales. It is a region inclined to austerity, and occasionally achieves bleak gauntness, but it is a pleasant enough run up the higher Clun Valley through Newcastle, past "the last house in England," The Anchor Inn, which a choleric M.F.H. once bought as the only way to get a drink at the hours he wanted. There is a staggering prospect into Wales from Kerry Pole's 1,555 feet, and just below there is a scraggy little fir-wood where you can or you could eat your fill several times over of the most enormous and delicious wild raspberries—though this may be a few yards inside the actual frontier of Wales.

We can now face eastward for the twin basaltic Clees —the well shaped cone of Titterstone with its dhu-stone quarries and high-lying coal-mines among dreary little settlements; and farther north the bulkier mass of the Brown Clee, in itself a twin, and at 1,792 feet the highest point of Midland England. They are the centre of a wide upland region, including a secluded hill-district round Clee St. Margaret overlooking the fine field-stretch of Corve Dale, backed by the undulating hills of Wenlock Edge, which in imagination we have already traversed. A small part of the western view from the flanks of Brown Clee is illustrated in our frontispiece, in which Miss Pitt has recorded a section of the north-west stretch over Dale and Edge to the Wrekin in its impressive isolation. The Brown Clee can be encircled by a 1,000-foot shelf road which affords a dramatic contrast in sweeping views; no description can convey any idea of their splendour, but no one can claim to have seen the English landscape at its most impressive till he has

rounded the hill. Miss Weale's vivid sketch of the
western prospect is, it is worth remembering, applicable
to all the views into Wales from any of the principal
Salopian heights:

"Westward hills of all shapes and sizes: mighty piers
jutting out into the sea; giant fists and breasts; mammoth heads, shoulders and buttocks; monstrous
barrows, bivouacs and saddles; cones and pyramids
all in wild, jostling profusion, with their crests of
forest like the manes of flying steeds or elfin streamers
in the wind, and in between the ranges elevated
valleys like wave-troughs in the sea, waiting in everlasting suspense for a fall of the black sea-horses into
their depths."[1]

The hamlets in this remote hilly pastoral stretch can
be eight miles from a station and four from an inn; a few
years ago the farms used to bake their bread and the
little girls curtsied to the visitor. A stream flows
merrily a good way along the street of Clee St. Margaret,
to the consternation of the ultra-cautious motorist, who
may prefer a twelve-mile detour. The vicar of Hopton
Cangeford, with eighty inhabitants, was also rector of
Cold Weston, a parish of thirty-two people. The way
between them is two miles by a footpath under a 1,000
foot whaleback; the four miles of roundabout road are
steep even for Shropshire. One Easter Sunday the old
clergyman arrived at Cold Weston, and in his shirt-sleeves
pulled the oldest bell in the county, while a visitor
knocked up people from the scattered cottages to get a
congregation of seven, nearly a quarter of the parish
population. The damp had got into the harmonium, so
the visitor whistled the hymn-tunes, selected by the
congregation themselves. It was at Hopton Cangeford
that this vicar's daughter devised a novel and chaste

[1] *Through the Highlands of Shropshire on Horseback*, Magdalene Weale.

51   A GLIMPSE OF STRETTON DALE FROM THE LONG MYND, SHROPSHIRE

scheme of harvest festival decoration, consisting entirely
of masses of the mauve autumn crocus. But a deputation
of indignant farmers declared themselves unable to thank
the Almighty for His bounties amid one of the vilest of
poisonous weeds, so the pale blooms had to give way to
the usual assemblage of marrows, turnips and such-like.
Now there is no one in separate charge of the parishes,
round which a neighbouring cleric hustles in his small
car, taking in the little untouched Norman chapel of The
Heath, where the minister would in old pre-heating days
of winter sometimes transfer the service to the comfortable warmth of a neighbouring farm-house kitchen.
These tiny remote parishes nowadays present no end of
a problem to the ecclesiastical authorities.

The southern edge of the Highland country is formed
by a sort of lozenge, defined by the four points Ludlow-
Brampton Bryan–Kington–Yarpole, thus following the
"grain" of the hills. It is a quite individual little region
of complex ridges, densely forested, enclosing round
Wigmore a triangular stretch of actual fen; yet after
swinging up through the fine oak woodlands of Bringe-
wood Chase (if you are motoring, that is, or trudging
steadily up the 600 feet if you cycle), the eye is met by
the well-known landmark of the three Downton Hills,
bare save for a thin little crest of pines apiece. A member
of the Historical Monuments Commission staff once came
here to record the antiquities—which incidentally, if
unpretentious, have many-sided attractions—but was so
gripped by the scenic loveliness that he has been back
most years since to a fifteenth-century farm in a woodland
stream valley, with memories of the Lollards. In
London Wigmore Street is universally known, but about
the actual place which gives it the name few have the
haziest idea. It leads into Mortimer Street, and the seat of
the mighty medieval family of Mortimer was for centuries
at Wigmore Castle. Besides its scanty ruins there are

remains of an Abbey, a fine church and a half-timber shop, but Wigmore has lost the chief of its amenities, the Georgian "Castle Inn," recently burned down and replaced by a tin garage. It was a real old English inn, not a hotel or roadhouse, where with cheery fellowship they made you comfortable, fed you royally and charged little. Once there was a placard in the bar with the startling heading: "*Wanted* 10,000 *Lovers*"—and underneath in very small print: "of our ancient church." The vicar's lady had prepared an illustrated booklet to be sold at 4*d*. towards the repair of the roof, from which lumps of plaster would fall disconcertingly into the nave, so that services were relegated to the aisle. A party of hikers who attempted an inspection one Sunday afternoon pencilled their impressions: "The church is kept locked, but the roof can be seen from the outside and anyhow what does it matter: it's your money we want!"

Not far away the great earthwork of Croft Ambrey affords a view of incomparable extent over leagues of quiet, flat-seeming vale country to the pale contours of the Malverns and the Black Mountains' long line. One early Whitsun the narrow path under the high ramparts was a green thread among far-spreading primrose masses, a real "primrose path," but another time when the same season was late and hot, a walk over the war-cut oak woods flushed clouds of brown fritillary-like small butterflies, while a stranded fledgling curlew called plaintively for its parents. The steep, smooth green wall of Croft Ambrey towers above the little hamlet of Leinthall Earls, and Tudor Gatley House sits in its park on the slopes across the valley, up which a rough byway twists through the hills to Woofferton. On one occasion, travelling in a local Ford, the petrol was too low in the tank to carburet on the steep Wylde bank, where the car stalled, and it was an awesome experience to plunge down backwards in jerky brakeful spasms.

South of the Highlands, from the spacious red sandstone plain of Hereford rises an irregular series of lesser wooded heights that straggle roughly south-west into Monmouthshire, which two counties between them have managed to retain as English the wall-like eastern escarpment of the Black Mountains, and a stretch of the Llanthony valley, as well as some foothills and the agreeable area of the parallel Golden Valley, with its outer bounding ridge rising sharply above Wye vale.

So we must reluctantly bid good-bye to the Welsh Border, with its wide stretch of high country thrust into the English plain from Mersey to Severn out of the massed plenitude of the hills of Wales. Infinite in its attractions, it may one day be more widely appreciated; may it still keep the unspoiled country quietude which is among the finest of its many admirable features.

III. THE COTSWOLDS

We have already glanced at the Cotswolds from our standpoint on the Malvern Hills. Now the time has come to make their better acquaintance, and if we are to meet them for the first time, there is little doubt that we shall be looking forward avidly to the experience. For no lover of England can have failed to have read much of this tawny band of wold that reaches diagonally from the Wiltshire Avon by Bath to the Warwickshire Avon by Evesham, from thence sending out limestone fingers through the rolling country of North Oxfordshire, Southern Northamptonshire and Rutland, to taper to a point in the Lincoln Ridge almost within sight of the North Sea. But since "Hills and Wolds" is the chosen title of this chapter, we shall here content ourselves with a scrutiny of the wold proper, roughly from Bath to Evesham; for though the continuation of the geological belt across the Midlands produces an almost identical architecture in the native oolitic limestone, save that the stone slates of Cotswold building are here generally replaced by thatch, this country of broad rolling fields and quiet villages has nothing of the hill character and little of the wold about it.

Those who have read of Cotswold but never seen it will approach the district with certain preconceived notions which, it must be frankly stated, may sometimes lay them open to disappointment. For writers on the subject have a habit of presenting it as it must have appeared around the year 1860. Certainly, little has been done as yet to touch the flawless miniature architecture of the villages, strung like beads along the steep, winding, wooded little valleys, nor have some of the townlets, such as Chipping Campden and Burford, suffered much harm. But the privacy of this small private world has inevitably been much invaded. Great main roads now make bluish weals over the grey-brown face of the wold. The quiet perfection of small farm-houses has been distorted by enlargement and adaptation for "residential" purposes. Village shops have blossomed into art and craft centres or tea-shops kept by faded dimity ladies. In fact, the hypersensitive might be aware of a faint sense of tea-shop sophistication invading most of the loveliest corners of this little world, a sophistication which is partly due to the number of weakly sentimental books and articles that it has called forth during the last twenty years, and also partly to the extraordinary fascination which it seems to hold for American tourists. Though there are fewer of them nowadays at the end of these lean 'thirties, the boom period of the 'twenties produced them in their shoals, and there was seldom a day that several large, hired limousines would not draw up outside one or other of the larger London hotels, to rush their parties on the stock sightseeing tour through Oxford to the comfortable portals of the Lygon Arms at Broadway,

53   SNOW AT STANTON, UNDER THE COTSWOLDS

54   A FARMYARD AT DUNTISBOURNE ROUS IN THE COTSWOLDS

55   FORD VILLAGE IN THE COTSWOLDS

with a detour to take in Chipping Campden on the way, thence on to the no less comfortable portals of the Garrick or White Swan at Stratford-on-Avon.

The several Cotswold examples presented in a great architectural book published under the same imprint as this one, Garner and Stratton's *Domestic Architecture of the Tudor Period*, must have produced a generous progeny in such districts of the New World as Long Island and Connecticut, to say nothing of Oshkosh and Kansas City; while the writer has even seen a genuine Cotswold manor-house transplanted with uncomfortable effect to the rather barren environs of Philadelphia. Until quite recently a roaring trade was done in the beautifully weathered stone slates of demolished Cotswold barns and cottages for the roofing of new houses in the United States.

What, then, is the particular Cotswold charm responsible for these manifestations? Firstly, no doubt, the delicious local architecture of the sixteenth and seventeenth centuries, whose tradition was strong enough to be maintained even in some measure up to our own day. Its beauty is due in no small degree to the fineness of the oolitic limestone, which you have but to scrape the surface of the wold to find, and which is easily fissible and needs little of the ordinary labour of quarrying. Then there is the fact that during the peak period of building the district was enriched by a boom in wool, at a time when the wolds, wild and unenclosed, were virtually a vast sheepwalk, and a brisk trade was maintained by stalwart graziers and staplers in the wool markets of little towns such as Chipping Campden. These facts provided the wherewithal for building; but the wherewithal would have been little had not the district produced a worthy body of craftsmen, who were able to transform this wealth and this stone into a local craftsmanship which informs almost every building of their age, from the great "wool" churches such as Cirencester, Northleach and Campden down to the outbuildings of the ordinary farm-house; from the rich man's house, such as that of the merchant Grevel at Chipping Campden, or Icomb Manor, down to the adorable clusters of habitation along any typical stream valley such as the Coln, the Evenlode or the Windrush.

One could fill all the available space in this chapter in writing of Cotswold villages: of Upper Swell and Lower Slaughter, Wyck Rissington, Naunton and lovely Bourton-on-the-Water, with its little streams spanned by miniature bridges. Bibury, in full summer, is like a green pocket amongst softly wooded slopes; Arlington Row, England's perfect cottage group, now happily acquired for the nation, stretches its great sweep of lichened stone slating beside the stream, broken by a range of miniature dormers; and from the grey bridge by the Swan Inn you can watch lazily for the trout which slip in and out of the reeds beneath the clear water. From the main Oxford–Worcester road which bestrides the range you can choose a quiet side turning which leads you down in a steep zigzag through flowering woods to emerge on the perfect Elizabethan manor-house of Chastleton, complete with tiny church in the grounds and dovecote in the field beyond, and a cluster of little grey-brown cottages straggling away behind.

The grey-brown of the buildings and the green-grey of the wold are the colours by which you chiefly remem-ber the Cotswolds. Habitation—villages, farms, houses—is generally secluded in the wooded valley pockets, and the wold itself ripples into the distance empty, and at certain times of the year a little bleak, networked with the dry-stone walls that are one of the achievements of the district and broken by an occasional thin fringe of beech. Here and there a stretch of ploughland breaks the monotony of the pastures, or in summer a stubble-field shines out from the distances of sun-browned turf. In autumn there is the flaming splendour of the beech-woods, in the valleys and along the steep westerly escarpment, with its long, sweet views over the hedge-chequerwork of the Avon vale to the outlines of other hills in the distance.

To sum up, it is not by any means easy to set down in cold print the sway which Cotswold undoubtedly exercises over many from both home and overseas. The whole district is fashioned of the oolite, and yet there are exhilarating contrasts between the sweep of the high, open wolds and the great elm-patterned stretches of a piece of enclosed vale country on which you may suddenly happen, like the great expanse from Bourton-on-the-Hill, or the unending varied vale views set out below you from the great northern bastion above Ilmington. There is the same effect with smaller-scale intimacy when you drop off the bare, rolling brown fields into a small, tree-dotted river dip, as above Burford to Little Rissington in the Dikler Valley; it was strange to find in a few months' interval that the great empty fields had been covered with all the paraphernalia of a huge aerodrome lay-out. One feature of the region is the rich depth of its green colouring in late summer, especially in the blue-green of the vast woodlands that run for miles along the sky-line, when your lane is decked in purple and gold with cranes-bill and yellow bedstraw. Each can find here his own pleasantness, scenically or architecturally, and if to the farming eye Cotswold seems forlorn and forgotten, there is a measure of rejoicing that, except for its fringes and the scattered military settlements, it escapes the full flood of building desecration.

IV. THE MENDIPS

From the Cotswolds we must hurry on to the Mendips, not even stopping for Dundry, the impressive whaleback with its slender church tower, which at some states of the atmosphere almost seems to overhang the houses of Bristol city. It is really the most westerly and the most detached of the Cotswold outliers, six miles away from the main range round Bath.

The Mendips face the parallel but rather smaller Quantocks across some fifteen miles of stark fenland. Though near neighbours, they are in every way an entire contrast, as we shall see; geology, like dress, does make a difference. The Mendips are a level-topped range of mountain limestone with all the characteristics of their formation—cliff-sided gorges winding up from the plain, vast caverns, swallets, potholes and underground rivers; their affinities are with the barer parts of the Peak district, as though some earth-builder had snipped off the tail of the Pennines and dropped it down to dominate the flattest part of the Somerset plain. It cannot be said that on the top of their four-to-six-mile wide plateau the Mendips are an attractive range—the bare, rough pastures are divided by stone walls, there is no impression of the 800-foot height, and to be outside one of the lonely high-lying inns, such as the Miners' Arms or the Castle of Comfort, on a drizzly Sunday morning in winter, is an experience to chill the spirit. There are slightly higher knolls of sandstone as at Black Down, and remains of Roman lead-working, where pigs stamped with the mark of Hadrian have been unearthed, and ancient camps and old tracks are scattered over the plateau. Priddy is the one village which clings to a hollow high in the centre of the hills; its inhabitant who, after his first visit to London, exclaimed, "Gie I Priddy!" may be commended for his heroic choice, and not many might be found anxious to rob him of the desire of his eyes. But if the high levels are in all but full summer gaunt and bleak, there are superb views over sea and country to the south, where the range towers a sudden 800 feet above the fenny levels at its foot; or to the north over lower outliers towards the Avon. The smaller gorges are impressive at Burrington Combe and Shipham—the latter rather spoilt by quarrying—but at Cheddar Gorge the high, plunging cliffs and piled-up masses of grey limestone are austere and gravely majestic whenever free from massed chara-banc invasions, and are happily detached from the con-fused huddle of modernist cafés with swimming-pools, and cheese and trinket shops at the cave entrance below. Axbridge and Shepton Mallet are nice enough little towns, and there is always the riot of Jacobean woodwork in Croscombe Church, but the pleasantest spot in Mendip land is where the old village town of Wells is pressed close against the combes, and the three towers of the cathedral stand out against the wooded slopes. It is equally delightful to look over this smallest of cities from the heights above, with an endless stretch of the tor-dotted grazing levels beyond.

V. THE POLDENS

Everyone is rude to the Polden Hills. If noticed at all, they are stigmatised as "mounds" or "hillocks," and more scorn is poured upon them than even the insignifi-cant Gog Magog ridgelet near Cambridge. And yet there is something to be said for this 200–300-foot lias ridge that pushes itself through the alluvial flats. It is pleasantly wooded, and so far as one's acquaintance with England goes, it is the only rise anywhere that stands up above a stretch of flat fenland on either hand. Conse-quently the expanse it commands is quite out of propor-tion to its mild elevation, as you will find out if you travel not too fast by the road that runs along its slight crest. It is made of the same stuff as the conical tors which dot the marshland, and everybody remarks upon the dramatic suddenness of *their* uprising. The stones of the Poldens, in the form of large flat slabs, are used as sides to barns, floors to farm kitchens, or even street pavements, and there is one bed of white stone which makes fine chimney-pieces and was used for mosaic pavements by the Romans.

VI. THE QUANTOCKS

The Quantocks have almost all the admirable qualities which can be demanded of a range of hills, and yet their attraction is not to be explained by a mere faithful enumeration of excellencies; there is an elusive charm, a subtle *Stimmung* which attracts to them again and again; it is perhaps partly physical and partly psychological; they impose a comforting restfulness. Dorothy Wordsworth, who had all her brother's insight into a landscape, summed up thus happily her local impression: "Wherever we turn we have woods, smooth downs and valleys with small brooks running down them through green meadows hardly ever intersected with hedgerows, but scattered over with trees. The hills that cradle these valleys are either covered with fern, or bilberries, or oak-woods. Walks extend for miles over the hill-tops, the great beauty of which is their wide simplicity." For though their dimensions are so slight that an average motorist can encircle them in less than an hour, to explore the recesses of the combes he must leave mechanical locomotion behind; the hill-sides entice to an infinite pattern of pedestrian ramblings. Though the western side holds the steep escarpment, the modelling here, as everywhere on these hills, is exceedingly subtle, and the mantle of woodland well diversified, till the height fades to a half as the tail of the range sinks into vale and fen. On the other side the hills are cut by the lively swift streams into a cockscomb of deep combes, each winding far into the hills, densely wooded and yet with its separate

56 THE BRENDON HILLS NEAR NETTLECOMBE

57 WEACOMBE IN THE QUANTOCK HILLS

58   THE POLDEN HILLS OVERLOOKING THE SOMERSET LEVELS

individuality. There is no need for a strict itinerary on the Quantocks; they are a paradise for aimless yet ever-remunerative wanderings; always the colouring is rich and varied, till the whole region glows in early November in a diverse harmony of brown and russet and gold, with oak and bracken, whortleberry bush and dark heather. From your guest-house or inn you can push up the level green floor of the combe or strike up the steeper ascent of a side valley to a spur, lingering in a hill-side copse on the way, and glimpsing far below a distant fan-shaped expanse of rich hedge-crossed vale country. Later you reach the main ridge, along which a track runs for the whole of its length; unlike the Mendips, the upper parts of the Quantocks are devoid of human habitations. There are views over the expanse of Taunton Deane and across to the ramparts of Exmoor, Dunkery-crowned, and usually on one hand is the lead-grey sweep of the Bristol Channel. It is equally heartening to push up the steep escarpment behind Crowcombe Church with its varied woodwork, and quickly reach the main ridge. The writer will never forget the experience of crossing the Quantocks on a dark autumn night, guided by an Ordnance map read by a torch. There was an intense stillness, and it was startling to realise that the impudent red eye winking steadily in the distance was a lighthouse in mid-Channel. Then it was possible to hold straight along a spur and drop right down on the house where one was to stay the night.

The output of poems by Wordsworth and Coleridge during their Quantock stay is memorable, but their sojourn was short, for they attracted the suspicion of a Government spy, and the agent refused to let Alfoxden House for a further term. Coleridge was regarded as a harmless nitwit, a "crack-brained talking fellow," but "that Wordsworth is either a smuggler or a traitor and means mischief. He never speaks to anyone, haunts lonely places, walks by moonlight and is always *booing* about by himself." At Alfoxden occurred the disastrous picnic when the cheese was stolen by a beggar, Coleridge clumsily smashed the brandy bottle, and they were reduced to bread and lettuces without salt. Coleridge's cottage at Nether Stowey is preserved as a memorial museum, but the little town was visited far earlier by a versifier of a very different calibre when John Taylor, the royalist "water-poet," had his tremendous battle with Egyptian hosts of fleas at the Rose and Crown.

VII. THE BLACKDOWNS

The Blackdown Hills face the Quantocks across the Vale of Taunton near Wellington, which gave its name to the Duke. A tall triangular tower is set up on one of the highest points of the hills as a monument to him. The range really consists of a plateau of greensand, the same formation which provides the bold bluff on which Shaftesbury is built. It is rather bare and treeless, but where at the back of the main ridge the rivers, such as the Otter and Yarty, have cut through to the marls, the valleys are cultivated and fertile, and the hill formation is left as separate ridges which to the south thrust out long fingers right down to the sea. The town of Honiton is really in the middle of the Blackdowns, and the Southern line to Exeter struggles through a small piece of them. Some concretions are found in layers which make excellent hone-stones for sharpening scythes; these are ground down to the right shape and sent all over the kingdom.

Roads have strangely enough been taken along the main edge of the Blackdown Hills and along the tops of the majority of the ridges, and it is an exhilarating experience, which probably few have enjoyed in full, to ramble up and down them. The London road runs along

an outlying part by Windwhistle Inn, and there are fine
open views over leagues of fair country, while from
some favoured spots it is possible to see the English
Channel and the Severn estuary at one time. The most
westerly of these ridges above Exmouth affords at
Woodbury Common a dominating point over the sea
and the Exe estuary, but the Haldon ridge west of
Exeter is perhaps even grander. Finely wooded, it
towers up before the traveller on the way from Exeter to
the south-west, and it is possible to keep to the high
ground from the typically Devon-named villages of
Dunchideock and Doddiscombsleigh to the sea by Teign-
mouth. But there is an aerodrome at Little Haldon, and
a certain amount of unfortunate, if possibly inevitable,
building vulgarisation disfigures the ridge.

VIII. EXMOOR OUTLIERS

From Dunster to Porlock Bay extend two twin whaleback hills, among the pleasantest in all the West Country.
Grabbist or Grabhurst rises immediately from Dunster
village, and while everyone should encircle it by the shelf
road by Wootton Courtney, any extent of time is well
spent on the ridge above, even though the woods have
been savagely hacked down. The sea view takes in the
whole of Bridgwater Bay, across to the Welsh coast, the
Vale of Porlock is laid out green and smiling at your
very feet, while the ramparts of Exmoor with the slight
swelling curve of Dunkery fill in the western sky-line.
The northern twin, which stretches from Minehead, and,
though one hill, is called successively North Hill, Selworthy Beacon and Bossington Hill, overhangs the sea,
and under its landward slope is placed the church of
Selworthy, with all the varied prospect of hill and vale
laid out from its high churchyard, and the idyllic thatched
cottage-almshouses placed restfully round the green.

IX. DARTMOOR

On Dartmoor a book, or rather a whole series of volumes, could be written. It is the greatest self-contained granite area in the United Kingdom, and it is curious that a comparison is not more frequently essayed with the Wicklows, the other great granite mass across the Irish Channel. Its 130,000 acres are practically all of unredeemed wildness, and according to your temperament, the time of year and the reception it affords you, you will either loathe it as a whole or come under its spell. It carries the highest elevation in England of any ground south of the Pennines, if we except the stretch of the Black Mountains eastern escarpment which Hereford-shire has managed to filch from Wales, which brings into England one or two bits 300 feet higher than Yes Tor. The loneliness and mystery of this great region, wild and almost untouched since the coming of man, can both attract and repel, and it has undoubtedly exercised a profound influence on the thought and lives of the folk who dwell on its margins. It can be heartening in the delicate freshness of early spring or under a summer sun, when a brisk breeze chases the cloud-shadows over the purple heather and the bright green by the stripling streamlets, but eerie in clinging mist, and sinister under heavy rain or deep snow. It is the source of nearly all the principal rivers of the county, has grim morasses to show, and the tors, or granite outcrops which crown so many of the higher points, are weathered into strange fantastic shapes, in which they parallel the Prescelly hills of Pembrokeshire, to which the prehistoric folk preferred to go for the monoliths of Stonehenge. There are peat-hags slashed by the rain into trenches almost reminiscent of a battlefield, and all but impassable except in the driest weather, and piled up "clitters," or boulder-strewn hill-sides, of which the ascent is a major penance. The

59 SHEEPTOR VILLAGE UNDER SHEEPTOR, DARTMOOR

60 A WOODED STRETCH OF EXMOOR FROM NETTLECOMBE

higher bastions, Yes Tor, High Willhays and Cawsand Beacon, face the north, but it is necessary for a tramp over the former two to select a day free from artillery practice, for the gun and the bomb-dropping aeroplane have now largely taken possession of the most desolate places in England. To the east and south are winding densely wooded river valleys; any view of Buckland in the Moor is sure to show massed trees. Apart from the artificial settlement of Princetown, Widecombe is perhaps the place which is set deepest in the Moor, and the tall, austere granite tower rising in the midst of the wide, shallow, hedge-crossed valley makes a scene familiar to many. The inclemency of the moorland, in all its grimness of cold and storm, mist and snow, was far from daunting prehistoric man, the remains of whose settlements dot the rough slopes. Only one of the great dolmens remains, in Spinster's Rock, Drewsteignton, but there is an abundance of hut circles, standing menhirs, stone avenues and many other relics. Princetown is a fittingly forbidding spot which seems to attract all the mists and rains that are about, and it is a satisfaction to know that there is some prospect that after some century and a quarter its career as a penal settlement, which commenced with the Napoleonic Wars, may finally be ended.

A curious little volcanic out-thrust runs out on the west side between the Tavy and the Tamar Rivers. Near here is Lydford, to the parish of which the whole of Dartmoor is supposed to belong, and on the abrupt knoll at Brent Tor, possibly, and if so very appropriately, named from the colour of its igneous rocks, is the tiny gaunt Early English church used for an occasional service in summer or for a wedding—for some of the neighbouring farmers can claim the right to be married in what is probably, in the physical sense, the highest church in England. In contrast to this last defiant rock tongue, the Lyd Valley by Coryton and Lyddaton is as soft and wooded and smiling as anything Devon can show.

X. EXMOOR

Of the two vast wastes which under the title of forest fill a considerable area of Devon, it has been suggested that Dartmoor might be considered the masculine and Exmoor the feminine. The latter is certainly the less grim, but it cannot be said that there is anything particularly smiling about it. Exmoor is really a series of grassy ridges intersected by the valleys of infant streams, among which are the Exe and the Barle. It is crossed by far more roads than its cousin to the south, and cars even push up over most of the 1,700 feet of Dunkery, which is a flattish dome, a gently swelling breast—we emphatically decline to call it, with the geologists, a monadhock, a word suggestive of some extinct Red Indian tribe. The real splendour of Exmoor lies in its coast, and the wooded river combes which bound its margins. The motorist may be excused for pressing on his accelerator pedal as he drives across the centre of it, for his road will probably be bounded by high, built-up banks surmounted by beech-hedges, in themselves attractive, but forming an endless double green line which excludes all but an occasional view-glimpse. The steep, wooded combes of the coast are impressive, but anything but accessible; some are private, but unless it is pouring, it is always an exhilarating experience to follow the twisting path from Porlock Weir round the coast to Culbone, and it is unforgettable when the trees and hedges are a riot of every conceivable autumn tint. The late Dr. Cox, who had an affection for it, maintained with hearty emphasis that Culbone was the smallest complete church in England, and it is certainly intriguing to find a House of God tucked away in such a situation. The coast culminates in the Foreland lighthouse, the most northerly point of Devon, and just inland at Countisbury is a grey little weatherbeaten church surrounded by the graves of shipwrecked sailors.

It is perhaps arguable whether the coast west of Lynton may still be reckoned part of Exmoor, but the mighty jutting headlands are the same, and surely the finest coastal spot in the kingdom is the arc of Woody Bay, with its dense oak-woods running down to the shore, followed by the cliff path or higher top road that leads to the sudden gash of Heddon's Mouth and the headlands of the Hangmans, Great and Little, beyond. Above the Lynton–Barnstaple road is the ridge by Chapman Barrows which, if inconspicuous, is nearly as high as Dunkery, and commands a sweep across mid-Devon to the northern bastions of Dartmoor and the whole coastline to Hartland Point, a scene of great extent and, on a grey day, of melancholy grandeur. Close by is Challacombe, where Bishop Hannington, as a stripling curate, arrived on his Exmoor pony dripping wet an hour late for service one Sunday morning, having lost his way in a dense mist. The aged clerk told him in a loud voice that he had better put on his "surples," as they wanted to go home for dinner, so he robed himself over his soaking garments and read them a short matins.

The broken country of hill and combe, copse, river and farming land which lies to the south of the forest can be fairly well gauged from the Barnstaple–Taunton road or rail between South Molton and Wiveliscombe. But in the writer's opinion at least, the most attractive part of inland Exmoor is round Dulverton, where is the winding wooded river valley of the Barle; perhaps under present-day conditions it is a matter for congratulation that it is roadless nearly all the way. Just below Dulverton the Barle joins the Exe, but eastward there is an equally delightful but far less-known little stretch of wooded country where the River Haddeo curves in a deep cleft round Haddon Hill past the typical little Devon hamlet of Bury, where we leave the Forest and the county.

XI. UPLAND CORNWALL

The granite moorlands, of which Dartmoor is the most conspicuous out-thrust, are continued through Cornwall in several patches, with gradually diminishing height, as you proceed westward, till the land gives up the struggle with its last slight upheaval in the 166 feet of the Scilly Isles. The main area of the Cornish moorlands is the large eastern stretch known as Bodmin Moor, which is crossed by the main road from Launceston to Bodmin. It is usually described as bleak, but can have a breezy open attraction of its own when the heather is in purple bloom and the marshy spots are starred with white cotton grass. Brown Willy, the highest point, is a rounded dome, and but little lower is Rough Tor, which stands up conspicuously with its twin-cairned ridge. From the number of stone remains around or leading up to it the place is adjudged to have been a sacred mountain of great veneration. If Cornwall lacks the fantastic tors of Dartmoor, with the exception of the Cheesewring by Callington, it exceeds in the number of prehistoric relics, which make the moorlands a happy hunting-ground for the archaeologist over what may be considered in a mild way a minor English Carnac. There are hut circles, stone avenues and beehive huts, barrows or burial-places, and standing stones or menhirs, on many of which the cross has been cut in the age of the saints. The legend that St. Sampson rebuked a crowd of pagans merrymaking at a stone on Laneast Down, and at the risk of his life cut a cross on the stone, probably has a foundation in fact, and was an oft-repeated incident. It is, however, impossible here to do justice to the saints of Cornwall,

whose names are as euphonious as their legends are endless and extraordinary; the county has a vast distinct
hagiology of its own. But all this time we are forgetting
the great dolmens in which Cornwall is supreme in
England—Lanyon Quoit, which the mechanical resources
of 1824 were inadequate to replace in its original form,
Trevethy Quoit and many another. Nearly all the Holy
Wells of Britain are in the county; some are of decided
architectural character. Ireland of course parallels Cornwall in the number of them it possesses, a possible sign
of intimate connection in early days. Near the beginning
of the moors is the church of Altarnun, frequently called
the cathedral of the moor, with its tall granite tower and
splendid series of carved bench-ends, which, with such
paintings as those of St. Christopher and Christ of the
Trades, are characteristic of the county's craftsmanship.
Nevertheless, perhaps the most remarkable feature is the
wide use made of the native moorland granite for the
arcades of the churches, both in West Devon and
throughout Cornwall. They are cut into an almost uniform design of chamfered arch and plain capital. This in
itself is something of an achievement, but what can be
said of the delicate patterning with which the sixteenth-
century builders have covered in this stubborn and
intractable material the whole of the great walls, the
tower and the porch of St. Mary Magdalene, Launceston?
It would be interesting to compare such a work with the
Calvaries which the Bretons, the Cornishmen's opposite
number, have produced across the Channel, but surely it
is a matter for rejoicing that, thanks to the munificence
of Sir Henry Trecarrel, so remarkable and exuberant a
tour de force has been patiently chiselled out and be-
queathed for our enjoyment and admiration.

J. Fairfax-Blakeborough

MOORS AND FELLS

Sing hey! for the moorlands wild, lonely and stern.
Where the moss creepeth softly all under the fern.
Where the heather sweetens the lone highland lea,
And the mountain winds whistle so fresh and so free!
To sing the grand anthem of freedom to me!

EDWIN WAUGH

There you may see a viewe, the like of which I never
saw, or thinke that any traveller hath seene any comparable unto 't, albeit I have shewed yt to divers who
have paste through a greater parte of the world, both by
sea and land. The vale, rivers, great & small, swelling
hylls and mountaynes, pastures, meadows, corn-fields,
parte of the Bishoprick of Durham, with a new porte of
Tease lately found to be safe and the sea replenished
with shippes, and a most pleasant flatt coast, subjecte to
no inundation or hazarde, make the country happy.

MS. Cott. Lib. Int. F. VI.

THE early writer quoted above was impressed by the
panorama from conical-shaped Roseberry Topping,
which like a cameo stands out in the Cleveland range.
There are an unlimited number of other heights from

61 GORDALE SCAR IN THE YORKSHIRE PENNINES

62   THE HEAD OF BISHOPDALE IN THE YORKSHIRE PENNINES

which the view of surrounding hills, apparently boundless moorlands, sequestered valleys and fertile plans
might equally have stirred his imagination and enthusiasm.

> Variety without end—sweet interchange
> Of hill and valley, river, woods and plains.

It is not easy to put into words the charm, the fascination and the allurement of the wild uplands of the North
Country. Their appeal varies according to the vagaries
of human inwardness and soulfulness. Beauty they say
is in the eye of the beholder, and it is a truism that the
eyes of few men behold alike. Equally few have in
their ego the same response to the culture, art and
poetry latent there. Thus it is that wold, moor and fell,
attract, inspire, uplift and rejoice from entirely different
angles.

Just as there are wide and obvious physical, geological
and scenic differences between the wold country of
Lincolnshire and of East Yorkshire, and the moorlands
which stretch across Lancashire, North Yorkshire,
Durham and the Northumberland country to the Scottish
Borders, so there are equally marked variations in the
character of the fell country in Westmorland and Cumberland; so, too, do these differences exist between one
range of hills and another. The wold and fell countries
have their own essential characteristics just as have the
heathlands, whilst each eminence with those with eyes to
see and mind and soul attuned to appreciate possesses
a distinctiveness, and often lore and legend which marks
it as a joy, a picture, separate, yet an integral part of a
wondrous whole.

Perhaps one of the most potent lodestones of the
uplands of the North Country is the relief they offer from
the industrial towns they shelter. So soon as we begin
to climb there is a consciousness that we are leaving the

everyday world of rush, hustle and petty restrictions, and of things mundane, for one in which there is not only unfettered, boundless expanse, with only in rare places creations of man to offend the eye, but also a world which is different in almost every detail. This does not only apply to the wild and rugged grandeur of the scenery, with all its variety and unlooked-for surprises; not only to coloration, which changes from hill to hill, and everywhere season by season; not only to the wonders of rock and gill, bog, and isolated homesteads and buildings upon which we come at intervals. These uplands in other respects constitute another world. The contacts and economy of life, the outlook, customs, speech and life itself of the "fell-heeder," "the moor-ender," and "the woldsman," differ from those in the vale. It is true that this is much less so to-day than it was in even the recent past, for inter-communication is nowadays much easier and more general. Indeed, many places hidden in the fastnesses of the hills, are now regularly visited by motor-buses, whilst their roads have been modernised out of all recognition. The dales and hill countries between the Trent and the Border country in far Northumberland are now in the main accessible by motor-car and bus, and are becoming known to ever-increasing numbers of tourists, who discover that we have in our fair land mountain scenery comparable with any abroad. These hills and fells are in very truth "a wilderness of sweets" in which one moment we find ourselves on the edge of a rocky precipice, and the next looking down into a gill, dell or valley with bracken breast high, with slopes covered with heather, or golden gorse, and with close-cropped patches of grass below. Surely if ever fairies danced anywhere, it was in such places as these, to the silver music of the streams (which in winter, however, can become angry and turbulent). Everywhere there are these hidden and unexpected slacks and gills to discover, the homes only of fox and badger, and black-faced mountain sheep; the nesting-places of hawk and raven, and here and there a buzzard. Some of them have their caves, all have their own river or stream and an individual beauty and character. Each is to the naturalist, and to the lover of nature, a veritable paradise in which to linger, there to speak in subdued tones, to feel taken out of oneself, and for the nonce to revel in the experience of truth—truth in the Ruskin sense. And when we tear ourselves away, and climb the farther side of one of these many pockets amid the hills, it may be to find ourselves transfixed with what we see below and all around us. It may be the sea—so near that the brine's tang is in the air we breathe, and with the naked eye we can watch the billows and see vessels sailing on the marine horizon. Much, of course, depends on the atmosphere of the day. One hour a view which thrills may be before us, and the next there may be rolling mist-clouds—marvellous in themselves—which enshroud everything. If it is not the ocean, with abbeys, historic ruins, villages and picturesque churches between us and the water, we possibly find (as at Gillamoor near Kirby-moorside to mention only one place) a "surprise view" in the shape of a dale, one side bathed in brilliant sun-shine, the other in a mighty shadow of clouds such as we have never before seen. Farmsteads are dotted here and there, and stone walls enclose fields stretching away until they meet a thousand acres of heath, and bracken-covered moorland, rich in colour be the month what it may. Incidental mention of stone walls remind me that they are an essential feature of our northern uplands, an integral part of its character. They are in keeping with the solidity, ruggedness, colour and character of all around. Though man-made, they blend with and even relieve the vast heath, and bracken-covered areas on which, as far as the eye can see, there may be scarce a tree or a bush. There are those who love the moorland country in all its variations who will tell you that the miles of dry-stone walls are amongst the chief attractions. To them such walls are a component part of the landscape and add to its picturesqueness and completeness. These walls fascinate them, appearing as they do to be great spinal cords and ribs stretching across, dividing, supporting and defining tremendous stretches of country and descending too into the valleys as a connecting link. In themselves they tell of the skill of the men who built them. Without lime for support these walls stand up for a generation—often longer—against the wild winds and storms which sweep over the hills. The blackface sheep, of ancient lineage, which can jump like stags, occasionally dislodge one or two of the topmost stones, and here and there, especially in localities in which mining operations are conducted, the walls may sink at their foundations and so cause breaks in the boundary line. Generally, however, the permanency of the moorland walls is remarkable. Miss Price in *Shadows on the Hills* (p. 195), refers to this when she writes:

"My eye was satisfied with infinite variety; everywhere I saw edge, angle, zigzag, spot, splash; even the walls make a patchwork pattern over hill and dale. I marvel at these walls; they are an outstanding feature of the fells, sprawling over them and along tracks which men have cut over their sides, but a disconcerting sign that he must be limited and protected, No part of this walled map that stretched before me was built in man's living memory. Some will tell you they were built two hundred years back; other say 'Lang afoor then,' and that the men who built them earned a shilling a day; to-day many a farmer has had to mortgage his farm for the upkeep of them. The stones hold firmly together with no cement, yet the

63   WINTER IN A YORKSHIRE DALE

64 MOORLAND HUNTING WITH THE ROOKWOOD HARRIERS, YORKSHIRE

65 A MOORLAND STREAM: DOE BECK, WEST YORKSHIRE

fierce storm buffets them in vain. No one knows who was responsible for these unending stone walls. It is said the Devil himself built that which runs from Dunmail Raise to Helm Crag."

It has been imagined by some who are not familiar with this upland country that artists are too generous with their colours—the red roads, the deep green or golden tints of bracken, the seas of purple heather, the blue and red shale-heaps, the lichen-coloured rocks, the olive of plantations, and the wondrous shadow effects. But Nature here is more lavish in her colouring than any artist, and more suddenly and constantly capricious here than anywhere. She seems to change her mood from gay to grave, from a silence one can feel to tumultous music, to play tricks with wind and sun, as nowhere else. Even those who know the hill-land best and love it most find that the picture they saw one day is changed the next, and that they are ever making fresh discoveries, finding new delights, and having their affection deepened, their marvel increased. Most tourists know the hills only in their spring and summer clothing and colouring, but those who are intimate with them in all seasons and under all conditions readily admit that even they have only a superficial, nodding acquaintance. There is such immensity, such vastness, that it almost seems beyond the power of our finite minds and conceptions fully to appreciate all there is in the external make-up of a limited area of upland. The extent of a typical moorland area which comes within the scope of this chapter may be gathered from the introduction to Frank Elgee's *Moorlands of North-eastern Yorkshire*, in which he says:

"The region forms one of the most natural divisions in Yorkshire, possessing its own special physical and geological features, and being well defined by distinct physical boundaries. In a general sense the district is an elevated tableland, nowhere attaining a greater altitude than 1,489 feet above the sea. In the south, this tableland is separated from the Chalk Wolds by the fertile plain of Pickering; in the west it is bounded by the Vale of York; in the north it is defined by the plain of Cleveland and the lower valley of the estuary of the Tees; and in the east it terminates in the grand sea cliffs from Saltburn to Scarborough. Within these lines the great moors occur, extending about thirty-two miles from east to west, and sixteen miles from north to south, and containing between three hundred and four hundred square miles of land more or less covered with heather."

The highest point on this range is on Urra Moor (Bilsdale) being 1,489 feet above the sea-level, but there are hill-tops of lesser elevation from which one may see farther. However, I doubt if from anywhere on the Cleveland Range the eye can see so tremendous a stretch of country as from the top of Cheviot. From this hill, when the day is clear, one may see the hills of Soutra in Midlothian on the one hand, and on the other conical Roseberry Topping, a landmark (by no means the highest) in the Cleveland Range. And from Roseberry itself one may view the panorama of hill and vale which so impressed the early writer quoted at the outset. Sometimes, in their rapture, in the intoxication of soul-stirring scenery, of exhilarating mountain air, the feeling of freedom and the wonder of it all, visitors marvel at the apparent matter-of-factness of the resident hill-folk. The tourist in a rhapsody bares his soul to the rough-hewn native and is astonished, irritated, dampened, by some such reply as, "You want to be up here in winter when the snow comes, and then, mebbe, you wouldn't think it so beautiful"; or, "You've got to winter these

hills and summer 'em, and winter 'em again, just as you
have to winter and summer people, afore you really
knows 'em." There is a good deal of truth in this charge
of apparent lack of enthusiasm, but it must not be
imagined that the hill-folk do not love their moors and
fells. Indeed their roots go far back and deep into the
soil, making them in many respects a race apart, to whom
the hills mean what the sea does to those born on the
coast-line. I was born a hill-man, and I know intimately
the temper and mentality of those who live on the heathlands and in the dales which run through them. I know
that the everlasting hills are to them life, and that they
love them with an intensity which possibly they could
not explain, or themselves do not understand. I have
before me notes of what one moorland farmer (whose
days have all his long life been filled with hard labour on
a beggarly moorland farm) said only a few months ago.
I call it an epic, and I know that his thoughts and feelings
are not singular, though few hill-men have the gift to
express themselves as he did. These are the very words
my friend spoke:

"As you gaze across the undulating country, you
see the heather is changing a few tones. If we were
nearer we would see the rugged, irregular patches of
crow-ling, or bell-heather, the latter now very bright,
really more brilliant in its hue as a twig than the true
heath. It comes earlier and lasts longer. It is the
great mass of the more common heath in its full
bloom, and as it slowly fades, that appeals to the soul
of the artist. Those great breadths of purple, edged,
or broken into by vivid green patches of bracken or
grass, make a background to the picture unexcelled
by either sea or sky. Soon after sundown, when the
lights are gently, slowly fading into night, it is entrancing. We feel the scents undefinably mingled.

If the honey-flow is on (seen in the dust of our shoes) we cannot quit ourselves of the honey in our nostrils. There are others, but the sweetest of all we may get is a whiff from the wild thyme. The bees are very busy on it just now before the bloom has come to the heather. But, finest of all the sensations on these wild, open hill-sides, is the feeling of freedom, with the winds blowing, as we think, untainted, fresh and pure, straight from the heavens. We open our arms, we meet the wind and let it blow round us, through us, we gasp it down into our lungs; it means the breath of life, the wind of our hills."

Those, then, were the words of a moorland farmer. As I have said, he was not an exceptional case of a hillman upon whom environment has an elevating influence. One finds this poetic sense, this love of the uplands strong even amongst those who complain of the manifold disadvantages associated with farming in such areas. This naturally brings one to the much-discussed question of cultivating some of the hill-sides, to increase England's reserves and make her more self-dependent. Previous experiments to this end have proved that there are tremendous obstacles to be overcome by scientists before upland heath country can be made over into the productive farmlands imagined by theorists and visionaries who picture them yellow with corn, giving remunerative employment to thousands of people and ensuring England's food-supply should sea-borne traffic be impeded and imperilled. Miracles have been performed; changes of which our forebears never dreamed have been effected in agriculture. The tilling of the moorlands, however, is a problem yet to be solved. Certain it is that the landowners of this generation have not the capital to tackle it as did some of their forebears, who in Yorkshire did so much as pioneers of afforestation and of a greater agriculture. To the hills we lift our eyes in admiration; from them has come great mineral wealth, and on them have lived, and still live, a sturdy race in a world almost apart, and under conditions demanding abundant faith and fortitude. But from the point of view of agricultural development we regard the moorlands with little faith as to their future.

Lincolnshire has its wolds as well as its fens, and we pass on to the wolds of East Yorkshire, then to the moors of North Yorkshire, Durham and Northumberland, and from there to the fells of Westmorland and Cumberland, on to the better grazing lands on the Cheviots, regarding which there is an old couplet:

> Though Cheviot's top be frosty yet
> He's green below the knee.

The varying terms for these northern uplands are often confusing to those who have looked upon such country as being hills, without having paused to examine the geological, topographical and agricultural differences which are very real, and often very obvious. It will perhaps clarify what is to follow if we briefly analyse the terms proper. In East Yorkshire the wolds form an extensive and important area. Locally they are spoken of as "t'wauds," a colloquial pronunciation which old documents prove was common in the thirteenth century. A wold may briefly be described as an elevated but often flat expanse of country. The derivation is still disputed amongst etymologists and both the Anglo-Saxon and Danish schools would seem to have good grounds for their contentions. The early authorities claim "wold" to have come from the Anglo-Saxon WEALD or WALD, signifying a treeless, bleak and unprotected upland, with wildness connoted, as in the case of the wealds of Kent. There was much excuse for arguing in favour of this origin of the word, especially prior to afforestation and

cultivation schemes. Then, too, local parish registers
show that the district was so wild as to be one of the last
in England to be infested with wolves, for the destruction
of which payments regularly were made. The late Rev.
M. C. F. Morris, who spent his life in the wold country
and recorded so much of its lore, recorded that up to the
middle of last century many of the long-haired, curl-
tailed greyhounds were to be found about the district.
Later authorities connect the word "wold" with the
Danish *vold*, a field or mound or rampart. Marshall, one
of the earliest writers on Agriculture, said in his *Rural
Economy of Yorkshire* (1796):

> "The wolds of Yorkshire appear as if, during some
> convulsion of Nature, they had been severed (by the
> sea-like Humber and its broad, rich banks) from those
> of Lincolnshire. In the present state of things they
> may be considered as the main link, broken off from
> the chain of chalky hills, which is thrown irregularly
> over the more southern provinces. The Yorkshire
> wolds are the Downs of Surrey on a larger scale.
> They are the most magnificent assemblage of chalky
> hills the island affords. The features are large; the
> surface is billowy, but not broken; the swells resemble
> Biscayan waves half pacified. The ground in general
> is peculiarly graceful. Wood and water would render
> it most beautiful. Water is forbidden, but wood may
> be had at will and it is extraordinary that the spirit of
> planting should have broken out so late. Utility as
> well as ornament calls loudly for this obvious improve-
> ment."

Forty years later, Charles Howard, of Melbourne,
York (he was secretary of the Yorkshire Agricultural
Society) wrote of "that elevated chalk and limestone soil
called 'The Wolds,'" and pointed out that as compared

66 LEVISHAM BECK ON THE PICKERING MOORS, EAST YORKSHIRE

67 SIMONSIDE SEEN ACROSS COQUETDALE, NEAR ROTHBURY, NORTHUMBERLAND

with the flat country of Holderness and the plain of York, the wolds are "essentially distinct in soil, cultivation and climate." He went on to define the extent of the Yorkshire wolds by an imaginary line of about thirty miles from north to south, from Malton on the Derwent to the village of Brough on the banks of the Humber. In breadth from east to west they vary much, but average about twelve miles. In 1812 Mr. Henry E. Strickland drew up a summary of the East Riding of Yorkshire for the Board of Agriculture, and in it he said of the wolds:

"The climate, in consequence of their great elevation, and their almost total want of wood and shelter, is severe and variable; the winds being extremely violent and penetrating, and by promoting a rapid evaporation, greatly aggravate the cold of the climate. The district has great uniformity in its general character. The northern and western fronts are towering and precipitous, from which it gradually sinks into the low country of Holderness. It may in general be said to have a moderately waving surface, intersected with numerous deep, narrow, winding valleys. The soil of the wolds is, with little variation, a light, friable, calcareous loam from three to ten inches in depth, and on the hills covering a chalk rubble from twelve to eighteen inches thick, below which the chalk rock lies to unknown depths."

The authorities just quoted wrote prior to the full fruits of afforestation and agricultural schemes of Sir Christopher Sykes (d. 1801) having been realised. Sir Christopher planted considerably and, indeed, was almost the pioneer of upland afforestation, and before he set about the development of the wolds it was possible to ride, on grass, the whole distance from Driffield to Malton.

16*

The moorlands of Lancashire, Yorkshire, Durham, Northumberland, and the Border country appear almost limitless in comparison with the wolds. Moor at once connotes land on which heather (colloquially "ling") is largely found. In *The Moorlands of North-eastern Yorkshire* (p. 31), Elgee rightly says that the word "moor" is in all essentials identical with the Old Norse MOR, signifying peat, turf, heath, or ling, and if we look at its meaning in the Gothic language we shall find that it is everywhere the same, though with some elasticity in its application. The Danes, who gave so many words to Yorkshire, topographical and agricultural, used the word moor, or mor, as being places on which turves could be cut. The Anglo-Saxons employed the word mor to define waste-land, a moor or heath. Elgee goes on:

"Many names are of Scandinavian origin and more or less describe the character of the particular moors to which they refer. Such is MURK mire moor near Egton, the name of which has been derived from Old Norse *myrkr* signifying dark, and *myrr*, a moor or boggy place. Again, the word "swang" is of frequent occurrence—Glaisdale swangs, and moss swangs, a word originating from the Old Norse *svangr*, a hollow usually more or less boggy. Then we have "syke," another term for swampy localities; "rook," or "ruck," piles of stones or turves; "slacks," shallow valleys; "haggs," wild and broken ground; "skews," small twisted valleys such as Hole Skew near Free-borough Hill. All these are probably derived from the names bestowed by the Scandinavian settlers of the eighth or ninth centuries."

In Yorkshire we rarely hear the word fell, though some of the moorland country could accurately be described as such in accordance with the significance the word has in Westmorland and Cumberland, where it is in common use, and where "moorland" is a term not so frequently heard. E. W. Prevost in his *Glossary of the Dialect of Cumberland* (1889) defined FELL as meaning (1) unenclosed or common land, whether hill or not; (2) a mountain, applied to particular mountains such as Scawfell, Caldbeck Fell, and (3) to a mountain district generally, which is termed "The Fell." . . . "In the north-west of the country the open commons were all distinguished by this name (pasture), and the lands since enclosed from the common still retain the name. In other parts they are called Commons, Moors, or Fells." Brockett, in *North Country Words* (1829) gives a fell as meaning "a rocky hill, a mountain or common, scarcely admitting of cultivation—frequently used for any moor or open waste, though palpably a high or alpine tract only." Camden, though hinting at other terminology, refers to only "moorland" in connection with the Pennine Chain.

Many of these hills, and adjoining lands, covering wide areas are described on old (and some modern) maps as "forests." To the average man this word suggests extensive woodlands, the absence of which has often occasioned both surprise and disappointment. Thus the explorers of Bowland Forest will encounter little woodland, except in the delightful Hodder Valley. Bowland is a district mainly of bleak fells and for sheer remoteness there are few routes to compare with that between the village of Slaidburn and the Ribble Valley. But Bowland is not all bleakness. There is the walk into the forest proper from Clitheroe, with the climb into Stanridge, and from here the view into the valley which goes (as all Bowland routes should) into Slaidburn is one of delightfully compact contrast between wood and bracken and heather. Apart from the Bowland, Inglewood and Rossendale Forests, Yorkshire alone has had as royal forests Galtres, Hatfield, Knaresborough, Pickering and those in Wensleydale and Richmondshire. In Norman, Plantagenet and early Tudor times the term "forest" defined an area of extensive waste-land which, to serve its purpose, necessarily included woodlands and pastures for beast of the chase. Thus the term "forest" which still obtains, means waste-land rather than wood-land, which makes clear the application of the term to Dartmoor, Exmoor, and the High Peak of Derbyshire. Pickering Forest in North Yorkshire was one of the most extensive of these royal game preserves; it comprised a considerable area of moorland, over the hills to Whitby and Goathland. In 1616 Pollard, late head constable of the libertie of Pickering Lythe compiled "certaine notes or marks whereby a forrest most propperlie mai be know and first what a forrest is:

"(1) A Forrest is a certain territory of ground en-vironed round about with immovable marks or boundaries.
"(2) It ought to be stored with Vert and Venison,
"(3) With all beasts belonging to a forrest.
"(4) A Forrest contains forrest, chase, park and warrant."

As a matter of fact Pickering Forest contained a wide area of moorland, and it also had a stretch of woodland, this being given in the Domesday Survey as being about twenty-four miles in length and six in breadth, but this was an exception. Inglewood Forest in Cumberland was another exception. There is an old saying in that county that in the days when Inglewood Forest flourished, so closely planted were the trees that a squirrel might travel from Carlisle to Penrith without ever touching the ground. Some of the traditions of this forest still remain, including that of the "Wild Huntsman" whose

68 THE ROMAN WALL ON THE GREAT WHIN SILL, NORTHUMBERLAND

restless astral and those of his phantom followers and
hounds still haunt what were once famous hunting-
grounds:

> Though Inglewood vanish mid chimneys and smoke,
> Her thickets uprooted, and felled her last oak,
> Our spirits shall haunt her, and men yet unborn
> Shall quake at the blast of the Wild Huntsman's horn.

There are also a number of terms in use for sub-
divisions, or particular parts of hills, fells and moorlands,
which will frequently be heard in use, and seen on maps,
and which may require elucidation. Indeed, a lengthy
and interesting glossary of words descriptive of the
topography of the uplands, could be compiled. It will,
however, suffice to give the meaning of those most
commonly encountered. "Slacks" are narrow, shallow
valleys or hollows; "haggs," wild and broken ground;
"moss," a boggy place; "gill," a narrow glen with rocky
banks and a stream (or "grain") at the bottom; "howe,"
the site of a tumulus, of which there are hundreds on the
northern moorlands. Elgee tells us, "It cannot be
questioned that the Howe builders had a preference for
the moors as burial-grounds, the highest points being
the favourite sites. The reason they had for this selection is not at all clear, but it may have arisen from a fear
of ghosts—especially those of dreaded chiefs. Probably
the ashes of important men only were interred in most
Howes." A "skew" (or sceugh), a rough, steep bank;
"dyke," in Northumberland, a wall or bank fence, in
Yorkshire the term usually refers to a ditch; "haughs"
in Northumberland are low, flat or marshy grounds.

Although the redoubtable Dr. Johnson in his
Dictionary defined a peak as "a sharply pointed hill," the
Peak proper is a district and includes Derbyshire and
parts of Cheshire, Staffordshire and, of course, Yorkshire
has a hand in it. Where Johnson erred, Old Camden

many moons earlier was, as usual, right in saying that ". . . it was called in the Old English tongue Peac-Land and at this day the Peak." In these days tautology is (or should be) a grievous sin, and it is difficult to understand the persistence of the phrase, "The Peak District."

In this lovely country of mountain, moor, dale and limestone stimulated pasture, there are countless walks that will not unduly weary your feet. But also, if you wish, you can take the difficult paths of Kinder Scout, Bleaklow and Derwent Edge, and this is serious business. Here you walk mostly on peat. Countless names occur to me of routes that each adherent ranks the best. Hayfield to Edale and along the Mam Tor ridge: Glossop, Doctor's Gate, Snake Inn, Edale. Then there is grand Kinder Scout himself, a mountain of heather and rock, much of it 2,000 feet above sea-level. Its sides are steep, but take you quickly and suddenly away from the industrial nearness. Other mountains of the Peak are Bleaklow, Derwent Ridge and Margery Hill. To know them intimately you must be a climber of experience and skill, but there are other moorland routes which will bring the grandeur of the mountains near, and also offer a beauty all their own.

One such is into Doctor's Gate and a good point to start is Glossop. From there you soon can leave the Sheffield road (just past Shire Hill) and at Mossy Lee encounter one of the main Roman roads across the Pennines. Here you get the best of Seal Edge, and Fairbrook Naze, and beyond Alport Bridge to Woodland Valley, Kinder Scout's plateau accompanies your road, which you should take for Win Hill. I like to see Kinder Scout's awe-inspiring frowns suddenly. So when I can I leave New Mills, and climb its hill, to the old Mellor Road on top, from which you look down on the Goyt. From Cobden, near by, go down to Mellor and skirt the

Ethrow Valley on the way to Sandylane. Past Coombs
Edge you climb to see magnificently (and suddenly) a
distant Kinder Scout. You won't want to rush back
townwards, but it is useful to know that via Rowarth
and Lantern Pike to Birch Vale, a train or bus will take
you there.

On some parts of the Yorkshire moors, as I have said,
there can be real (not chance) remoteness and for miles
no anchor of civilisation in sight. Farther north, this
lost feeling is more common. But in the Peak, if you
beware of the mountains, there are homelier and more
intimate possibilities—you are always striking a farm or
hamlet. These valleys have a soft and pastoral beauty.
In particular, some of the dales of the Dove Valley, or
between the Wye and the upper Dove, remind me of
the moorland dales of North Yorkshire. If you are in
the mood for some such "peace from life's fresh crown"
Buxton is a good place to start from. Make for Dowel
Dale and soon the quiet of Earl Sterndale will make you
sojourn there since it is peace you want, and ease. If
the climb of Hitter Hill invites, your labour will be well
rewarded by the grand expanse of the Dove and its
meadows. Descending via Aldery Cliff and High
Weeldon you reach Hurdlow Town and some two miles
distant is the old-world village of Monyash. Lathill
Dale is near with its green and compact beauty, and
Conksbury Bridge, Haddon and Bakewell (of which
more later). Now this can be called the limestone
country of the Peak. The uplands have no great elevation nor are they ever changing their contour. Here
and there your view will be interrupted by a lime quarry
or a disused mine. There are "swallets" to explore, and
the inquisitive will find romance in the underground
caverns, a legacy of the now disused lead mines. There
is a variety even amongst limestone valleys. In Chee
Dale, for instance, there is a splendour of white massed

rock which watches over the river below and makes walking as far as, say, verdant Miller's Dale, heavy and tiring. It is here that the Wye takes command of the picture as it assumes its wide course through scenery more wooded, and passing Monsal Dale on to Ashford, until, via lovely Bakewell (a Saxon town the original name being Baddecan-well, the be-diked well) the river finds its home (and its rest?) in the waters of the Derwent. Other walks abound, well known and otherwise. Amongst the former there is, of course, the often-praised walking country of Dovedale, which offers the same ingredients as the one previously outlined—woodland, and river, and limestone rock—and indeed Dovedale is as lovely as its name.

In the foregoing few sketchy itineraries my aim has been to indicate contrasting features of the countryside rather than to act as a guide on a walking tour. But before going east over the Pennines for Yorkshire hills, I must ask you not to miss the grand sight of Jacob's Ladder whenever you are Edale way. You reach it by Upper Booth; it had its origin as quite an unimportant footpath, but the years which have brought increasing armies of trampers have fashioned it into the 300-feet landmark (and ladder) it now is. It is a grand point from which to view the Peak, and if Hayfield is your destination you get there best, I think, by way of Coldwell Clough.

The northern upland scenery is indeed the greater part of the northern landscape, and the traveller from the south meets it when he reaches the mountains of the Peak and its hills. From here the Pennines run in a continued ridge to the Highlands of Scotland; from Ashbourne in Derbyshire to the Roman Wall, and on that route there is Appleby, Muker, Brough, Ilkley, Middleton-in-Teesdale and Buxton to note for headquarters when you go exploring. The great Pennines divide Yorkshire

from Lancashire, and Durham from Westmorland.
They may not properly be the backbone of all England,
but they are the mother hills of the north and give life
to all its rivers.

The Hambleton Range extends from Easingwold to
near Helmesley; the highest point is near Kilburn where
the White Horse (cut 100 yards along the side of the hill
in 1857), a gliding club, and the curiously situated Lake
Gormire annually attract thousands of tourists. The
lake covers an area of about sixteen acres, and is about
one mile in circumference. It lies at the very foot of the
white stone cliff (1,056 feet above sea-level) and, as with
Semmerwater in Wensleydale, many local legends are
associated with it. Below stretches the fertile vale of
Mowbray bounded in the far distance by Penhill in
Wensleydale and Great Whernside in Coverdale.
Hambleton for time out of count has had a very close
and important connection with the turf. Indeed, by
statute law horse-racing was at one time allowed only at
Newmarket, York and Black Hambleton, as the early
turf recorders (and others) persisted in calling it, despite
the fact that Black Hambleton proper is a hill some miles
away from the old race-course and present training-
grounds. At the foot of the Hambletons lies Coxwold
(with its associations with Sterne, not to mention its
being the legendary burial-place of Oliver Cromwell)
and Byland Abbey, and nestling in the hills close by the
River Rye (which here turns into Ryedale proper) are the
ruins of beautiful Rievaulx Abbey. They stand in
sylvan setting on the borders of Duncombe Park with
its many deer, confined in wild and natural surroundings
by a wall which stretches for some miles by the side of the
Thirsk–Helmsley road over the Hambletons. Another
road (once used by toll-escaping drovers) leads from
Hambleton to Cleveland. It must be travelled on foot
and literally takes one off the beaten path into grandeur

and solitude, and past Chequer's Inn with its curious sign bearing the advice and promise:

> Be not in haste, step in and taste
> Good ale for nothing to-morrow.

This hill-top hostelry has gained wide fame because its peat fire has been continuously alight for well over one hundred years. Many a moorland farmer will tell you that there is nothing really remarkable about this as for quite as long a period there has always been sufficient red-hot peat-ash left in the morning to restart their fire on their own kitchen hearthstone. Nowadays, however, the big open fireplaces are giving way to modern grates and modern cooking which rules out the once popular "turf-cakes." Even on the hills coal-lorries find their way to far-off places. Thus there are fewer peat "rooks" seen on the moorlands and sooty rather than sweet blue peat-fumes issue from many a farm-house chimney. The tang of this peat-smoke has been referred to by Donald Boyd in his excellent book, *On Foot in Yorks*, as

> ". . . a perfume indescribable to me, but one which smells as though all the sweetness and vigour of the moor had been torn out of it and were presented in one trickster's potion by the deed of fire, the smell which is the memorial of half the great tragical stories of our tongue; peat-smoke of the Covenanters drifting over the graves of the martyrs; the smell of the fires of Ireland burning in wretched cabins which still could house the hope of revolt; the smell of the ancient north country ravaged by every invader who crossed the sea; all these like the peat, silent under the coat of grey ash, but waiting for the breath that would fetch the red glow up again."

Duncombe Park previously referred to, is owned by

70 BUNSTER HILL, NEAR ILAM, STAFFORDSHIRE

71 IN DOVEDALE, DERBYSHIRE

72 THE VIEW FROM HEY TOR, DARTMOOR

the Earl of Feversham, one of the most extensive hill and moorland proprietors in the North. Farndale, famed for its daffodils but now partly given up to waterworks, is his. So is little-explored Bransdale, tucked away between Farndale and Bilsdale, which latter is also part of his estate. From the Hambletons by Helmsley, over Harriet Aire, down Newgate's steep bank to Bilsdale, through its twelve winding miles, either branching off at Chop Yat and continuing through Raisdale to the Cleveland Range or meeting it by continuing along the Stokesley road, almost every acre is owned by Lord Feversham. Of these dales perhaps Bilsdale is the most delightful, the most accessible, and certainly the best known. It was here, so says tradition, that George Villiers, second Duke of Buckingham, whilst out with his hounds caught the chill which resulted in his death. On his retirement from the court of Charles he lived at Helmsley Castle and established, if not the first, one of the very earliest packs of foxhounds in England. His country was that which has been hunted by the Sinnington, Bilsdale and Farndale packs ever since the gay Duke died (*not*, as Pope says, "in the worst inn's worst room," but in the still standing private house of a tenant at Kirbymoorside). These northern hill packs—there are many others which go far back in history—the Goathland and Staintondale in Yorkshire, the Ullswater, Coniston, Melbreak, Blencathra (the original country of John Peel, of whom the world would never have heard had it not been for the song) and others on the fells, the Haydon and Border in Northumberland—are part of the life and tradition of the hills. Their roots are far back in the story of the past and are so connected with the lore and legend, not to mention affections, of the folk on the heathlands as to be part of their inheritance. So intimately do foxhunting matters enter into their lives that it is not so very long ago that the local Hunt fixtures for the week were given out amongst the Sunday notices at some dale churches.

Reverting to the point at which the Earl of Feversham's extensive moorland property joins the Cleveland Range, it is there one begins to see in the red and blue shale-tips evidence everywhere on the hills of the extensive workings which took place in and beyond Cleveland (Whitby way) for jet and alum. The jet trade was killed by the importation from abroad of inferior material (which changed its colour and cracked), and killed, too, by the fickleness of fashion. The more extensive and far more important alum industry in the locality came to an end when other and cheaper means were discovered for its production. Just before his death last year Major R. B. Turton wrote a book (posthumously published) entitled *The Alum Farm*, in which he brought incontrovertible evidence to show that Sir Thos. Chaloner of Guisborough did not, as has for long been believed in North Yorkshire, discover alum on the hills on his Cleveland estate. It was John Chaloner, father of Thomas, who first found and worked alum, not in Cleveland but in the Isle of Lambay. Major Turton's book suggests that when Thomas lost his lands and was deprived of the Isle of Lambay, his cousin, the younger Sir Thomas offered him asylum at Guisborough and called his attention to the geological treasures in the adjoining hills. Thus does the author of *The Alum Farm* destroy local legend:

"The discovery of alum is attributed to Sir Thos. Chaloner, who was undoubtedly the Governor of Henry, Prince of Wales, and who is usually described as a distinguished naturalist on the strength of a book called *A Shorte Discourse of the most rare and excellent virtue of nitre*. This book is attributed to him in the Index of the British Museum (no doubt on the authority of Anthony Wood in his *Athenae Oxoniensis*) but a very cursory examination of its contents should have convinced the compiler that Wood's information was unreliable. The story runs that during his travels in Italy Sir Thomas remarked the similarity between the delicate green tint of the vegetation near Guisborough and that of the alum-producing district of Puteoli and that he bribed some of the Pope's workmen to accompany him privately to England, whither he smuggled them in casks. This so exasperated the Pope, who had a lucrative monopoly of the alum trade, that he fulminated an anathema against both the seduced and the seducer."

Major Turton then proceeds to rob Cleveland at any rate of the distinction of originating the alum trade on its hills, though not of the importance which later was attached to the industry there. But notwithstanding exposure, it is almost certain that when strangers remark upon the red road leading from Chop Yat in Bilsdale through Raisdale to Carlton in Cleveland (one of the most picturesque of all the villages under the shadow of the Cleveland hills) and upon other similar roads, or ask the origin of the red and blue shale-heaps along the hillsides, they will continue to be told the Chaloner legend, perpetuated by an old Cleveland poet, who thus opened his verses nearly a century ago:

> Time was when alum was the staple trade
> Of Cleveland, at our feet appears to be
> Some old volcano's crater. Industry
> Of alum-worker's muscles 'twas that made
> That huge abyss—the only monument
> Remaining of their toil.

Yet not only for alum, jet, or its iron-stone mines is the Cleveland Range famed. At the village of Marton was born Captain James Cook, who as a boy walked from Aireyholme Farm under Roseberry (where his father was hind) to Great Ayton school. On the pack-roads over this same range the first of the wonderful Cleveland Bay horses carried heavy burdens. They were originally known as "Chapmen's horses," and were bred on and around the Cleveland hills. As roads improved they were dosed with the blood of the best thoroughbreds of that day—horses which had won long distance races, carrying heavy weights. And so the horse of the Cleveland hills came to be in great demand to draw the mail and stage coaches. They are still bred and still in demand all the world over for grading-up native breeds and, because of the density and quality of their bone, their activity, courage and prepotency, are used as a foundation for hunter breeding. Roseberry has been incidentally mentioned. This conical-shaped hill stands out as a sentinel in the Cleveland Range, and can be seen, as already shown, from Scotland. From its summit a remarkable panorama can be seen on every hand. Its name has passed through many forms, and its shape and beauty has been marred in recent years by mining operations under its base. These are now discontinued, but not before Roseberry Topping suffered much. It is steeped in legend and has a special place in the affections of Yorkshire folk who never tire of its story. Northwards, and a long way below Roseberry, there is the varied country of Tees-side and county Durham. To the north-east and south-west the Clevelands extend almost without a break. The general level rises to the west, but eastwards there is a gradual descent until the limestone ends in steep cliffs along the coast which shelter beautiful bays and fishing villages such as Runswick Bay and Staithes and southwards to Whitby. Here the full glory of the Vale of Cleveland falls gently away into the Vale of Pickering, interspersed with rolling moorland, expanses of heather, and occasional stretches of woodland. What the naked eye cannot see are the many deeply entrenched streams which are so characteristic of this limestone country.

Only a mile or so away from Roseberry stands Easby Hill with its monument to Capt. Cook; from both summits it is possible on a clear day (and when there is no smoke-screen from Tees-side) to see the Cheviots, in dim outline. These hills vary in character from the Clevelands, the Hambletons and other ranges within the scope of this chapter. There are much greater areas of grass on their sides; heather and bracken do not seem to have made the same inroads as they have on most Yorkshire and Northumberland ranges. One speaks of Northumberland to-day in its restricted county application and not of the Northumbria which extended from the Tweed to the Humber. There is, of course, abundant wild hill country both on the hills stretching Otterburn way to Carter Bar and the Borders over the military road from Chollerford Bridge into Cumberland. This same military road takes one into the region of the world-famous Roman Wall—the most interesting feature of the Northumbrian hills, indeed one of the most remarkable examples of Roman culture we have in England. Mr. R. G. Collingwood, M.A., F.G.S., a recognised authority on Hadrian's Wall, rightly says in his book:

"The part that is most worth seeing is the section twenty-five miles long, between Halton Chesters and Birdswald, and of that section the really spectacular part lies between the North Tyne at Chesters and the Tipalt Burn at Thirlwall. Here, and here alone, the actual Wall stands high above ground for miles together; elsewhere the earthworks that accompany it are plain enough, but the Wall itself seldom is visible except to the eye of faith."

Originally this Wall was seventy-three miles long,

stretching from Wallsend to Bowness-on-Solway. It takes us back to the second century, but even so is not "as old as the hills," as the common simile has it.

If the Wall transports us almost to the very beginnings of our island's history, the Borders have seen the making of much more history in which the hard-bitten hill-men played no small part. These Northumbrian hills seem everywhere to breathe of the Percys, of battle and of raids, forays, attacks, and moss-troopers. The late Mr. Howard Pease in *Northumbrian Decameron*, speaking of the time between Edward I to James VI tells us the Northumbrian folk were never free from terror and nightly attack. He says:

"The first thing a Northumbrian did when he woke in the morning, it has been said, was to put his hand to his throat to see if it had been cut in the night. On either side of the March line the conditions were alike—either nation lived by taking in each other's cattle, and the 'Fire the Fells' and 'Hard-riding Dicks,' loved the life. The Robsons might run a raid into Liddesdale in order to 'larn' the Armstrongs and Elliotts that 'the next time gentlemen came to take their sheep they were no to be scabbit.' . . . After 1603 the occupation of the moorland Othellos was gone. The lance of the moss trooper not infrequently became the pick-axe of the pitman."

There is peace on the Border hills now and though times and conditions, and life itself change, though there are pylons to disfigure, roads, and ugly houses in unexpected places, here and there man-made excrescences to jar, the hills and vast moorlands remain constant. Even when man has destroyed the beauty of one hill-side there is always abiding comfort in the knowledge that we have only to walk or drive on a mile or two, to again be amid beauty undisturbed.

E. F. Bozman

MOUNTAINS AND LAKES

THERE is magic in the place-names of the English Lake District—Scafell, Helvellyn, the Old Man of Coniston, Wastwater, the Langdale Pikes, Esk Hause, Black Sail, Seatoller, Dungeon Ghyll—and no one with adventure in his blood can contemplate the distant sky-line as seen from the east side of Lake Windermere, comparable on a much smaller scale to the famous views of the Alpine Chain from Bern or Zurich, without a tingling in the toes and an itching to be among the mountains. These are mountains right enough. Green and smooth and harmless they may be on a fine summer's day, their precipices visible and easily avoided except by the fanatic who actually chooses them for ascent or descent of his own free will, yet they can be grim enough when mist swirls round them, luring the walker to unjustifiable excursions among rocks and clefts that seem to assume gigantic dimensions in momentarily revealed glimpses, or when snow and ice have bound the rock ridges and hoared the grass slopes; or again when a gale buffets and volleys over the cairns on Great Gable and its neighbour Green Gable, shrieking through Windy Gap, so well named, between them.

An approach almost equally popular with the famous Windermere one is from the Keswick end. The situation of Keswick itself is more dramatic than that of Windermere or Ambleside. It is more like a Swiss mountain village, set right among the hills with the huge Skiddaw group shutting it in from the north and the foothills of all the other important groups stretching invitingly to south-west, south and south-east. Before motor-cars were so popular it had in detail the characteristics of an alpine village, and even to-day in spite of sophistication it retains something of this quality—a quality that seems to be imposed on villages by mountains that hem them in. Steep streets, tumbling water, modest well-built cottages, the sound of nailed boots, an ever-present skyline silhouette, felt even when the clouds are down— these are among the features. And always a pervading smell of fresh air.

Windermere and Keswick are the official gates to the lake district; in addition there is a sort of tradesmen's entrance, the approach from the sea-coast via Wastwater, a way that should be reserved for the initiated because it leads so directly to the secret heart of the fells, Scafell itself; and another beautiful side-entrance, very private, is by Ennerdale.

Like all great mountain districts, the Lakes keep their secret hidden from the casual observer. Their secret is Scafell, and the key to the inner temple is Esk Hause. Scafell, alone among English mountains, is somewhat inaccessible by the easiest route, and its steeper approaches on the northern precipice offer some of the finest rock-climbing in the world. Baedeker, usually so reliable, is wrong when he conducts the tourist to Scafell Pike, the higher of the two summits, and says that the view from

73 THE HEAD OF WINDERMERE, BACKED BY LANGDALE PIKES, FROM ABOVE AMBLESIDE

74 TARN HOWS NEAR CONISTON IN THE LAKE DISTRICT

Scafell does not differ enough to "repay the trouble" of a visit. Actually Scafell is incomparably the finer of the two peaks. And in spite of their height (about 3,200 feet) the summits of Scafell and the Pike are not visible from Keswick or Windermere. They withdraw behind or lose themselves among their satellites, the Gable, Bowfell and the Crinkle Crags, and leave the more showy work to mountains such as the Langdale Pikes and Glaramara. It is an admirable technique, characteristic of the truly great.

Helvellyn and her companions while not exactly within the inner sanctum are yet not subsidiary to Scafell. If Scafell is thought of as the King of the Lake mountains, then Helvellyn is more like the Queen than the Prince. (Perhaps burly Skiddaw, the only other peak to over-top 3,000 feet, is the Prince.) She is of equal importance with King Scafell in the general scheme and below her spreads like a train the beautiful lake of Ullswater. She is more accessible, too, as a Queen should be, than Scafell, and on her Striding Edge, that famous dizzy walk, she offers the adventurous tourist the slightly spurious thrill of a danger that looks greater than it is. For if on a fine day you fall off, or on a day of gale and rain are blown off, the Striding Edge, you will not roll down to Red Tarn on one side or down to Grisedale on the other, though you may feel as if you will; you will in fact stay more or less where you are and have only yourself to blame if you cannot find your way back to Grasmere or to Patterdale. If, however, you over-step a precipice on Scafell, or on any of his lords-in-waiting—Great Gable or Bowfell or Pavey Ark or the Langdales—then nothing will save you except your two hands and feet; if you fall you will be killed.

Although the area of the Lake District proper is so small, some thirty miles north and south by twenty miles east and west, that in theory it can be traversed during a long day's walk in either direction, it must not be thought that two days on foot will suffice to explore it. Certainly two days so spent will give the tourist a far better idea of the lie of the land than a week in a motor-car blazing over Kirkstone Pass or Dunmail Raise, and bowling along the lake-sides, but they will not begin to do the district justice. One of its chief charms is its extraordinary variety within so small a compass, and merely to know the main outlines is to miss the trees while being aware of the wood. Supposing uniform weather conditions (most rash to pre-suppose uniformly fine weather—and needlessly gloomy to expect uniform wet weather, for the rain changes in quality and quantity from day to day, almost from hour to hour), but supposing for the sake of argument uniform weather, one of the first things the walker or climber will notice is the kaleidoscopic changes of scenery. It is possible by ascending 100 feet, by turning a hairpin bend in a zigzag path, or by crossing one of the thousand torrents, to change the panorama so radically that one seems to have walked into a new country. No other mountain district has this quality in so marked a degree; the most widely travelled mountaineers, hardened in landscape sensation, have remarked the point. There is in fact no "typical view" in the Lakes—not bare mountain-side, not gleaming lake, not green shoulder, not forest, not rock precipice, not scree-shoot, not cowering slate-roofed farmstead, not narrow valley studded with boulders like sheep, not feathery waterfall; none of these are typical, though all are to be found in profusion by their admirers. Water is perhaps the most typical commodity of the area—I suppose the sea-lover would say the same of the Atlantic—fresh bubbling water which the pilgrim to the district first meets in one of the full rivers, the Esk or the Duddon or the Cocker or the Derwent, so clear and hurrying as English rivers go, then in one of the big lakes, Windermere or Derwentwater or Ullswater or Crummock

Water and Buttermere, whichever way he happens to come, then in the lovely dashing mountain torrents and waterfalls that fill the big lakes, then in the high tarns like Grisedale Tarn under Helvellyn or Sprinkling Tarn above Styhead Pass or Stickle Tarn below the Langdales, then, as the climber raises himself under his own steam, in more secret and inaccessible places which he has to hunt for because he is thirsty; until at last he is at the top of one of the high mountains, above the water-level of the district and out of reach of the springs. Water too is characteristic of the district because it is usually raining in the Lakes; driving mist or big thunder drops or most often plain, teeming, soaking rain from an apparently inexhaustible sky.

But when it is not raining in the summer-time and the sun comes out it can be blazing hot, hot enough in a dry season to make the walker parched with thirst as soon as he is above the tarns and to make the rock-climber, plastered against the sun-baked rocks of Scafell pinnacle, curse himself for leaving his sack at the foot of the climb; hot enough to make a bathe in the shallows of one of the lakes more enjoyable than the average English sea. Such conditions are rare, just as in winter hard ice and deep snow are rare; but the very hot days and the very cold days come and are all the more enjoyable by contrast with the prevailing wet.

This variety of feature makes it exceedingly difficult to identify the mountains and lakes in the landscape at any given moment, even when they are old friends well known by close acquaintance. Their appearance changes rapidly and completely with the observer's progress, and it is not proper to claim to know the Great Gable, for example, until it has been seen from a number of different aspects, in which it will change in shape from sharp to smooth, in colour from green to black, and in texture from hard to soft. Thus the only way to learn the district

18

is in detail, by a number of eccentric walks, not great ridge-striding walks, but carefully arranged expeditions from one valley to the next via the intervening mountain-tops. Consider, for example, three adjoining valleys, Buttermere, Ennerdale and Wasdale. These dales are utterly different in character and each gives an entirely different impression of the great mountain group—the Scafell and Gable group—which they drain between them. A good plan of reconnaissance would be to start from Buttermere and walk up to Scarth Gap, then over High Stile and down to Ennerdale and the Angler's Inn. Next day the astonishing views of High Crag and the Pillar can be absorbed during the walk up Ennerdale again, over Black Sail Pass, or possibly including the Pillar mountain (not the Rock) *en route*, and on down to Wasdale Head Hotel. Such a circuit will put the tourist in a state of mind proper to approach Scafell and the Gable themselves, and will greatly enhance his appreciation of their grandeur. Similar expeditions can be planned all round the compass of the Lake District, and they can easily and safely be worked out from the Ordnance map with a little first-aid, especially as to the time factors (for as in all mountain districts journeys must be planned in time rather than in space), from local informants, or from one of the many guide-books. Ascents of all the big peaks can be included in these traverses from dale to dale, or better still can be offered the tribute of a separate expedition each, which will mean that the tourist will have to stay at least two nights at each of his inns or cottages. I say "have to stay"; I am writing only of this plan; it will be no hardship to the mountain-lover to spend his whole annual fortnight or month in Wasdale or Buttermere or Seatoller or Gras-mere or Coniston, and the rock-climber will need several such visits before he begins to know the numerous routes in each district. This detailed knowledge of

75 THE UPPER PART OF CRUMMOCK WATER, LOOKING TO HONISTER CRAG

the mountains must be acquired in order to be able to enjoy the great day-walks that can be made through the district from north to south or from east to west.

As I have suggested the one-inch Ordnance map, carefully used and supplemented by local information, is the best possible guide to the district. Baddeley's guide is also useful and detailed, and there is a whole mass of literature of a more or less practical nature, mostly of comparatively recent date, that is to say, written during the last hundred years or so, when mountains have changed gradually from public menaces into fashionable objects of sport. Fortunately the climber, or the walker, or the hiker may still rove the neighbourhood untrammelled by any literary associations, and he need not even bother to read or carry any of the legions of guides and handbooks. The one-inch Ordnance map is better than all the guides put together and the district is safe at all times of year if certain obvious precautions are taken. The best descriptive book in prose as far as I know is still A. G. Bradley's *Highways and Byways in the Lake District*, published in 1901. Another very good book, and of more practical use as a guide, is *The Lake Counties*, by W. G. Collingwood, and more recently H. H. Symonds has written a very useful guide to walkers called appropriately *Walking in the Lake District*. The rock-climbers have their own special climbers' guides, published by the Fell and Rock Club, and these must be consulted by anyone attempting the crags—it is folly to be without them unless there is an experienced climber in the party. There are five volumes dealing with Doe Crag, the Pillar Rock, the Scafell group, Great Gable and Borrowdale, and the Langdales respectively. In each the climbs are graded in difficulty from "easy" or "moderate" to "very severe" or some would say "verging on the suicidal." These guides are very reliable, but the climber of experience may be inclined to explore on his own sometimes without necessarily following the elaborately scheduled routes to the letter.

For the mass of creative literature that derives from the lakes it is hardly fair to hold the district responsible. There is good, bad and indifferent reading to be found, ranging from the famous names of William Wordsworth and the Lake poets through a whole gamut of writers, professional and amateur, to our well-loved Sir Hugh Walpole to-day. It is amazing, evidently, what the scenery there will do for the writing man. This galaxy of talent must often have been a source of wonder to the agricultural inhabitants of the hills who were trying to make a living out of sheep and farming. Wordsworth, as the most famous and as a native of the counties, was loved and idolised locally, but he must have been an object of curiosity striding round the fells. An old stone-breaker at Rydal is reputed on being asked "What's the news?" to have replied "Why nowt very particlar, only old Wudsworth's brocken lowce ageean," and the house-wife of a Rydal cottage once said that "he goes booin his pottery about t'rooads an' t'fields and taks no nooatish o' nobody."

Wordsworth's inspiration is shown truly when it comes indirectly from the mountains, in writing such as the *Ode on the Intimations of Immortality*:

> The cataracts blow their trumpets from the steep;
> No more shall grief of mine the season wrong;
> I hear the echoes through the mountains throng,
> The winds come to me from the fields of sleep. . . .

His direct description, of which so much has been preserved, as, for example, the following lines about the reflection in Lake Windermere, is far below the standard of his great philosophical poems, and often descends to banality.

And yet 'twas but a shepherd's boy
  That watched the wind's uncertain turn,
Apply'd the spark with wanton joy,
  Blowing the turf to make it burn.

On blooming heath, on furze, on brake,
  The crackling torrent feeds for miles:
The boatman on Winander Lake
  Sees the inverted blaze, and smiles.

At a time when England is in danger of losing her
countryside the value of the Lake District is paramountly
that of personal refreshment for the wanderer in the
solitude of mountain and valley. Books and literary
associations are best left behind, and for this reason even
guide-books are suspect. The Lake District is so small.
It could be spoiled if literary and historical associations
were to be pinned to each crag and boulder. Let the
tourist find what he needs in it for himself, not the second-
hand discoveries of his predecessors. That is primarily
what this safe and accessible jewel offers. Let us assume
that the tourist has acquired some detailed acquaintance
by the apprenticeship I have suggested. Then let him
take one of the great through walks, say, for example, the
shortest and perhaps the finest, the across way west to
east, from Wastwater to Grasmere.

*   *   *   *   *

It is a fine morning and the tourist and his wife, or
failing his wife his friend, leave the inn at Wasdale Head
after breakfast. As soon as they are outside the door they
begin to forget the cold and shabby but romantic dining-
room, for Yewbarrow and Kirk Fell tower steep and
green on the left, and to their right the Scafell massif lies
hidden, waiting to disclose itself as a reward for height
gained. It is a dappled morning perhaps, with a fresh wind
blowing and whitish clouds racing across a background

of blue sky. The mountains are sometimes clear, sometimes wreathed. The walkers saunter to Burnthwaite. through a stile that seems to have been designed to pass only the thinnest sheep-dogs, and they are on the rough track to Styhead, their nailed boots scraping and crunching musically. The path mounts steadily and new views of the hills begin to unfold. The walkers settle down to their uphill rhythm, slow and sure, and for the most part they look down at the stony track, selecting the best footsteps. After half an hour or more they pause to take stock of the situation. A few minutes ahead of them a party of men and girls, with two or three coiled ropes among them, is leaving the path on the left and plugging up the hill-side to Kern Knotts. They will climb the chimney, a steep and cheerful place in fine weather, but black and forbidding, especially on the slabs above the chimney when the wind is shrieking and tearing the mists over the Gable; probably when they have done the chimney, they will unrope and go on up the mountain to the foot of the Napes above, a fine precipice which offers numerous rock-climbs of varying degrees of difficulty. On the Napes is to be found the Needle, that sensational and often photographed rock-climb which is really a sharp detached boulder on one of the arêtes of the precipice. It is a short climb (but long enough to be dangerous), and A. G. Bradley reports a non-climber as looking at a photograph by his friend who was trying to convert him to the pleasures of rock-climbing and asking:

"What's that thing?"

"The Needle Rock," replied the enthusiast.

"And who in thunder's that d——d fool on top of it?"

"That's me."

When their climb on the Napes is safely over they will be able to look over the valley and get a side view of Scafell Pinnacle itself, that miracle of firm rock.

The walkers resume their way. They are not on a rope

77 THE ROOF OF THE LAKE DISTRICT FROM CONISTON OLD MAN

and are free to meditate on the scene around them. They are beginning to feel their height now; the going is easier and the wind stronger. The path rises continuously until they are at Styhead, the top of the pass between Wasdale and Borrowdale. The mountains open up finely now. Ahead the stony track leads down to Seathwaite, to the left is an inviting path to the large and invisible Gable summit; the walkers turn right, continuing upward over grass and mountain-side to the beautiful green plateau that is called Esk Hause. Here they pause and take off their sacks. The view is a thrilling one, comprising "the whole of Borrowdale and Derwentwater, with Skiddaw in the rear, visible from his base to his cope";[1] it is better in some respects than a summit view because the shapes of Great End and Bowfell are seen to better advantage from below. The day is clearing, and the wind is sweeping away the cloud from everywhere except the major summits, the three-thousand footers which are still distinguished by their smoke-wisps. The air is fresh with the smell of wet grass and rock, and perfumed with a faint scent of thyme drawn by the sun. The main features of the district are all visible from here, the central mountain group and the radiating valleys each with their characteristic lake. The Langdales look particularly fine; they are a good mountain shape; they rise immediately ahead of the walkers, between them and their destination at Grasmere, and will be passed later in the day either on their left shoulder or much lower down on the right slopes.

These hills that look so smooth and innocent on this dappled day conceal fearsome precipices, which must be avoided by the walker, and on which routes up to the limit of human achievement have been worked out by rock-climbers. The most famous are Scafell, the Pillar Rock, the Napes and Doe Crags. Scafell, to which a

---

[1] C. Mackay, *Scenery and Poetry of the Lakes*, 1846.

cairned track on the walkers' right hand now leads invitingly over hidden Scafell Pike, is the finest in natural splendour and its northern precipice brings the triumphant climber right out on the top of the mountain. There are many sound routes, such as the Slingsby chimney route, well within the power of any athletic party under proper leadership, and for the adventurous the face of the pinnacle provides many elegant fine-weather routes, climbable only in rubber because of the small footholds which will not take a clumsy nailed boot; the pinnacle routes are steep and sensational and dizzily exposed but essentially safe because of the quality of the rock. The climbs on Scafell compare favourably in every way with such famous Alpine climbs as the Chamonix Aiguilles, and Scafell pinnacle catches the eye in this district as inevitably as the Matterhorn in Zermatt. The Pillar Rock as a cragsman's hunting-ground is hardly less in stature. The crag is not quite on top of the mountain—it is on the Ennerdale side—but for sound and (once begun) unescapable routes no two could be finer for ordinary folk than the North Climb and the New West on the Pillar Rock. The feature of the North Climb, after a series of steep and amazingly varied pitches, is a nose which leads the climber out along a delicate traverse until he is poised over a drop of hundreds of feet into Ennerdale when suddenly all holds seem to desert him. Actually he has only to grasp the smooth nose with his palms and pull up, and he will arrive. But it is impossible to believe this at the first attempt unless there is a strong rope firmly held from above. Therefore leaders on this climb must be experienced. Fortunately the obstacle can be turned by a detour, and only the roped members of the party need actually take the nose "direct"; the leader ensconced safely above and firmly belayed, can play them on the rope, watching their struggles and hesitations, and

79 A LAKELAND FARM AT LITTLE LANGDALE, WESTMORLAND

80 THE HEAD OF WASTWATER, CUMBERLAND

81 WATENDLATH VILLAGE, NEAR KESWICK, CUMBERLAND

irresponsive to their cries for mercy, with the knowledge that one good pull on the rope will bring them to safe and easy ground above. The feature of the New West climb is its general steepness of angle, its soundness of rock, and its exposed slabs near the top at a point where the leader realises in a flash how much vertical ground there is immediately below him. The list of climbs can be extended to a long one, and nowadays a number of severe routes have been worked out by the experts surpassing in difficulty even the great Central Buttress climb on Scafell which, when it was discovered by means of cunning rope-manœuvring at the critical point, was thought to be the limit of possibility.

The walkers put on their sacks again, and make their way past Angle Tarn to the steep and slippery track which plunges by Rossett Gill to the inn at the head of the Langdale Valley; here they hesitate, perhaps because they are considering a detour to visit the famous Dungeon Ghyll Force, or perhaps because one of them wants a glass of beer.

The morning walk is done now. The walkers eat their lunch and the weather is so warm in this sheltered valley that they lie in the sun listening to the music of the torrent gurgling and tinkling over its rocks. The way ahead of them now lies over the shoulder of Harrison Stickle to Stickle Tarn, and when they begin to climb the grassy rock-strewn slopes views of the Coniston mountains will open out on their right, and Lake Windermere will spread out her long silvery train to the south; Windermere is the pearl of the Lakes, and in my opinion the most beautiful, though others may prefer wild Wastwater or solitary Buttermere or the more surprising Ullswater.

If the afternoon is really as warm as it seems to be, and if the walkers have a coat to lie on (and if there has been beer at the inn) they may be well advised to rest for two hours or more; partly because to rest in such surroundings is to renew the appetite for scenery, partly because the early evening is one of the most beautiful times of day in this district. In the swift alternation of hill and valley lovely shadows are cast, and as soon as they begin to lengthen the harmonious shapes of the peaks are silhouetted on neighbouring green hills. The water noises, too, are particularly delightful towards evening, increasing in a steady crescendo to their maximum at nightfall when other sounds are hushed. The evening is not to be recommended for the high summits—the big mountains seem to ignore the climber as dark approaches as if warning him that he is there at his own risk and that his proper place is among human habitations in the valleys—but this evening's expedition is not intended to include Pavey Ark or the Langdale Pikes; it is, however, certainly worth mounting the necessary thousand feet to Stickle Tarn so as to see it and Easedale Tarn by evening light, and to approach Grasmere by the true descent into its valley to the accompaniment of the music of Sour Milk Force.

The descent into Grasmere may be *ad libitum*—it is a curious fact about mountain walking, provided that the weather is fine, that a way can always be made at choice downhill (except, of course, on crags); it can be picked out and followed irrespective of tracks and maps; going uphill is another story altogether—then the track should *always* be followed, for it is sure to be easier and quicker in the long run, and the map should be consulted at regular intervals. As the walkers saunter down towards Grasmere in the evening light, they see its lovely trees and lake. The wind has fallen, and the morning cloudrace has given way to a stately procession of cloud masses marching above the distant horizon. The short grass is still now—only the longer grasses move lazily. The light is fading when the travellers reach the houses, and perhaps after a late cup of tea in the village they may feel like another stretch of walking—their feet are unharmed by a day among the mountains, and most of the motors have gone. In the dusk they swing out along the road, the always beautiful road past Rydal to Ambleside, and thence on to Windermere to catch the night train for the south.

Geoffrey Clark

SANDS AND HEATHS

THE English Heaths stand out from their cultivated surroundings like gipsies resting in a market-square. They are highly coloured and untamed with a touch of something older, more primitive, than the golden corn-field or the fragrant water-meadow. Some, it is true, have become little more than public exercise grounds and others have been captured and held by the Army, but there remain large tracts of the countryside which retain much of their original character. The whole English landscape must have presented the aspect of a common with oases of cultivation before the Acts of Enclosure and high farming reduced all but the most hungry and intractable soils to a hedged orderliness. To-day the heaths are found only on the gravelly subsoil of the Bagshot beds or the less accessible or cultivable outcrops of sand.

The scene is invariably the same in kind though it may differ considerably in detail or emphasis. It consists of wide open expanses of heath punctuated by dark groups

82 ON MIDHURST COMMON, SUSSEX

of Scotch Pine. It may be flat or hilly, afforested or bracken-covered, purple or brown with heath or ling, or yellow with a profusion of gorse. On the gravel it is flat or rolling with little sharply outlined hills; on the sand often high above sea-level on a plateau or clinging to a steep hill-slope. In basic colour it is bronze, deep green and yellow.

The English heaths of any size or beauty are distributed largely over the south-eastern counties, though they break out as far north as Sandringham in Norfolk, and are even found in Cheshire in the well-wooded region of Delamere Forest. Their greatest concentration is in the neighbourhood of Bournemouth, where William the Conqueror created the New Forest, and where the beautiful heaths round Poole Harbour stretch for many miles in a wide circle. Londoners, of course, are more familiar with the Surrey and Sussex heaths and commons which lie so conveniently placed for Sunday picnics. In Kent they are less well defined, being rather incidents in the general scene than open unfenced areas with names. In Berkshire the commons stretch from Newbury to Windsor and link up with the North Hampshire commons near Basingstoke, which in turn meet the Surrey commons at Farnham.

The New Forest is undoubtedly the best known and in many ways the most beautiful of all the English heaths. It is roughly contained in an irregular quadrilateral with Bournemouth, Fordingbridge, Romsey and Southampton Water at the angles. Lyndhurst may be said to be the centre. From here it is possible to enjoy the most delightful walks along grassy tracks, across bracken-covered commons or between thick woods of oak, birch or beech. The whole landscape has the freedom of a moor without the moorland exposure, for the Lyndhurst region of the Forest is sheltered and warm. It is possible, too, since Lyndhurst lies at the meeting of five important roads, to explore by car or bicycle the whole of the Forest without difficulty. The road to Beaulieu lies over Denny Lodge Walk through woods and across the open heaths so typical of this scenery. It ends in the charming and characteristic village with its ruined abbey, mellow brick buildings and tidal river. The combination of heath and river scenery is delightful, for the river destroys the feeling of sterility so prevalent in the open heath landscape and is itself enhanced in beauty by the proximity of the heath. Bucklers Hard, two miles down the river, is an ancient boat-building settlement with a broad street of Georgian brick houses fronted with grass verges to the roadway. At the end of the street is a grassy slope which leads to the river with its sharp bend; on the opposite bank a thickly wooded estate stretches for a mile in either direction; the rest is open country. It is a unique settlement, as architecturally satisfying as Milton Abbas in Dorset, but with a queer flavour of boats and smugglers.

Beaulieu Heath is the familiar level expanse of heath backed, as always in the New Forest, by a thick woodland setting. The little road which runs south to Exbury with its magnificent parks and plantations, and its vast Georgian mansion, is unusual since it emerges from the Forest and runs along the margin of the Solent. Here we find one of those lovely stretches of the English coast where an enclosed water runs between low foreshores backed by a ridge of hills. In early spring the scene is silent and lonely, with the immense flats of mud at the mouth of the Beaulieu River extending to the main channel and the long, low outline of the island shore blocking out all sense of the open sea. It is a fitting coast to the Forest. The return road through Fawley to Hythe and Marchwood is made exciting by occasional glimpses of the funnels of those huge liners which lie in the Southampton Docks and seem to dominate the landscape far more in a distant view than in the dock itself.

The Highland Water, which leads to the Lymington River, with the other tributaries in this extensive catchment area, have created a low-lying landscape, where reeds and rushes join the heath and gorse. It is an area where the variations of colour are richer than in the more arid upland stretches.

It is impossible to describe the Forest tints in autumn. They form a harmony of all the browns, reds and yellows in an artist's palette. Beeches with their copper leaves and their moss-grown boles—for in the Forest a certain dampness seems to destroy the clean silver trunks found in chalk country—combines with the lemon-yellow of oaks and birches and the almost crimson colour of the damp bracken to create a fairy-like scene made all the more striking against the carpet of deep umber provided by the dead ling. In spring, too, when the sap is rising, the wine-coloured shoots of the birches which occupy low-lying stretches of the river valleys as well as the fringes of the thicker woods, add a new note to the grey-brown winter background, and herald that outburst of glorious fresh colour when the buds burst and each tree is clothed in a different shade of green.

The Forestry Commission control the policy of afforestation and the result of their activities may be seen at many places in the vicinity of Lyndhurst and Brockenhurst. Woodland craftsmanship is visible in the neat piles of fencing posts which are stacked near the roadside or in clearings of the wood itself. The shaggy Forest ponies, too, which wander at will in the open heathland, add a characteristic touch. It is a delightful experience to spend a day or two at the Compton Arms, which stands beautifully placed in the open Forest, and waking in the early morning to find, beneath the bedroom window, a group of ponies feeding in the foreground.

The road from Ringwood to Romsey, familiar to all motorists, runs on high ground and affords long views across the open heath to the blue hills of the Isle of Wight and Purbeck. The Forest looks its best on one of those warm, cloudy days, when a freshening wind sends the cloud shadows chasing each other across the brown carpet on the hills and the sunlight picks out the woodlands in patches of gold and orange or models them with deep blue shadows.

As we have already mentioned, this great area of heath scenery extends in a wide semicircle with Bournemouth and Poole Harbour as centres till it reaches the ridge of the Purbeck Hills in Dorset. Here, with the cold green of the chalk hill as background and the exquisite reaches of Poole Harbour as a foil, the heath landscape attains its greatest beauty. No one who has stood on Nine Barrow Down can ever forget that immense panorama of crimson heath and torquoise water which stretches away to the yellow cliff near Bournemouth, with the purple outline of the New Forest as the distant background. And this tremendous view is only one of a whole series which may be obtained during a walk along the ridge of the Purbeck Hills. Farther to the west, where Flower's Barrow rises above East Lulworth, it is possible to look to the north and watch the shadows deepen over Coombe Heath or turn to the south and overlook the sea as it stretches away to the grim shape of Portland.

The Dorset Heaths can be divided into two sections, the one surrounding the inlets of Poole Harbour, the other extending in open expanses of heath landscape till it meets the cultivated country to the north and west. The Poole Harbour section is bounded by the road which runs from Bournemouth to Wareham and from there to Corfe Castle and Studland. Within this boundary there exists one of the most beautiful tracts of country in England. Arne Heath, which forms a conspicuous height

84 ON BERE HEATH, DORSET

85   BIRCH AND BRACKEN IN THE DUKERIES, NOTTINGHAMSHIRE

to the east of Wareham with a crown of pine-trees, shelters the small agricultural village where cows make the approach to Gold Point almost impassable in winter. Shipstal Point, on the deep Wych Channel, is a diminutive fishing hamlet which commands a low-level view of the harbour itself and of the islands which add to its beauty. Visitors who know this area leave their cars at Arne village and walk on a sandy path between woods to the shore at Shipstal. The whole harbour is flat and muddy, with reedy margins and green-covered islands forming at points where the mud is held in position by the roots. It is a remarkable region for birds, and the call of the curlew is seldom absent from one's ears. Swans swim in the deeper waters and fly inimitably with necks outstretched and wings beating with that strange and characteristic squeak, till they glide with a long splash on to some inland lagoon. A night spent on one of the small inhabited islands is an education in natural sounds.

At the eastern end of the Heath, at Studland, sand-dunes protect the lower Little Sea from tidal invasion, and here the motor road crosses from the ferry at Sandbanks and runs through the heath to Studland village. The Knoll House Hotel, sited in an elevated pine-wood, is a delightful vantage-point from which to enjoy Studland Bay and the rough wooded country round Little Sea. In fact it is one of the privileges of Dorset to sit on those well-kept lawns on a warm summer's afternoon and lazily watch the colours change on the brown heath with its fresh green birch-woods or on the cerulean sea.

Between Studland and Arne, the two accessible horns of this section of heath, there is a large open area of ling-covered landscape where access is possible for the walker or rider alone. The tracks begin bravely as roads but, as the heath is penetrated, disappear into boggy holes beyond which only the most experienced tradesman's van

20*

or the farmer's own vehicles can proceed with safety. On foot, however, it is a delight to wander along the sandy paths and explore such interesting objects as the pier at Goathorn, Ower Passage or Russell Quay. Fitzworth, again, commands splendid views across the harbour to Green Island or Furzey Island and, more than any of the other promontories of the heath, possesses the charm of complete isolation from the disturbing outer world. Slepe Heath, Middlebere Heath and Wych Heath complete, with their dry, heathery hills and their adder-ridden, boggy valleys, our survey of this highly coloured margin of Poole Harbour. In it may be found in addition to the hills and valleys and the short, gnarled woodlands, farm-house groups with the attendant cottages, built in brick and stone and roofed with Purbeck stone tiles. They are essays in harmonious building for they stand in a wide, open scene where any ill-chosen material would utterly destroy the whole landscape.

The outer Dorset Heaths are wilder and more wind-swept with their tawny surfaces relieved by groups of thin, tall pines. Bere Heath, Puddle Heath and Affpuddle Heath are characteristic, where the brown and purple foregrounds sweep up to the higher ridges leaving little tree-covered islands like Millicent's Clump or Gallows Hill. The Forestry Commission have taken over a large acreage near Bloxworth and will turn the heath scene in this district from a world of brown open spaces to a dark world of thick pine-woods.

It would be impossible to describe in detail all the varied scenes which occur in this unpeopled region, for the general character is the same: river valleys with meadows bordered with heathy slopes; conspicuous land-marks like Pallington Clump or Woolsbarrow; planta-tions of rhododendron like those which glorify the little road which leads near Hyde House to Philliol's Farm or farther to the east, Holme Lane—these, and a hundred others like them, help to make up a landscape of the richest colouring. Indeed it is difficult to think of a more intoxicating scene than the magenta world to the north of Binnegar when the heath is in bloom and the setting sun has cast its ruby light over the whole landscape.

Gravel pits and clay pits are conspicuous features of this landscape and are both picturesque and untidy. Abandoned gravel pits, like the one on Black Hill, near Bere Regis, can be impressive features, for the bright orange of the surface contrasts vividly with the dark green of pine. Abandoned clay workings have created those uncanny but beautiful pools of which the "Blue Pool" is the most universally known. In this region, south of Wareham, the fine outline of Creech Barrow dominates the whole countryside and combines with the wooded grounds of Creech Grange to form one of the most beautiful and secluded corners in Dorset. In the early summer when the bluebells are in bloom the whole landscape seems bathed in that inimitable blue haze. The grounds of Lulworth Castle, where peacocks strut on the splendid terrace of this towering ruin, can also be claimed as part of the heath landscape.

But it is time to leave the Wareham Heaths and move farther to the west to where the Hardy monument stands up, a familiar landmark seen for many miles, on the summit of Black Down. Here we have an island of gravel in a sea of chalk and limestone. Gorse and bracken dispute with the ling for the complete possession of this elevated site, from which are obtained long views to the Isle of Portland and down the coast towards Devon.

In West Dorset and East Devon, including a portion of Somerset, the greensand has formed a series of long, elevated ridges. Here, once again, can be seen the characteristic groups of pine-trees and flat heathlands. But cultivation disputes with the wilder heath for mastery. It is only on the steeper slopes, or on the arid summits of the ridges, that the open heath retains its hold. It is nevertheless a conspicuous component of the Devon scene, providing in this area its most striking features.

Dumpdon Hill and St. Cyres' Hill, above Honiton, are striking examples of sand-topped ridges capped by conspicuous woodlands. There is no resemblance between them and the Dorset heaths save the common clothing of bracken, gorse and pine-trees and patches of ling. The Dorset heaths are spread out in a comparatively low-lying plain, whereas the Devon sands are raised high above the sea-level on the tops of splendid ridges which run for miles at a time. East Hill, above Ottery St. Mary, is a typical ridge of this nature with a steep escarpment to the west and a level top. Here it is possible to walk for five miles along a level, dusty track through thick woodlands of pine or fir till Beacon Hill is reached. The Blackdown Hills in Somerset provide a further example of the same type of scene, but in this case the ridge runs east and west, forming a fine southern background to the Vale of Taunton Dene.

Great Haldon, near Exeter, is the most westerly example of heath scenery. The high roads to Plymouth and Torquay climb to the summit of this grand hill, with its level top and race-course, from which some of the finest views of Dartmoor are obtained. Here again are the wastes of heath and bracken, the pine-woods and the thickets of gorse, but whereas the East Devon ridges break up the heaths into a series of primitive survivals in the midst of cultivated fields, Haldon has preserved them intact. It is a pleasant experience to spend a day on Great Haldon enjoying the views over the mouth of the River Exe on the one side and Dartmoor on the other, with its curious tors and grim outline so forbidding in all but the finest weather.

It is impossible to mention all the areas where the out-cropping greensand provides a typical scene, for it forms

86 A WEALDEN HAMMER POND, BALCOMBE, SUSSEX

87 PITCH HILL, ON THE SANDY RIDGE OF SURREY

a fringe to the chalk scenery over much of England. It will be sufficient to mention such conspicuous features as Duncliffe Hill, near Shaftesbury, a wooded, isolated landmark conspicuous to all travelling to and from the west, and near Semley and East Knoyle in Wiltshire a group of sandy hills which form a fine area of typical scenery. Here a whole hill-side purple with willow herb is a feature not to be forgotten. The same band of green-sand carries our scenery along the foot of the chalk escarpment above Westbury and the Lavingtons to meet the gravel heaths which begin to appear near Hungerford in Berkshire and which form such large heath-covered areas round Newbury.

From Newbury eastwards through Hampshire, Surrey, Sussex, into Kent there is an almost continuous band of gravel which carries on its surface a whole series of commons and heaths. Crookham Common and Greenham Common form a level ridge of high land made beautiful by heath and gorse which overlooks the well-wooded country round Highclere, with its beautiful park, and beyond that to the chalk hills above Kingsclere. This is a fascinating region, hilly and secluded, where it is possible to enjoy a surprising variety of landscape in a single day's walk. It provides, indeed, a most enlightening lesson in the effect of geology on scenery. At Newbury itself we find the alluvial valley of the River Kennet, with lush-green water meadows and a series of locks, bridges, weirs and channels where the canal and the stream intermingle in a bewildering system of give and take. Above the valley the gravel-covered hills rise sharply on both banks, enriched with pine-woods on the higher ground and birch, beech and oak where the soil is deeper. Open spaces covered with the omnipresent heath contrast with well-grown woods and thickets of rhododendron. Beyond this is a narrow strip of thick clay, where pasture fields, oak woods and hazel coppices combine with an occasional brick field to change the landscape. Dominating the whole of the scene and closing all southern views we find the steep escarpment of chalk down which runs in a continuous wall of hill from Kingsclere westwards. It is a landscape rather for the discriminating walker than the normal tourist. It is intimate and friendly with pleasant brick villages and small hospitable inns never too distant. At Hampstead Marshall, where the hill-side approaches the broad stretch of the Kennet, thousands of swifts fly screaming along the dark surface of the water, over which trees cast deep transparent shadows. Above this enchanting pool on a high plateau there once stood a great Palladian mansion in a formal setting: this has disappeared leaving only a series of finely proportioned gate piers standing, like forlorn outposts who have been deserted by their general.

Bucklebury Common, Silchester Common, Alder-maston with its unspoilt street and splendid park-land, Stratfield Saye with its avenue of Wellingtonias and the great pine- and bracken-covered landscape at its eastern gate all help to carry the heath scenery across the south of England. But although these commons are in a sense individual there is a similarity about the scene which palls. Flints cover the surface, gravel lies just beneath it, water is absent and thickets of gorse make walking a penance. It is only by contrast with the more fertile woodlands on the London clay which generally surrounds the gravel deposits and provides green pasture fields and deciduous woods that the scene retains its charm. A desert of flint, gravel and sand could overpower us with its arid infertility.

In Surrey, however, this is no longer the prevailing character. Here nature has raised a series of high, sandy hills which command even the chalk downs to the north and look out boldly across the Weald to where the South Downs run in a blue silhouette to the sea. Here the rich

relief of colouring in the woods and of the hills themselves helps to create an entirely different picture from
the flat aridity of the Hampshire Common.

Leith Hill, Holmbury Hill and Pitch Hill cover a wide
area of heathy land, thickly covered with pine and birch.
On Leith Hill the summit rises to more than nine hundred
feet. Everywhere the roads are deeply sunk in the soft
sand, with the hedgerow trees clinging to the banks by
tangles of exposed roots. Towards the higher contours
of the hill, oak or chestnut are replaced by birch and pine
and patches of heath take the place of cultivated fields.
Here and there shallow quarries have exposed the yellow
sandstone rock. "Hurts," brambles, gorse and bracken
intermingle in gay profusion. There is no harsh or
masculine note in the whole scene.

Ashdown Forest in Sussex, on the other hand, is
windswept and severe. Here is a heath scene reminiscent
of the higher stretches of the New Forest, where coloured
hills stand high above the surrounding countryside and
look at the sea or the distant chalk ridge. The landscape
at Forest Row is wooded, but the high road soon rises
sharply on to the Forest top at Wych Cross and runs in
an unfenced world of brown hills and elevated pine-
woods. Here it is possible to walk for miles along the
rough tracks, enjoying the freedom almost of an open
moor. We say "almost" because there is a fundamental
difference between a moor and a heath. The moor is on
higher ground and extends for many miles: the heath is,
generally speaking, confined to well-defined areas or is
merely an incident in the general scene. The moor is
associated with mountains, the heath with hills or uplands. Even in the New Forest, where the heath occupies
a large area, the whole aspect is different in kind. The
moors smell of peat and heather and have little brown
streams gurgling in peaty valleys to add music to the
sighing of the wind and the barking of the grouse. The

heath is scented by pine-trees or the smell of burnt gorse, for the heath is so dry at certain times of the year that extensive fires are only too frequent. The moor, on the other hand, seldom catches fire, except at those times of the year when a whole hill-side may be seen with lines of flame creeping along, like the burnt patches on the "fern paper" Christmas fireworks.

But we must not be drawn away from our southern heaths to wander in the unconfined space of the northern moors.

The heath gains its effects entirely by colour, and this is enhanced on thundery days when the sky is inky grey and the orange trunks of the pines with their blue-green tufted tops stand out in clear-cut groups perched on the tops of little prominent hillocks or ancient barrows. The foreground is either pale green or copper with bracken, or intoxicating with the scent of gorse in full bloom. The clear yellow of broom is found in patches, or the pink or purple rhododendron. Birches grow happily in certain stretches, contrasting their slim, cool trunks with the hotter colouring of their surroundings. The climax of the heath landscape comes when the little bells are in full bloom and, in a promising year, flood the whole surface with their inimitable magenta red.

In Surrey, where for a fleeting moment, we glanced at the three sandy hills of Leith, Holmbury and Pitch Hill, it is possible to study the difference of scene when a heath is supported on sand or carried on gravel. On the sand woodlands predominate and the scene is one of great variety and beauty. The greensand outcrop usually occurs at a considerable elevation, and the woodlands sweep up the sides of the hills like surging armies. Hindhead and Haslemere are centres of such a world, being treeless where the Devil's Punch Bowl forms the superb foreground to this well-known scene, or well wooded on the western slope towards Grayshott and

Bramshott. Near Haslemere there is yet another Blackdown Hill, which forms a magnificent landscape feature
when seen from the Weald, for it rises abruptly from the
low-lying valley of water meadows and grassland—a huge
pine-clad bluff. Near Godalming, again, there is a group
of hills of the same nature, Hascombe Hill and Hambledon Hill with Highdown Heath and Munstead Heath.
Here again we have the deeply sunk road with its tunnel
of trees, the pine-clad slopes and the sudden views across
the lower country.

A study of the geological map of the south-eastern
counties is extremely interesting for it shows a kind of
hairpin-shaped band of greensand surrounding the heavy
clay expanse of the Weald and separating it from the
chalk downs. Along the whole of this band at Maidstone
or Sevenoaks or running down past Ashford in Kent to
the sea at Hythe we find hills covered with pine-woods
standing up against the fruit orchards. In Kent it is less
continuous than in Surrey, but the character is always
there. To the east of the Wealden clay, again, we find
an outcrop of sand and sandstone forming the elevated
area of Ashdown Forest, and the hilly landscape round
Tunbridge Wells, and Mayfield. To the unskilful
amateur these variations of sand and gravel which appear
on the surface over so large an area in all parts of the
country are bewildering in their complexity. We have
seen them appear on the hill-tops in Devon as a level
plateau on a ridge or a mere cap to a detached hill. We
have found them in Dorset, spread out like a carpet
beneath the narrow ridge of the Purbeck Hills or as
fringes of pine and gorse along the edge of the huge
central chalk mass. In Hampshire we have enjoyed their
presence in the glorious woodlands of the New Forest
and its wide, open heaths. We have followed them along
the rather arid ridges in Berkshire to Surrey and found
them in their greatest glory on Leith Hill, or Hindhead.

And finally we were studying their characteristic landscape in Kent under the new name of the Hastings beds.

We propose now to leave the southern counties and go to Norfolk where they help to form one of the most delightful landscapes of their kind in England. Surrounding the King's home at Sandringham, with its superbly wooded grounds, and fringing the wide, sandy waste of the Wash lies a compact area where the well-grown trees and richly coloured sands, alive with the colour of gorse in bloom or rhododendron in exotic masses, create possibly the finest sand landscape of them all. Nowhere is the warmth of the sandstone so striking—almost overpowering when seen in the estate cottages or village streets. Nowhere, save perhaps in Scotland, are the pine-woods so well kept and mature, and the sudden openings so blessed with exciting views across the sea. The Wash itself, with its bird life, its mysterious quicksands, and its wind-ridden marshy shore, is a glorious foil to the thickly grouped woods with their parallel trunks, bursting into puffs of dark green foliage on their lofty branches. All this can be happily observed from the little road which ties itself into a lover's knot near Wolferton. Along it we drive or ride on a sandy surface with wide grass verges backed by thick woods: at intervals we gain those exhilarating glimpses of the marshes or the sea itself. Wide grassy cuttings open out woodland vistas and thick banks of rhododendrons close them. There is no solider mass of shrub than the grouped azalea which rises and falls like a miniature range of mountains made glorious by the pink, cerise or crimson blooms.

The whole county of Norfolk is dotted with little heaths and commons, especially at the rear of Sheringham and Cromer, where they are, like many of those in Kent, incidents of wildness in the midst of cultivation, rather than extensive landscape features.

In the south, however, near Attleborough and Thetford, there is an extensive region of heath landscape, made beautiful by bracken which grows in tremendous level stretches of waving green or still copper. This can be seen in all its beauty from the little road which leads through Hockham and Tottington, past the lovely estate of West Wretham. Deep blue meres and circular dewponds are a feature of the scene. It is the breadth and openness of this landscape that is its greatest charm. Newmarket Heath, a little to the south, needs no introduction, though here we find a mixed landscape made up of the features of chalk as well as heath. Ascot, another famous heath race-course in Berkshire, is entirely on the gravel, and surrounded by miles of gravelly subsoil. Here we are in the presence of the Army which has planted itself firmly, with Aldershot as a centre and Camberley as a dormitory, over thousands of acres of the once open heath. It is in many ways an admirable use for this type of land, for it is dry and infertile, open enough for manœuvres and hilly enough to provide ample cover. Furthermore, the landscape is not entirely destroyed for pine-woods hide the hutments, and the hills are too hard and resistant to be badly damaged, as Pirbright Common can bear witness. The Chobham Ridges, with their view across Bisley Common to Woking, is a fine example of a gravel ridge, flat on the top and flinty and dropping suddenly to the lower level in a steep escarpment. Near Farnham again, within reach of the Army, but free from its occupation, Frensham Common with its strange abrupt hills and its ponds provides the finest example of the open heath scenery found on the greensand. Instead of the thickly wooded hills, we have long stretches of flat heath rising, as we have said, to the sudden humps with little feathery groups of pine crowning their summits. The road from Frensham to Hindhead passes directly across this landscape, skirting the shore of Frensham Great Pond with its bathers and its reedy margin, and rising finally to the wooded heights of Grayshott. From here it is interesting to proceed due south, skirting the lovely lake at Shotter-mill, and the little secluded valley of Kingsley Green, and passing over the steep hill known as Hatchfarm Hill, drop into the river valley with its meadows at Fernhurst. This little valley lies peacefully between two high green-sand hills; Hatchfarm Hill to the north and that splendid ridge to the south up which the Chichester road winds with a magnificent sweeping curve to Great Common before gliding gently down to Midhurst. Here the valley of the Rother separates the fine hilly country of pine-woods, heaths and sandy wastes from the foothills of the South Downs. There are few more beautiful sights than the herds of deer, apparently without number, which feed in the grounds of Cowdray Park on those green spaces between the plantations of gigantic trees. The road from Midhurst to Petworth after leaving the Cowdray gates runs along the north bank of the Rother among thick woods or the familiar bracken wastes. Instead of the open heath, in Sussex we find these thick woodlands and, in the clearings, the unsuppressible bracken.

It is interesting as we come to the end of this rambling study of the English heath scenery to consider the contribution which it makes to the English landscape as a whole. The most typical English scene, I suppose, is the pastoral scene, cut into a patchwork of small fields by living hedges, and relieved by the deep shadows cast by the hedgerow oaks, or elms or the common ash. In this simple setting an old grey church tower will raise its pinnacled head with a cluster of harmonious buildings, cottages, farms or barns, grouping themselves at its base. Cattle graze the meadows, or lie munching contentedly in a hollow as far removed as possible from the gate of

89 ALDEBURGH HEATH, SUFFOLK

exit. Second only to this gentle rural scene must be placed the downland scene of sheep moving across the open hill-side modelled so softly by the long blue shadows cast by the evening sun. The open down and the enclosed valley make up the greater part of our landscape. In the north and west there are high hills and in the centre a huge elevated platform of heather. Beyond these features little remains but the river valley with its wet meadows and the dry, untamed heath. Its contribution, therefore, to the English scene is one of variety and colour. The gipsy compared with the farmer; the red handkerchief on the bronzed neck.

Thomas Hardy described the heath with insight in his *Return of the Native*. He felt that strange quality inherent in the wilder stretches of the heath of being older than civilisation; of being witch-ridden. Crossed in a modern car the heath has lost much of its power to frighten, but in the past, on a winter's afternoon, when the clouds are low and fleeting and the rain drives horizontally across the unprotected slopes of Wool Heath, it must have been a grim adventure to walk from Wareham to Puddletown. Here are the wilder heaths, even to-day, little known to any but the poacher or the man on horseback.

Highwaymen, too, were once associated with heaths. The lack of habitation and the cover afforded by plantations of pine and birch or thickets of gorse and bramble, enabled him to accost his victims with little fear of disturbance. Hartley Flats near Camberley is a wild upland of heath that still retains this feeling of a threat hidden somewhere in its level surface.

In contrast to this harsh aspect of the heath scene, we might end our chapter with a description of a little-known region between Mere in Wiltshire and Frome in Somerset. Here, at Stourton, is to be found a secluded scene of exquisite beauty. The long lakes at Stourhead, fed from Six Wells Bottom, which form the source of the beautiful

River Stour, lie embowered in immense woods. Rhododendrons in spring are reflected in the tranquil surface.
Little "Belvederes" stand above steps on the lake-side
and sloping lawns cover the well-kept banks where huge
trees cast the deepest shadows. It is difficult to think of
a more perfect example of landscape gardening come to
maturity. Grottoes of fantastic stonework carry on this
artificial but entirely satisfactory landscape. An inn with
battlemented walls, a village green, stone houses and a
grey church combine with the walls of the manor garden
and the stables to add a further human touch. If, after a
tea at the hospitable inn, the enterprising visitor cares to
explore farther he should take the little lane which runs
through Castle Wood to Aaron's Hill and then turn due
south and proceed along the boundary between Wiltshire
and Somerset. From the openings in the woods to the
west he will look for miles across the Somerset meadows
to Glastonbury Tor and Mendip. The exposed band of
greensand which is responsible for the Stourton landscape
continues northward to Longleat Park where once more
great woods enrich the scene. The Shear Water near
Warminster is a well-known beauty spot visited by the
inhabitants of Frome and Warminster during the summer.

It is not easy to describe the heath country without
appearing to repeat endlessly the same sentences and the
same adjectives. It is only where a strong county flavour,
as in Devon or Dorset or at Sandringham in Norfolk,
adds a subtle overriding character to the familiar groups
of trees or yellow patches of soil that we distinguish a
different aspect. In Devon, too, the long beech hedges
which distinguish the whole of the uplands help to
change the prevailing note. It is impossible to remain
unimpressed in East Devon, in the crumpled landscape
of deep valleys and long ridges, where villages lie hidden
away at the ends of narrow, winding roads, and where
the uplands stretch to the sea on the one hand and the

Somerset vale on the other. It is emphatically a country for walkers and riders, not for tourists, for it has a remoteness from, a rabbit or fox-ridden indifference to, the more normal life in the populated districts of the county.

There is a perfect road which runs across the open heath on Gittisham Hill after a steep climb from Ottery St. Mary. As it drops down the long slope to Honiton it overlooks a wide expanse of this upland country picked out in light and shade, and coloured by the warm brown of the lower slopes. Here the greensand caps to the hills with their thick, dark woods stand out boldly, and add immensely to the beauty of the scene. And so we end our chapter on a note of splendour, rather than on the harsher, though often no less beautiful, tone of a landscape on the widespread gravel heath.

Adrian Bell

FENS AND LEVELS

IN describing the Fens one is describing a man-made country. Every type of our landscape owes its character in more or less degree to human habitation: even in the wild and hilly regions men have built walls. But no other part is so completely determined by the hand of man as are the Fens. The earth is there simply the raw material of an industry: it has been taken out of the sea: it is a little world which was not, until man brought it into being; and he has moulded it according to his needs. The spirit that shaped the hills may have been that of the eternal Poet; the hands that shaped the Fenlands were concerned with daily bread.

This sounds as dull as a back garden; and yet, on the great scale on which the thing presents itself to the view —on the road, say, between King's Lynn and Spalding; or from the banks of the Ouse between Littleport and Southery—the effect is exactly the opposite. I do not know when I have seen a more exciting prospect than when I first saw that great expanse on a sunny spring

91 WIND ON THE FENS

92 THE OUSE NEAR WICKEN, IN THE CAMBRIDGESHIRE FENS

93 TULIP FIELDS NEAR HOLBEACH IN THE LINCOLNSHIRE FENS

morning. It was a teeming landscape, typified by a
rosy old lady near at hand in a sun-bonnet (though the
wind was icy) and a pinafore and gum boots, digging
lustily on the edge of a dike. In the next field three
people were sowing broad beans by hand, walking up
the rows, sowing from baskets with an abbreviated
version of the sower's traditional cast. You could not
see the seed falling; it was just a rhythmic movement to
the eye; and in that vast space had a ritualistic look. A
machine drawn by horses, which had a superficial
affinity with the medieval plough, being mounted on a
frame, was closing the ridged earth over the sown beans.
The beauty of that earth was a thing one could have
watched all day: the share divided it exactly; it fell away
like finest garden mould. As indeed it was: a hundred
and fifty pounds an acre that land is worth, which used
to lie under the sea. It is the sheer goodness of earth that
is the beauty of the Fens. That and the sky. The few
acres being tilled close to where I stood were moated
by dikes, narrow and deep, whose sides were so clean
and steep they might each have been gouged out with
one stroke of some great instrument. These were what
made the earth so tilthy and workable early in the year.
From here to the sea, invisible over the horizon, the fall
was hardly eighteen inches. By that small margin acres
and acres of land were kept drained. The spot on which
I stood was the earliest attempt by man to hold back the
sea—the old Roman bank which still runs intermittently
along the former coastline, and in this place bears a
modern tarmac road. An elevation of just these few
yards gives a view and sense of height.

It is impossible in writing of this land to leave out the
activities of men on it, for they are essentially involved
in it. It is a populous view you get from the road to
Spalding; it is, perhaps, the Fens ("marshes" they call them
in Lincolnshire) at their richest and most characteristic.

I am not forgetting Ely; but here too are little Elys—
churches dominating the landscape, on ground maybe
a foot or two above the rest of the Fen, which seems to
exaggerate their height and give them a cathedral-like
prominence, all their proportions and detail enhanced
against the blinding sky. Gedney and Terrington stand
out particularly. Beside them, the box-like houses of
the farmers look essentially mundane. But never mind,
the soil is so dynamic in its fertility that such staring
contrasts, even, can be resolved into terms of human
life.

There is the earth, great patches of it and little,
rectangular with clean-cut dikes. It is not the black peat
soil of Ely, but brown silt-land, dried light by the east
wind and the sun. There it lies below the slight eminence
of the raised road, big and little trays of earth like something poured into a mould and set. Men, women, horses,
tractors, carts, swarm all over it. There are, perhaps,
dozens of farms in view, yet the whole might be one
great farm; the only division other than the dikes is in
the diversity of cultivation, again entirely rectangular;
one set of ploughs making dark lines across the view,
another set along it. There are repetitive small groups
of trees dotted about the level space, each marking some
homestead and its home meadow. For the rest, the
diversity is in colour and movement. In one place the
earth has been limed: it has a roan look there; and a pair
of grey horses are ploughing it, and another is drawing
an orange-coloured wagon across the field. All the carts
and wagons are painted—freshly, prosperously painted—
this bright orange-colour, the colour of a ripe mangold;
and they shine out from a long way off, such is the
clarity of the light. There are little charlock-coloured
tractors too: the air is full of their bumbling. Aeroplanes
go overhead—and they are all part of it: pylons stretch
diagonally across the land, and they are part of it too.

The very sun itself seems to have a pulse in its shining. There are square houses standing out in space, and buildings all neat and angular, and here and there stacks, and here and there a gate standing up alone—no hedge —all miniature and exact; just like what man, bent on daily bread, would make of a virgin land. It is impossible to view it otherwise than in terms of human life and activity, and as such the sheer fertility and heart of the soil produces a synthesis of the products of all ages —from the Roman bank to the yellow tractor. It is an industrial landscape; land the raw material, the machines to work it, and where the machines cannot go, men and women with spades and hoes, digging and chopping and sowing. And it is real work: some have their coats off; some are down on their hands and knees. Flashing in the sun are glass-houses, through whose doors a glimpse of a sea of blood-red tulips may be had; in others potatoes are in piled trays preparatory to setting. In other fields, instead of corn, rows of grey-green daffodil spears, rows of strawberry plants, over which a man is going as carefully as over a garden bed.

When people speak of the Fens the impression is of a bleak and dreary, if not waterlogged, land. In the depth of winter this might be true: storms are as free of that land as of the sea; but as for floods, though the water occasionally breaks through, for the most part there is less flooding here than in hillier but less well-cultivated parts of the country, where ditches and water-courses have been allowed to become choked and rivers silted up. A little farther south, for instance, a moderately rainy spell is sufficient to drown all the meadows of Constable's country. But make land worth a hundred and fifty pounds an acre for cultivation, and the cultivators will take very good care to keep the water off it, even though it is but a foot above sea-level.

The moods of the Fen landscape, apart from man's

activities, are the moods of the weather and the sky.
But again, we cannot leave man out of it, for the weather
governs his activities as well, and on a day of sun at the
end of winter not only do the Fens lie bright and bask-
ing, but the land comes alive with men, horses and
machines, getting ready for spring sowing. And that,
whatever other aspects the flat country may wear, is an
optimistic and inspiriting sight. Gone are the will o' the
wisps, the weird wild-fowl cries, the meres and reedy
wastes that made it once a solitude for monks; nature
no longer wears a primordial, but a worldly and smiling
face. It is unique in England in being a bit of country
where farming is prosperous. It is worth going a long
way to see what that looks like. We do not know: we
have grown so used to a countryside of picturesque ruin
that we have come to imagine that it always looked like
that. But here around Spalding and Holbeach there is
not a picturesque weed nor a lapsing roof nor a bulging
wall. All is neat and plain and—if you like—ugly; but
actively, dynamically human. As a tradesman in Holbeach remarked, "Poor farmers, they can only afford one
Rolls-Royce a year." That is an exaggeration, but the
country has definitely a thriving and busy air. The
farmsteads venture right to the edge of the Wash, only
a ramp between them with their lonely trees and the tidal
flats. Solitary and mournful it looks—where the sea
meets that low-lying land of the Wash, yet a fair finds it
profitable to stay in King's Lynn market-square for a
fortnight. Not a matter of a roundabout and a few
booths either, but a fair that fills the whole space to
overflowing, replete with everything conceivable that
electricity can do to garify it. The noise, too, is deafen-
ing. Whereas in the old days the steam organ could but
blow its utmost, now by means of an amplifier an
ordinary gramophone record announces itself like the
Last Trump. Added to that the showmen bawling, also

through microphones; and a flaring fantastic light on the
old house-fronts. While just across Lynn channel the
lonely farm-houses stand at the end of marshland roads.
You can walk along the bank of the Ouse till it reaches
the Wash. But even here one is never far from life,
human life. The returning cockle boats come sailing
up to Lynn: oil-driven cargo boats from Holland pass
to and fro. Work on the channel is constant: there are
piles of reed and bush faggots built in great escarpments
for use on the banks and bed of the river. On the other
bank, barges and a tug and men are at work. The bank
narrows and ends in a point, the Ouse meets the Wash,
and there, abrupt after all this industry of man, is the
sad, quiet sea. To the right are creeks winding among
winter-grey marsh grass, and sandy mud-banks and
wafers of land straggling into the water. They are edged
—dotted white—with gulls; the only positive colour in
the evening light, like a still surf. More gulls are flying
out to sea; they come in endless procession; they keep
directly above the river. Out at sea, as they turn for a
moment, they are visible, white: next moment they are
invisible, grey among the grey. Silhouetted against the
sunset sky on the other bank is a man lifting a faggot.
Small and weak-looking gesture against such space; yet
that repeated thousands of times has kept the river clear
for traffic and has moulded the face of this land.

The sky impends over the Fens: it is our high, dry,
East Anglian sky—full of light. Spring comes with
mountains of cloud: the actual land becomes the least
part of the view; the eye is carried up into heights more
mountainous than solid earth can show, sun-fused. The
clouds have become very real indeed. Every weather
is visible in one view. You have but to turn on your
heel to see storm and shine, and the border region of
rays bursting fan-like from the brink of thunder. Or if
it is a clear day, the sun is a lonely light in space. In the

22

face of it the tree-clumps, houses, churches—all are in silhouette, forms of haze. Turning slowly you see all angles of light on things, till you arrive at the opposite horizon where everything is shone upon, every colour and edge picked out clearly. The sky is so bright, it seems to press upon the eyes. And when the sun sets, thin and tapering clouds against the glow mould exactly the forms of the land edging itself into the sea, indented with creeks of bright water.

On the edge of the sea, and just behind the embanked river, a cottage stands, and the very embankment is made a garden—here are those domestic touches of vegetable plot, orchard, sunny wall and fowl-run surrounded by their hedge, as though lying snug inland.

Wisbech was once on the sea: now ten miles inland, it used to stand at the mouth a great estuary. A typical Fenland town, the tidal river runs right through it, its industrial main road. The River Nene, conveyed by Morton's Leam straight to Wisbech, left its old course a more or less derelict river-bed—since canalised—the old Well Stream.

Although the Fens would seem to be a monotonous, flat expanse, they have their variations. The low country inland from the Wash becomes wilder, less populated, and not quite so intensively cultivated; though still much more so than ordinary arable land. There is more corn-land and less of that flower, vegetable and glass-house cultivation that characterises the Spalding district. Still the land is valuable enough for one to see horses and a plough being manœuvred in a half-acre plot which would be left derelict in any other part of the country. But, again, as one nears Wisbech, slightly rising ground (the rise quite imperceptible) makes orchards and fields of soft fruit begin to be more numerous. The orchards are all highly industrialised trees—sprayed and pruned to flat-topped umbrella-like or wide bowl-like shapes.

94   TRACTOR PLOUGHING NEAR SPALDING, IN THE LINCOLNSHIRE FENS

95   PLANTING POTATOES NEAR MEPAL, IN THE CAMBRIDGESHIRE FENS

96 THE RIVER BURE NEAR WROXHAM, ON THE NORFOLK BROADS

Heaps of prunings and trees that have been rooted out and discarded lie beside the orchards. These orchards have no resemblance to the homely orchard of tradition—to the old West-country orchard of long grass and lichened, leaning trees. The grass seems pale and poorly under these, and one wonders if that is due to the amount of spraying to which they are subjected. The orchards, the carts, the boats—there is no end to the details whereby one district differs from another. A tool will curve thus in one county and a little differently in another; and behind that slight difference lies a whole host of local conditions. It is so in the Fens, and it is to become aware of these things that is half the interest of a journey.

Again, one catches a glimpse in passing of an ancient house set in a park—a rarity for these parts—and looking at the contours on the map, discovers that that piece of ground must have been one of the islands in the undrained Fens.

Or the name of an inn, "The Woodman's Cottage," standing in an expanse where bare land goes to the horizon, makes one aware of another aspect that the country formerly wore.

"The Lathrenders' Arms" is another local inn—and "The Old Ship."

There are certain things that tend to repeat themselves in a flat landscape, and impress themselves on the mind as typical of any Fenland scene. Some are half-natural, like the great drains; others are small but no less significant, the sheet of tarpaulin stretched on poles, behind which stationary work, such as the riddling of potatoes, goes on. This wind-break is universal in the Fens. As universal as the great clamps that stretch, some of them, the whole length of one side of a field.

In the Wisbech district one is aware of being in more than just a flat arable country: one is aware of being in the midst of a feat of engineering. The repetition of straight, upheld dikes, great streaks of water going direct to the horizon, and there melting into the sky and seeming to cut the country in two. We talk of stream-lining—there is no stationary thing I have seen that gives such a sense of speed as these main roads of water: there is nothing to detain the eye; not a bush, not an indentation of the bank—the sight is flashed to the horizon. Sometimes two of the great drains meet: the junction is as clean as a junction of rails, and the power of distance is doubled to the view. Metal pylons pass across them on their own straight journey—much use is made of electricity in the Fens—and the two are complementary. Pylons, which are merely an eyesore in a "beautiful" countryside, here express just that aim and vigour which is characteristic of the land.

On the other hand, the old course of the River Nene, by-passed by these cuts, goes meandering through Fenland villages, with a trickle of water in it, given up to village ducks. Some of these villages are pleasant places —Outwell and Upwell, with gardens beside the water and a white mill turning at the end of the vista of its long river-side street.

One comes to Welney and, mounting a bridge, is standing looking along the Old Bedford River, and then in about half a mile along the New Bedford River, which runs parallel, and now takes most of the water. These great cuts go straight from Earith to Denver Sluice, which is the key-stone of the drainage of the Fens; twenty miles embanked above the land and dead straight, while the Ouse is going thirty-three, and meets the Bedford River again at Denver, and thence on to King's Lynn. Between these two artificial rivers is a tract of land easily flooded—the Bedford Wash. In the winter it is like an inland sea. A road runs across it only just out of the water, sometimes not, and to stand on that road looking to right and to left is to experience something of what the Fenland must have looked like before it was drained; a quiet, glittering sea, absolutely unbroken to the horizon. The strangeness is to see so great an expanse of water so still, just reflecting the sky and populated by sea-birds. The transition across the Bedford Rivers is thus startling—you exchange limitless earth for limitless water and then for earth again; and the road turns and runs along under the tall bank of the river. There, a small three-cornered patch of ground between the bank and a field-dike, which anywhere else would have been used as a tramp's camping-place and a dumping-ground for tins, is freshly dug and planted with rows of fruit bushes.

You exchange also the smell of marsh water which rots in the air between the two rivers, for the smell of newly turned earth.

The earth here is black, and gives a peculiar aspect to the day. The sky is clear and bright with spring sunshine, but the earth reflects none of it, it is black as night. It is a curious juxtaposition, the vast blackness of the earth under a sky so bright, as though the two were cut off from each other's influence. And there is another strange thing here; after travelling many miles through the Fens you see suddenly—a hill. It is not, of course, a hill in any real sense of the word, but the eye has grown so attuned to flatness that it meets that rise with incredulity, with a sense of mirage, and magnifies it involuntarily. And upon it, against the sun, a thing of mist, a bulk whose outline is not just the outline of trees, but of a more lucid grace—Ely Cathedral. It looks quite close; the rise of the ground seems to bring everything near. But a signpost says "Ely 9."

The Ouse is met with again at Littleport; and the road between Littleport and Downham Market affords a typical Fenland view. There is the Ouse, upheld between high banks: stepped down from that there is

the road following its course; and below the road again
lies the land. On either side of the river are farm-houses,
their roofs about level with the banks. They stand well
below the water, and thence stretch miles upon miles of
this rich, black land, a world of wealth, real wealth, all
dependent on those two green banks. Here you may
get at a glance the whole essence of Fenland—the
fertility and the science of it.

It is a characteristic of English scenery almost universal, that the distance of any vista resolves itself into
the likeness of a forest: it is a thing upon which foreigners
remark—you seem to be journeying always towards a
forest which you never reach. One of the differences of
the Fens is the absence of that background. The few
homestead trees never thicken and congregate upon the
distance; the atmosphere thickens first, and there are
places here where no group of trees, no stacks, no
buildings, intervene at all, and the eye travels over bare
black earth as over the sea, and nothing but the curve of
the earth or the limitations of human sight prevents one
seeing on and on. But the eye instinctively seeks something to rest upon, and turning aside from that clear
view may discover a group of stacks or a naked house.
The atmosphere is such that the tops of their shapes are
sharp and black-shadowed, while their lower parts seem
to float in haze. Nearer at hand one notes how the
orange-coloured carts glow out from the black earth,
and how the Shire horses harmonise with it. In another
landscape they would look quite black, but against this
earth there is discovered in their coats a rich, nutty brown.

A man is driving them on a roller: the clank of it is
borne on the breeze. There stands his house at a little
distance; some buildings, three trees. There seems no
reason why he should not go on rolling to the horizon.
One can stand on the bank in the teeth of the wind and
look at him and his horses and his house and buildings,

and try to get the feeling of what it is like to have that for home, and that space for company; and wonder what boundaries and landmarks his mind has picked out from that view, and whether long concentration upon things at hand have made him feel hedged-in and homely in space.

Now this is that part of the Fenland which originally approached firm ground. Hereabouts, if you can imagine yourself sailing in from the open sea when the Fens were under water, you could see islands begin to appear more frequently; there is Ely, Littleport, Southery. The name Littleport tells its own tale, and as you go along the Downham Road the river branches away to the right and the road mounts the quite considerable hill into Southery. The stretch of road between it and Littleport goes beside one of the oldest and most far-reaching pieces of interference with the course of Nature that the Fens have known. There used to be no River Ouse along that two-mile stretch originally. The Great Ouse went quite another way from Littleport: it did not have its mouth at King's Lynn at all but at Wisbech; it flowed into the great estuary there. The Great Ouse flowing deviously to Wisbech, and the Little Ouse to Lynn, came, at Littleport, to within two miles of each other. In the thirteenth century a cut was made joining the two rivers, with results that have altered the whole course of Fenland history, and still complicate the drainage problem. Chiefly, the first result was worse flooding than before, because there was not enough regular water to keep the great Wisbech estuary from silting up, so the flood water could not get away, while at Lynn the small channel of the Little Ouse could not take the vast increase of water diverted from Wisbech.

Southery on its hill has something of that antiquity one associates with an English village. In the Fens there are some pleasant houses among home meadows

and high trees—substantial eighteenth-century farmsteads which bespeak a thriving domestic life there and
not mere subsistence. But nothing earlier than that.
While in Southery and other "islands" you find some
medieval cottages. One old inn, now pulled down,
had the reputation of having been originally a lighthouse
shining across the Fenland sea.

Beyond Southery there is a more typically English
sort of country. The River Wissey has the appearance of
running in a valley rather than a fen: there is, however
slight the slope, an appreciable difference. Denver,
famous for its Sluice governing the whole drainage
system of the Fens, is as unlike a Fenland village as you
could imagine. You might be in the green heart of
England. For one thing it is a village of stone. A local
brown stone called Carstone has determined the architecture of the village: in some houses stones are laid
together, no thicker than Roman bricks; in others they
are in the larger blocks. The mortar between these
stones is frequently studded with smaller stones—
"garnetted." The village is umbrageous and has wide
green verges, spreading out into little commons. The
Sluice is a mile or more away, a mighty stone dam across
the Ouse where the Bedford River joins it, holding up
the tidal water from the sea sometimes high above the
level of the Ouse on the other side of the sluice. The
sun shining down the Bedford River makes one blinding
ray of it: beyond lie the bare Fenlands, while beside the
Ouse itself the pleasant water-meadows of Denver,
backed by the trees of the village, make a pastoral scene
that one does not associate, somehow, with the Fens.

And very soon then, you are out of them altogether
and into a different country. Just to point one of the
contrasts that English scenery affords, the road from
Stoke Ferry on the edge of the Fens to Thetford is only
fifteen miles, yet after being able to see to the bare

horizon, you are now so hedged in with trees that you cannot see more than a few yards. For on either side are the dull and endless acres of coniferous afforestation.

There is also in the fens the village of Isleham near Mildenhall, which in its buildings if not its lay-out, has more the appearance of a Cotswold village than a Fenland one. It is built—walls and farms—of what looks like grey stone, but is in reality a hardened kind of chalk called clunch. It is odd to see these grey walls and great church-like barns and no swelling wold rising above the village. Nor to hear, as one expects, the West-country dialect that goes with grey walls and buildings, but the clipped Cambridgeshire accent. And to reach the edge of the village and see the road become a "drove" going straight out into the fen, and a boy with a donkey-cart swaying along it piled with crates of spring flowers. Droves and lodes, earth and waterways cut direct to their mark; these are the ways of the Fens. Only one small region of original undrained fen remains, and that is at Wicken, the haunt of naturalists. The preservation of a wilderness is a curious anomaly, but there you can see it, the thickets of reed and coppice wood, intersected by water, humming in the summer with insect life; and you can understand William the Conqueror's difficulty in running Hereward the Wake to earth, with miles and miles of such undergrowth to conceal him. It is odd to be faced with "regulations" on entering this primitive sanctuary. The buildings near the Fen are small reed-cutters' huts, and reflect the difference between this old thicket life and that of the flower and glasshouse lands of Spalding.

This sedgy Wicken scene is reminiscent rather of another portion of East Anglia—the Broads. Properly speaking, much of Broadland is not flat at all, but good undulating arable country, with only a signpost to let you know you are anywhere near a broad at all. That and a frequency of notices against trespassers—non-existent in the Fens—which suggests the proximity of holiday country. Unfortunately it seems inevitable that the presence of holiday-makers even for a month in the year results in a kind of colonial-shack type of architecture, and temporary-looking erections of concrete and corrugated iron. Potter Heigham is a place of this kind, and in the winter looks about as forlorn as the holiday-makers themselves would if they stood there in their holiday clothes.

Horning is another example of a holiday village, with a kind of bungalow Venice towards the broad; with bungalows reached by bridges and little gardens trembling on the verge of inundation. In winter it looks a sad, subsided little place.

However, not much of the Broads, comparatively speaking, is tamed in this fashion; and if you get round to the south side of this chain of Broads you get a sense of their essential character of wildness and solitude. The domesticity of the good farming country around, its red earth out of which the red-brick cottages seem to have been born rather than built, its happy little dells, give no hint of the lonely waters but an occasional stack of reeds, built just like a stack of corn is built, only stiffer, brusquer in outline. Then you dip down, and leaving some grange-like buildings and cedars, find yourself suddenly in wild England—the country of Richard Jefferies' *After London*. Pale rush-plumes and their black reflections in the flood water, larches, a thickening of coppice wood all round. Moorhens calling. Absolute solitude.

The Broads are, of course, determined by the lie of the land. Its undulations have gathered the waters into these meres, which otherwise would have resolved themselves into fen. In any case there is a considerable margin of sedge and bog. In former days the Broadland rivers were the natural roadways of the district, and the

97 LOOKING ACROSS SEDGEMOOR, SOMERSET

98 GRAZING MARSHES AT CLEY, NORFOLK

90 GLASTONBURY TOR FROM THE SOUTH MOOR SOMERSET

management of water-craft of all kinds was as inborn as the management of the plough.

Out of the holiday season Ranworth is a picture of earth and water in old domestic neighbourliness. The inn with a seat round the roots of its pollard oak; opposite, the broad green staithe running to the water's edge, a few of those characteristic saucer-like boats moored there; the church tower overlooking trees and water from its hill. There is an old house or two beside the staithe with mossed reed thatch and ancient chimney. There is a quietness enhanced by the water, and a loiteringness in the neighbourhood of the staithe, which seems to have something to do with it. Soft puffs of wind scurry the water, little flocks of ripples are born and die: a bird sings in the dark wilderness on the other side, and the call comes clear over the broad; and other sounds near at hand seem to be amplified; murmur of anglers conversing; a man baling water out of a boat; the crunch of cart-wheels on the road, replaced by a long rising and falling of voices as the carter stops his horse and talks with a friend. Many a quiet grey afternoon subsides thus beside the inland waters, in the pursuit of small ends slowly, sociably, as has always been done. The accumulated wisdom of local life seems embodied in the shape of that small boat—so slight, so light a curve, a nimble slip of a craft. And an air always of expectancy beside the green staithe, looking out across the wide water for a brown sail that might at any moment appear as out of that thicket where the hidden river runs. Over its trees a far church tower signals some other sequestered anchorage.

Unlike the Fens, where the pumping is now nearly all done by engine, no view of the Broads would be typical without a windmill. Wherever you have a prospect there you may discern after a minute the turning sails, perhaps only one sail visible at a time, rising against the sky above trees and sinking into the brown landscape again. They are the continuous movement in the landscape, complementary to the summer sails of yachts gliding along it, just as the winter figures of anglers in a boat are the typical stillness. Sitting muffled in a monumental patience, they and their boat are part of the winter landscape: you may see them on every broad. They watch the water, and an old labourer, a bough of a tree on his shoulder, leans on the bridge and watches them. He tells of the decline in the numbers of wild-fowl, of the havoc caused by the breaking-in of the sea at Horsey, and the death of all the fish in those broads where the salt water has penetrated. You would think, while he stood he would have eased himself of his load of wood; but no, it rests there on his shoulder while he tells of the record pike that have been caught in that broad.

As one approaches the grass flats between Acle and Yarmouth the windmills increase from twos and threes till a whole host stand before one on the treeless expanse. It is perhaps one of the most curious views you can have of England in the twentieth century, to see so many windmills at one glance. All of the old traditional kind, near and far, turning fast and slow; but all turning —some fairly tumbling round, others turning so slowly you can hardly see the sails move, they go in slight jerks like the minute hand of a big clock. They are by no means uniform; some are white, some are black, some brown, some partly this, partly that. Some have gaps in their sails, a bit toothless-looking. Some are of brick, some of wood, some are tall, some squat: some bear their sails high, others' sails seem almost to skim the ground as they turn. Mills of every size according to their distance away—a giant at hand, the clack of whose turning is even louder than the wind, to a mere ant of a windmill on the horizon. All this variety of the same thing makes a harmony: as you travel the straight road, perspective draws several mills together till their sails make a tangled group of turning; then they separate again and lose relationship, and the speed of one ceases to compare with the speed of another.

As it was in the Fens—every weather is in the sky. A storm comes over and passes in a flurry of tossing gulls, sweeping sails, and the wild white smoke of a train. Beside the mills are houses, tiny by comparison: they seem half sunk in the green plain, as the green plain is brimmed with water. There is a vast and uneasy sense of water here; it shines level in every dike, all along the roadside too, while the mills turn ceaselessly. Ahead, mist-grey against the sky, stands up that mixture of industrial and ecclesiastical architecture which is Yarmouth—which is also to a lesser degree, King's Lynn.

Through the heart of Yarmouth runs a breadth of water like the river of a Continental capital, and fishing-craft packed close—a forest of sails and funnels. A huge pylon rears itself above the houses—a sort of Eiffel Tower of a pylon. You cannot escape this plan, this industry, about the landscape of the level, fertile, East Anglian country; it is in the very briskness of the air. And here on the Yarmouth quay as on the quay at King's Lynn one has the feeling of being at the heart of it. That Martian-looking pylon is somehow not out of context.

Looking back, as one dips into the wide Waveney Valley at Haddiscoe, which is roughly where Broadland begins—or ends—there is a moment as you go when one of these distant super-pylons seems to straddle an old windmill. It is worth stopping and protracting that moment: the stout-hearted, bustling little windmill, and the grey, graceful giant—for when pylons reach a certain size they have a curve in their outline, like the curve of a lighthouse, of a tree.

One of the characteristics of these level expanses is the

importance of small objects: everything is visible, every movement becomes a focus of interest—even a bird rising distantly.

North Norfolk, too, has its flats, far-reaching between firm land and the sea. Whether you are a naturalist seeking birds or whether you are a lover merely of wild earth and water, these flats that lie before Wells and Blakeney and Cley have an unforgettable quality. At low tide Blakeney lies stranded: at high tide the creek fills, lifting the boats from off the mud till they float and rise level with the little quay. The effect of the tide up the channel is of a river flowing backwards, it comes in with an observed current, it overflows and partially or wholly submerges the marshes, and then the place seems to stand on the verge of the sea. But actually the sea is more distant to reach than as the gull flies, for there lies the long bar of Blakeney Spit parallel to the sea, rising towards its limit where the river turns at last into the sea. More than one East Anglian river has this habit of running to within a matter of yards of its destination, then suddenly turning and flowing beside the sea for a mile or more.

There is a beauty of mud in the long sunsets on that Norfolk coast; it becomes luminous and reflective, and the birds give it a perpetual unrest. It is a Thule; and more than any scene banishes the sense of measured time. In the morning light the mud shines like an old mirror whose silver has gone blurred, with patches of clarity where water stands, with patches also black and withered. Where the early sun fuses on it, the mud shines like a rippling sea, only with the difference that there is no motion in it, but a sort of transfixed coruscation, as the scales of a fish glisten. The rest takes the light in a soft sheen; reflections of clouds lie in it, of distant trees, and old black stumps sticking up askew. Here and there patches of marsh green which can just struggle above water to live, look black also. Here by the creek the surface of the mud is moulded as subtly as a living body, with rippling tide-marks, swellings and sub-sidings, and the wet on it like a skin. There are pools where the blurred reflections suddenly assume the clarity of glass. Sometimes, at low tide, in the morning bright-ness you can believe that the water has not receded but been frozen still. It is a third tone of light, between the brightness of the sky and of the sea—the sheen of mud. It might almost appropriate the term used of Constable's paintings—sky-mud.

Birds are in continual movement, low over it, crying a medley of cries; sad whistlings, cackles, honkings—all with that mournfulness that none but the pewit brings inland. A flock of starlings deploys over it, higher than the rest, a gyrating cloud. Every bird's reflection is blurred and elongated in the mud: there, the flock is like a forest in motion. The richness of the mud is this indefiniteness and multiplication of reflection; the images are not clear-cut as in the water-pools—mere skin of mirage to one gazing across the expanse—but a hazy procession of colours.

Birds skim the surface like skaters—alight, splash and cry and wheel up again. The knots of marsh grass, seen against the sun, make cloddy black shadows at the verge of the tidal flat, where channellings small as wrinkles in flesh catch narrow silver gleams.

There are marshes at Cley, too; but so pertinacious is man the cultivator, that where the ground rises a little at last between the marshes and the sea he has made a field or two of good earth, and there you may see horses and ploughmen at work with the boom of the surf in their ears, on the sunny side of the sea-wall. It is mar-vellous how, with the salt water so close, the corn can grow, nourished by fresh-water showers and come to harvest. Characteristic, too, of that corner are the grey pebble-built houses, and the generous walls. And every wall is crowned with wild wallflowers, and they spring out of countless crevices. In early May the whole village is a-flower. This flowering out of the grey is equal to anything I have seen in the West, which has a genius for that kind of beauty.

The vitality of all this East Anglian country of marsh and broad and fen is the light. It is always changing: clouded even, it is awake. You realise it most startlingly if you happen to travel from west to east in midsummer, so that it is broad day both at the beginning and end of your journey. Over there a beautiful landscape is just objectively, a beautiful landscape—there are rich contours and restful greens and greys—but here in East Anglia a glance of sun on some distant tree or spire seems positively to pick it up and give it to you. And if you stand on the low ridge behind Cambridge and look across the Fens, they are a wash of deep blue, a sea of haze, with Ely Cathedral a small carbuncle breaking the sky-line.

The Fens have their counterpart, in the West, in the Bridgwater Flats and the lowlying lands that run to Glastonbury. Here, too, there is a great ecclesiastical tradition, when inaccessibility was the bulwark of civilisation. For that was a sea of islands like the Fenland sea that washed round Ely, Littleport, Crowland, Thorney. But it seems a sadder scene; for the fragmentary ruins of Glastonbury are unmitigated, as Crowland's are in the east by Ely still intact and crowning the land that has no line of hill. On the other hand, in the Somerset levels the Quantocks or the Mendips are often within sight, and the sheer richness of the pasturage has a beauty which is cumulative. Here, too, the local industry of the basket willow lends its own aspect, both bright and pensive; the brilliant flush of the osiers in the spring, and the quietude of willows. But grass it is chiefly, acres and acres of fine grass with villages hidden among thick West-country trees. It is indeed much more reminiscent of its former state than are the East Anglian Fens. They are patched with planted crops, or bare earth, brilliant here and there with bulbs like a gipsy garment: only at midsummer when the corn stands high and waves in the breeze is there a likeness to the sea. Sedgemoor is a sea of grass, winter and summer; and you are forcibly reminded that it once was water, by its level and unbroken green, but chiefly by the bold way the islands rise out of it. Hills here *are* hills—there is the feeling of hills all round. Even small hills are in a sense big hills—sudden, as, for instance, Glastonbury's Tor. The Polden Hills cut right across it and a whole series of headlands jut into it from the Quantocks side. Then, bounding it on the south there is the ridge that runs through Curry Rivel to Langport, whence you can go by way of Ham Hill, and through the Poldens to Glastonbury. One always seems to see this country in a sort of misty sunlight, the sunlight moving in a veil from headland to headland, then gliding over the plain. This West-country atmosphere seems most at home in the Vale of Avalon, and breathes the spirit of the old legends over the land. Being English one can never see it apart from its associations. There is also a considerable region of flat country between the Quantocks and the sea: country which seems to take half of its happiness from its juxta-position to the hills. After the lonely barrows of the infertile tops, the sense of rest and homeliness in the quiet fertility of one farm after another is grateful. Mixed land this—a good deal of it arable, where it is pleasant again to see the plough at work and the fields in human occupation. Nor must one omit a mention of that rich pocket of alluvial flat near Porlock, where the best barley in the world is grown. There is a sort of fertility there that is almost sub-tropical; and again, to gaze upon that ruddy patchwork from the heights as from an aeroplane is to be cheered by the beauty of rural domesticity that a fertile soil breeds.

The same aspect is that of the Bridgwater Flats—only it is in terms of cattle and grass. It is a peaceful, contented sight to see the herds of red bullocks feeding there or resting under the willows beside the ever-present water, knowing that they are actually fattening on that grass.

Another grassy plain there is in Cheshire, and that affords the same sort of view, but with a difference. There, in the midst of an industrial community, herds of dairy cows are the rule—and when one says herds of dairy cows, one means to-day only one sort of cow—Friesians. Now, one can never have enough of fat red bullocks on flat pastures: they look warm; they look comfortable. But somehow the same thing in terms of black and white Friesian cows becomes monotonous. The unvaried black-and-white looks cold under the grey skies: they need a livelier atmosphere than the motionless cloud that hangs low over Cheshire for days at a time. They can look well under a brisk and broken East Anglian sky sometimes, when the clouds are dazzling white and deeply shadowed: they have a place in that sort of day. But this Cheshire plain is a repetitive pattern—homestead, black-and-white cows and marl-pit pond. In the distance, a factory chimney, or a stack of them, keeps you aware of being in something of a pastoral island in the midst of industrialism.

As these green levels are with their cattle, so is Romney Marsh with its sheep. Here again, and especially in that alluvial stretch of country around Rye and Winchelsea you have the effect of a receded sea. The way the lawn-like pasturage positively flows out between the two old ports and spreads into a plain before them can be grasped by the lofty view that the old coastline affords. The "landscape," in the sense of infinite local variability of contour, suddenly stops, and in its place you look out upon just one thing—grass and sheep. Behind the sea-wall against which the waves rage, the sheep nibble the sweet turf as contentedly as though they were in some snug inland valley. The windy solitude, within sight of orchards and hop gardens and all that fruitfulness for which the district is famed, yet holds aloof from it. It has more in common with the sea than with the hinterland, and no amount of holiday camping even can domesticate it. It seems unbroken grass as you stand looking across its level, till you start walking and discover a network of watercourses, with bridges whose gates are a feature of these fenny pastures, standing up alone as though waiting for a hedge to grow beside them.

Other stretches of lowlying land England possesses, sometimes on the coast, like the peninsula between Chichester and Selsey Bill, sometimes far inland, like the wild tract of Otmoor which occurs in the midst of the comfortable country of the Oxfordshire borders, or estuary land like the Solway Moss. The characteristics of these fens and flats is their extreme variability, according to the success or otherwise man has had in controlling the water that surrounds them. In one place such as Selsey you get good corn-land, or even, as around Spalding, cultivation of a garden tidiness and intensiveness; in another such as Otmoor the effect is of wilderness untamed.

I have attempted to give an idea of the aspect and atmosphere of these amphibious regions in general. For though they are widely separated geographically, they have more in common with one another than with the various kinds of country that border them, and from which they are essentially aloof—both in their manner of cultivation—or non-cultivation—and the outlook of those who dwell upon them. Thus they talk of Fenmen, in East Anglia, as people of a common bond, whether they are natives of Lincolnshire, Cambridgeshire or Norfolk.

The Fens and Levels of England, besides those broad natural effects of distance and great skies, and the mingling of the cries of land- and sea-birds, possess monuments unparalleled to human effort—Ely Cathedral and the Bedford River, each after its kind.

100 SHEEP PASTURES ON ROMNEY MARSH, KENT

101   THE FORESHORE, ST. MARGARET'S BAY, KENT

Geoffrey Clark

THE COASTLANDS

COASTAL scenery is often dramatic, even startling, in its contrasts. The foreshore is the battle-ground, littered with debris, upon which the land and the ocean fight out their eternal battle: the one steadfast, grim and silent, the other restless and unrelenting. It is impossible to enjoy a coastal scene without, perhaps subconsciously, sensing the presence of a threat. Even the great migrant population of summer visitors, who know the sea only as a boundless bathing-pool and the shore as a soft surface upon which to lie and brown their bodies, must hear on their radios or read in their newspapers, of a lifeboat wrecked in a gale or of a parish flooded by some wind-driven tidal wave.

Considered statistically, however, the coastal scene on its grander stretches is a superb contrast between the wide horizontal plane of the sea's surface and the vertical face of the land: the one stretching away to a softened horizon line, its coloured expanse given a texture by the wind and a pattern by moving cloud shadows or submerged shallows; the other crumbling into a thousand shapes, tinted to as many shades by the rock from which it has been weathered, and framed between the sable beach at its base and the emerald or bronze field at its summit.

The sea has carved our coast into a series of promontories and bays, and, with the help of our rivers, has created deep or sandy estuaries; by the power of its tidal waters in alliance with the wind it has eroded one stretch of cliffs to pile up the debris in the form of sand-dunes or pebble-beaches elsewhere; it has, indeed, fortified the land against its own powerful incursions.

All landscape is changing from day to day: our trees are growing higher or being cut down and carted away; our fields are increasing their soil by absorbing decaying roots and vegetation; our rivers are carrying away their banks or piling up a barrier in their estuaries, but the whole process is slow enough to avoid general observation. On our coast, however, the rough and tumble of tide, wind and rain is altering the landscape before our very eyes: in a single generation it is possible to watch a coastal landscape change radically. The Dowsland landslip in Devon or the tumbled clifflands between Lyme Regis and Charmouth in Dorset are well-known examples; recently the population of a parish in Norfolk was forced to flee before a sudden onrush of the sea which broke down the weakened embankment guarding the lowlying meadows and rushed down upon the grazing cattle and farm buildings. It is possible that this land may revert to salt marsh with its characteristic coarse grass and sea-birds. Poole Harbour, too, thanks to the advent of a certain grass, is rapidly silting up: islands of mud are forming, held together by grass roots, very beautiful to see, with the pale yellow-green blades standing out against the intense blue of the water, but destructive to the grey mullet and its fishermen. All landscape, too, has movement. The wind gliding through a cornfield; trees bending and the smoke from a group of cottages floating in a blue swirl away down some gentle valley; but a coastal scene is vital with movement. The sea itself ceaselessly sweeps to the attack with wave after wave breaking gently on the shore or crashing with a thud against some granite cliff. Seagulls drift vigilantly cliff-high or swoop gaily down to catch an unwary fish; a cormorant flies quickly along the surface or, most beautiful spectacle of all, a gannet with wings closed, drops like a stone into the water to swallow a hasty bite.

To this tremendous picture man himself has added breakwaters and harbours, fishing villages and light-houses, and, less heroically, seaside resorts and holiday camps. The older works of man, which represent his brave attempts to curb the sea's vigorous onslaught on the land, his breakwaters and harbours, his stone piers and cleverly sheltered coves, or the weatherproof houses which sheltered his families while he faced the weather in his small fishing boat, have grown to be part of the scene. They were conceived in harmony with the natural laws of landscape building. The curve of a pier took on a line which resisted the onslaught of the waves; the houses of a village fitted their site like seagulls on a cliff ledge; a lighthouse stood up from its rocky foundation a perfect structure to resist the wind and the waves. The newer works of man, the seaside resorts, at first were built broadly and comfortably on spacious sites where idlers and searchers after health could walk without hardship and enjoy the invigorating sea breezes during the warm summer days. More recently, the craving for sea air in the summer has brought into being those haphazard collections of bungalows, shacks and refreshment-rooms which disgrace too many miles of our coastline and reflect the less hopeful side of our modern civilisation.

It is convenient, for the purpose of this chapter, to

classify the English coastal scenery into certain broad categories. At the one end of our classification we have the sublime cliff landscape where the hardest rocks stand out boldly in gigantic walls or jagged promontories, defying the wildest onslaughts of the winter storms. At the other end we have those dreary miles of low-lying cliff or shore which have been seized upon by the speculator and holiday-maker and turned into sordid slums of unrelieved squalor. Between these two extremes we have splendid sandy wastes, romantic and picturesque coves, unspoilt fishing harbours, ports grand in their scale, long pebbly beaches, deeply cut estuaries and old-established seaside towns; in addition there are islands large enough for life, or merely rocky isolated cliffs which form the breeding ground of sea-birds. Indeed, the English coastline is composed of a complex variety of materials, ranging from the hardest granite cliffs on the extreme south-west to the softest sandy wastes on the north-west and south-east. It contains cliffs of every colour, from the black cliffs of Cornwall and Northumberland, through the blood-red cliffs at Dawlish in Devon, the pink sandstone cliffs at Sidmouth, the grey limestone cliffs at Purbeck in Dorset, the superb golden cliffs at West Bay, Bridport, through pale browns, greeny-greys to the shining white cliffs at Beachy Head, Sussex. The sands can be grey, red, brown or gold, even white, and the pebbly shores of every colour under the sun. The Chesil Beach, that scythe-like curve of shingle on the Dorset coast, consists of many coloured pebbles graded by the tide from the brown sand at Burton Bradstock to the tennis-ball pebbles near Portland. It is a kind of coastal museum in which can be found specimens of most of the rock-formation of the south-west.

It is advisable, perhaps, in this comparative study of the English coastal scene to write off as it were the whole of the low-lying type of seashore which has been degraded by untidy shelters for summer visitors, ranging from the smallest wooden huts to large pretentious villas. In this category we must include the whole south coast from Bournemouth eastward round the Thames estuary to Southend, and the Norfolk coast from Yarmouth almost to Cromer. Here, with the exception of a few stretches to be mentioned later, a coast never in itself striking has been rendered aesthetically and sociologically pitiful.

At the other end of our scale of values must be placed those sublime stretches of the coast where the hardest rocks are thrust out like advance posts far into the sea, or stand like armoured phalanxes locked together with their shields forming a solid wall of opposition to the sea's tidal charges. Here, indeed, coastal scenery reaches its most striking form. From Minehead in Somerset to Studland in Dorset, and from the mouth of the Tyne to Flamborough Head in Yorkshire, except when our rivers have broken through and formed low sandy estuaries, the land presents a solid cliff-face to the sea. It is far from being an unbroken wall as a glance at any map will show; it has been formed into bays, points, harbours and estuaries, but generally speaking affords the grandest examples of wild, rocky coastal scenery.

Possibly the most striking picture of all is to be seen from the winding road which leads steeply to Hartland Quay in North Devon. The approach has been through a windswept landscape of fields and hedges, where dark stone farm-houses stand bravely against the wild westerly gales, and deeply cut valleys shelter the villages. It has passed the tall tower of St. Nectan's Church, which once carried a beacon light for sailors, and the row of colour-washed cottages at its base, and finally plunged down the hill leading to the battered harbour where, at a sharp bend in the road, it discloses an astounding medley of tortured cliffs, jagged reefs, and beating waves, stretching to the north and south as far as the eye can see. The whole scene portrays strife. Torn and battered promontories guard those little shallow but secluded bays which are so difficult of access. Streams tumble in falls to the sea. Sharp ridges, enjoyed by seagulls, project menacingly seawards and break the Atlantic rollers as they ceaselessly advance against the main cliffs. It is superb but restless. In contrast to this it is interesting to remember the sublime walk along the Northumbrian coast from the salt-flavoured village of Craster towards the forlorn ruin of Dunstanburgh Castle. Here a gentle grassy track leads easily along the shelving foreshore. The writhing torture of the Hartland scene is entirely absent, and in its place are low sloping cliffs of the hardest basalt, backed by softly rounded hills. The time to enjoy this scene is in the early spring, before people have realised that winter has passed, when the scene is empty of all life but the terns and kittiwakes or the cattle. The east wind touches our cheeks, making them glow with a tingling warmth, the gentle sound of the sea is in our ears, and on the hill, which forms the goal of our expedition, we can see the weatherbeaten remnants of the old castle, fading, like its history, into a misty background.

Hartland Point in the north and Land's End in the south contain between them a long stretch of wild and wind-swept coastline. Here the tempests of winter have laid low all vegetation. The whole aspect of the scenery is one of "standing to," of being, like a battleship, "cleared for action." It is a hard world of bent heads and breathless climbs.

Beyond Hartland Point to the east, where the change in the direction of the coast has afforded shelter, an entirely different landscape is to be found. Trees clothe the cliffs and descend to the very water's edge. Instead of jagged, naked rock scenery, we look upon a world of pink, sloping cliffs sliding in crumbled screes to a greyish shore, inter-spersed with thick woods. A storm may be raging at

Hartland or Padstow, but at Clovelly all is peace. This right-angle turn of the shore at Hartland Point is one of the most striking features of the whole English coast. The headland stands up boldly, its summit swept by all the gales of Heaven, with the Atlantic Ocean beating on its western shore and the waters of the Severn Sea sweeping the steep slopes below the lighthouse. Here, perched between cliff and sea, man has cut himself a ledge and built a home for the lighthouse keepers, surprisingly hidden from all but the closest approach. Lighthouses, generally speaking, stand up bravely for the world to see, sited as they so often are on low rocks or islands or on the higher points of headlands; but Hartland has hidden this lighthouse from all but seafaring eyes.

It might be interesting here to write a little further on the lighthouses of the English coast, as they fit in so happily with the character of the wilder rock scenery. Designed to resist the most violent storms, constructed by feats of the utmost skill and endurance, they stand out as superlative human contributions to the coastal scene. Who could fail to be thrilled by the spectacle of the two rocky islets off Land's End, the Wolf Rock and the Longships, each crowned by a slim granite structure, and each surrounded by miles of raging ocean? There is no more engrossing experience than to stand on the hotel terrace at Land's End, amidst the luxuriant dead man's finger which grows so rampantly at this particular point, and watch a storm approaching from the north-west and devouring the sunshine which had, to that moment, been lighting the surface of the sea: there is a malicious determination, an offensive power, in this remorseless approach of darkness, so patent in that wide, open space. Or again, who has not enjoyed the brilliant blue sea off the Farne Islands in Northumberland, when they have looked out from the magnificent ramparts of Bamburgh Castle and watched the white breakers baiting the foundations of the

Longstones. At Portland, too, where an astounding block of limestone projects for four miles into the English Channel, it is a delicious experience to lie on a grassy bank among the close-cropped turf, shot with the colours of tens of thousands of short-stemmed flowers, and watch the waters of the notorious race contend with each other in a series of convulsive swirls. In the foreground stands a large white lighthouse with a deep chocolate band round its circumference, brilliantly clear-cut against the blue of the water. In winter, on this selfsame slope, it is often only possible to approach the same structure on hands and knees, so exposed is the sloping headland to wild westerly gales.

It is natural and logical to find a lighthouse in a setting of dangerous rocks, and our coast is well equipped in this respect: indeed it must be considered a characteristic feature of our wilder coastal scenery.

On the whole south-west coast the power of the Atlantic gales is a dominating force in modifying the character of the landscape. Immediately the direction of the coastline exposes the land to this wind, trees disappear from the shore and on the hinterland crouch in agonised curves; when, on the other hand, there is protection afforded by such headlands as Foreland Point, or changes of alignment as at Clovelly or Lynmouth, the equable temperature of the West brings to life a luxuriant growth of tree and shrub. On the south coast of Cornwall and Devon this is well illustrated at such places as Lamorna, Torbay and Dartmouth. Swanage in Dorset can provide, possibly, the most interesting example of this change from exposure to shelter, for Durleston Head, like Hartland, is a point standing boldly out to sea where the coastal direction changes from east–west to south–north: here the grand limestone cliffs of Purbeck give place, on the east, to a thickly wooded, crumbling shore where it is possible to look through a vista of pine-trees to a rich blue sea.

102   DURLSTON BAY, DORSET

102   THE ROCKY CORNISH COAST AT TINTAGEL

It is convenient, after this generalised study, to take the English cliff scenery county by county. The greatest attention has so far been given to the South-west of England, since there we have found the most exciting scenery of all, and we propose to return to that region after studying the different types of cliff elsewhere. It has already been noted that the second most interesting range of English cliff scenery occurs between the mouth of the Tyne and Flamborough Head. Farther north, however, in Northumberland, that strange band of intrusive rock known as the Whin Sill is responsible for those lonely and impressive mounds of basalt on which stand Bamburgh Castle and, as already mentioned, the ruins of Dunstanburgh. Here indeed is a combination of hard volcanic cliff and sandy estuary, of wild bird life and romantic architecture, difficult to match in the whole range of the English coastline. The cliffs themselves rise into high mounds or slope in slippery shelves to the sea: the sands are clean and yellow and the pasture slopes glide gently to the shore or rise on to the mounds themselves, clothing all but the exposed rock-face in a soft green mantle. Seagulls sail through the air or sit on the wall of some dark stone pier, while a greater black-back gull tears a large decaying crab to pieces on the harbour-bed at Sea Houses or Craster. Fishermen, with rosy clean-shaven Northumbrian faces, in bright-blue motor-boats, glide swiftly in and make fast at the quayside, while in the quiet waters of the harbour itself eider-drakes and -ducks are seen tamely floating like soft feather balls. There is a salty freshness, born of the sharp east wind, which seems to have seasoned this section of our coast. The men, the houses, the cliffs, the whole slope and texture of the landscape have been polished by it. The flavour of the South-west is entirely different: there it is gale-swept not windswept. There the rollers approach with a wide-spaced rhythm born of the thousands of miles of the Atlantic

Ocean: here in the North-east the rhythm of the waves is shorter and quicker.

Farther to the south, between the Rivers Tyne and Wear the rocks belong to the magnesian limestone series, being softer and more liable to erosion. Deep caves occur, such as the famous cavern at Marsden which is used as the rear portion of an inn and at Blackhall Rocks farther south; or the sea has left islets and promontories, battered into holes which penetrate from one side of the rock to the other, as exemplified in the Marsden Rock itself and Holy Rock at Roker, Sunderland. The whole coast presents a bold face to the sea; the land is comparatively level and runs in well-farmed fields to the cliff-edge, which drops abruptly to a sandy shore or rocky, shelving beach, as at Souter Point near Whitburn or Salterfen Rocks near Ryhope, or the oddly named Featherbed Rocks. It is a coast where long lonely walks can be taken along the firm sand at low tide provided the points of access, which are not numerous, are known. Characteristic features which, in the less grimy past, must have added greatly to the charm, are the little valleys, known as Denes, which run out to the shore cutting into the wall of cliffs: Castle Eden Dene is a typical example. To-day, however, much of the greenness has disappeared before the smoke of the colliery chimney: in the place of a soft agricultural landscape, never heroic, but often pleasing with its red pantile-roofed farm-houses and grouped buildings, there stand vast modern collieries like Easington and Horden, highly electrified and gaining their coal from under the sea-bed. On a sunny day Horden Colliery, standing up boldly against a blue sky and a still bluer sea, makes a magnificent feature typifying the scale, order and power of modern industry.

The wide Tees estuary separates these limestone cliffs from the red liassic cliffs of North-east Yorkshire. On a clear day, standing on the immense sands at Seaton Carew, they present a superb background, stretching as

104   ROBIN HOOD'S BAY FROM THE CLIFFS, YORKSHIRE

105 ST. BEES HEAD, CUMBERLAND

they do in a long perspective of headlands to the climax of Flamborough Head. In the foreground lies a golden plain of sand reaching to a low stone breakwater. Above this the bold silhouettes of the Cleveland Hills rise deep violet in colour, accentuated by the deep indigo slopes of the huge slag-heaps of Middlesbrough and South Bank. Here, in this spacious setting, industry itself has added a new beauty to the scene. The Yorkshire cliffs begin to rise immediately to the south of Saltburn and continue almost to Scarborough. The bold mass of Boulby Cliff, the highest sheer cliff on the English coast, is seen to the greatest advantage from the sea itself, and indeed much of this rocky shore is inaccessible. It is, however, broken into by the lovely bays of Runswick and Robin Hood. At Runswick Bay the wide sweep of the sand stretches to the headland of Kettleness which projects boldly seawards. At Staithes, a little to the north of Runswick Bay, there is a narrow harbour protected from the violence of the northern gales by Colburn Nab. Here, perched on its rocky ledge only a little above the level of the sea, lies one of the most characteristic fishing villages in England, reminiscent of Mevagissey in Cornwall though smaller. It is difficult to think of any human colony so utterly dependent on the sea for a living and so dominated by a rocky background. The cliffs themselves are terra-cotta red with horizontal bands of brownish sandstone. Robin Hood's Bay, like Runswick Bay, is a wide sweep of sand, backed by a grassy slope covered in a thick vegetation of shrubs and small trees, stretching to a lofty headland. Beyond this again, proceeding southward, the cliffs become inaccessible and it is not till Scarborough is reached that we find sea scenery of more than ordinary interest. It should, however, be noted that the road to Scarborough runs across the wide Yorkshire moors and is of the greatest beauty. Scarborough will be described later, when we are dealing with those seaside towns which add by their architectural character and the siting of their streets and buildings to the beauty of the coastal scene. The setting of Scarborough is magnificent with its bold Castle Hill and its perspective view across the sandy bay to the cliffs which run southward.

The lowlying region known as The Charrs separates the high moorlands of North Yorkshire from the Chalk Wolds which meet the sea at Flamborough Head. Here, but for the speculative builder, is a glorious cliff landscape of grey-white cliffs buffeted by the turbulent North Sea and carved into coves and isolated pinnacles. Flamborough itself, with its memorial to some of its sons drowned at sea in one of those epic incidents of rescue common to the wilder stretches of coast, is an old-established village, but at the Landings and at Flamborough Head, huts and bungalows have destroyed the grandeur of the cliff-top entirely.[1] The feeling of open wildness has departed, and even though the sea will rage with all the accustomed fury, the head has lost its ancient harmony when the lighthouse alone stood bravely up against the wild winter storms.

No further cliff scenery of any real importance occurs till we reach Kent, where the North Downs run out to the sea between Folkestone and Dover, and where the chalk is exposed in the Isle of Thanet. Here, like Flamborough Head, man has intervened to take away the untamed aspect of the fine wild cliff. Nevertheless the scene looking along the beach towards Foreness Point has a certain grandeur where the solid wall of chalk provides an uninterrupted background to the shore. The well-known Shakespeare's Cliff at Dover, too, has a noble outline, but the whole of this white coast gives its noblest impression when approached by boat from the Continent. Then indeed it is the threshold of home.

Chalk again provides us with our two next impressive

[1] Since this was written the Bridlington Council have purchased the Head in order to preserve its ancient beauty.

stretches of cliff landscape, the glorious white cliffs of Sussex and the weathered rocks near Swanage in Dorset. Beachy Head, towering above the lighthouse, begins that fine range of Sussex cliffs which rise on either side of Cuckmere Haven and include the Seven Sisters. It is a coast seriously attacked by the sea where the main road itself has been endangered, but bold and impressive when viewed from the rocky foreshore at Burling Gap. The Dorset cliffs, on the other hand, do not form a solid stone wall, but project like a narrow finger seawards. From Studland they form the southern boundary of the glorious Studland Bay and end in the battered form of Old Harry, who recently lost his wife to the violent caresses of the sea. From Peveril Point, Swanage, they appear as a long, sheer, inaccessible cliff, crowned by soft green turf, with the perpendicular form of the Pinnacle standing out as a white obelisk in the morning sun. For those fortunate enough to live in one of the Old Coastguard cottages, the early morning view of these rocks is unsurpassable, for the rising sun sends a pink glow over the whole white surface, combining with the blue shimmering sea to form a world of transparent opal. The Dorset chalk reaches the sea a second time between White Nothe and Worbarrow Bay, and forms, with the reefs of Purbeck limestone, a series of coves, bays and striking headlands. It is a coast where geological students and lovers of landscape can study the effects of sea, wind and rain on a great variety of rocks, and witness the brave defence put up by the Purbeck cliffs between Durlston Head and St. Aldhelm's Head. Here the grey limestone cliffs rise sheer from the sea without foreshore, except where a small valley like Seacombe and Winspit has cut a way to the rocky shelving base of the cliff, and form one of the finest stretches of English rock scenery, bearing out the observation made earlier in this chapter, that the harder the rock the finer the cliff and the grander the spectacle.

At St. Aldhelm's Head, a great landmark capped by its little chapel and row of coastguard cottages, the cliff changes from cold grey to warm grey and possesses a sloping base where the limestone debris has piled itself in the characteristic form seen again at Portland. Here Emmett's Hill towers above the black depths of Chapman's Pool, where the underwater shelves of the Kimmeridge rock make bathing far from pleasant. The cliffs of Kimmeridge clay are black and dismal, and liable to fall at any moment on the unwary bather who is undressing beneath their overhanging brows. Gad Cliff, to the west of Kimmeridge Bay, rivals St. Aldhelm's Head as the finest individual cliff on the Purbeck coast. Both are of limestone and both possess the sloping base and the precipitous summit, but while the one forms a noble headland seen for miles, the other is part of a long, serrated, cliff silhouette.

The Dorset coast, unrivalled in many ways as it is, is made unique by the strange form of Portland which projects for four miles into the sea and is attached to the mainland by a narrow slip of road only preserved from inundation by the shingle bank known as the Chesil Beach. This, one of the longest shingle beaches in Europe, stretches for a distance of fifteen miles and guards the lowlying coastal plain at the rear from the onslaught of the sea. Behind it lie the waters of the Fleet, where the swans from Abbotsbury come at certain times of the year to feed. Seen from the high northern summit of Portland, it stretches in the most perfect curve till it is lost in the golden cliffs by Burton Bradstock. The contrasts, in form and colour, on this stretch of the English coast are astounding in their variety. Portland itself forms the climax of all views, whether seen from the high road above Abbotsbury, or from the coastal path on Flowers Barrow, Lulworth. Frequently it provides a grey background to the Fleet, when the dark forms of the warships

106 THE HEADLANDS OF THE GREAT AND LITTLE HANGMAN,
NORTH DEVON

107 ARISH MELL GAP, DORSET

108 THE CHALK PINNACLES OF BEER HEAD, SOUTH DEVON

lie like silent sentinels in Portland Harbour. The Isle of Portland is a solid lump of rock riddled with quarries. It slopes from the high ground above Chesilton gently down to the Beal where the cliff is only a few feet above the water-level. There, surrounded by the sea, it is possible to think oneself on the prow of a huge battleship, with decks cleared for action; for the landscape is entirely without trees or habitations save for the white coastguard station behind the lighthouse, with its black chimneys.

Farther to the west, beyond Bridport, the Dorset coast begins to assume the highly coloured mantle of Devon, and the softer cliffs of Golden Cap and Thorncombe Beacon, which rise in splendid silhouettes against a long-vanishing perspective of coastline, are truly golden in the afternoon sun. Here the beaches are invariably of shingle, and the sea is able to make that tearing, screeching noise as it pulls the pebbles down the steep slope with its undertow. Between Charmouth in Dorset and Seaton in Devon the whole coast has assumed a strange aspect owing to repeated landslips. At Dowsland the upper chalk and greensand formation, after an exceedingly wet season, broke away from the cliff and foundered over the inclined and slippery base of lias. The resultant landscape is a dark jumble of contour, with footpaths taking leaps of ten feet at a time to lower levels and where the vegetation assumes the oddest angles. The notices, too, which warn the wayfarer that he proceeds at his own risk, emphasise the restless nature of the scene. It must be added, however, that the walk along these sliding cliffs from Charmouth to Lyme Regis affords long views down the Devon coast and of the beautiful old harbour at Lyme Regis itself.

Beer Head rises approximately to five hundred feet above the sea and is topped with the soft green turf familiar to us on all the chalk downs: from the Coastguard Watch House there is a magnificent prospect of the coast from Portland Beal to Berry Head, a total of some sixty miles. The chalk formation continues almost to the River Sid and is penetrated by the deep valleys of Branscombe, Dunscombe and Salcombe Regis.

The English chalk, which is responsible for so much of England's characteristic landscape, has been followed down the coastline from Flamborough Head in Yorkshire, where we saw a pale grey cliff scene battered by the North Sea, by Foreness Point and Shakespeare's Cliff at Dover in Kent, past the glorious white cliffs of Beachy Head, Sussex to Ballard Point and White Nothe in Dorset. In Devon, at Beer, we look upon the most southerly outcrop of chalk, and in this well-quarried hill we bid farewell to the chalk cliffs of England.

Westward of this the coastal landscape takes on an ever-increasing degree of colour. At Sidmouth on a warm day it is a delight to sit on the front and look upon the pink cliffs to the east glowing in the sunlight. Between Budleigh Salterton and Exmouth the cliffs take on the well-known deep-red colour of South Devon, which is so surprising when met with for the first time. Here there are warm sable beaches backed by the soft red cliffs. At Exmouth the view along the coastline towards Straight Point is full of charm. The whole coastline in South-east Devon is pleasing rather than heroic. It glows in sunshine like the cliffs at West Bay in Dorset, but with a deeper shade of burnished gold. Erosion of the cliff is continuous and the effect is dramatically illustrated at Ladrum Bay, where the soft marl has succumbed to the attacks of tide and wind, which has left isolated pinnacles and islets complete with their turf caps.

Beyond the River Exe, which proves such a formidable obstacle to all who are proceeding westwards along the coast, the cliffs are of the deepest blood-red, clothed in gorse and making an almost overpowering impression in the heat of early summer, when the sea itself is a rich blue-green. The railway has interfered with the sea-front to some extent on this sector, but has at the same time provided protection from the onrushing waves. After crossing the estuary of the River Teign it is possible to follow the main Torquay road which climbs to some five hundred feet above sea-level and commands a wide panorama of the curve of Babbacombe Bay to its southern termination at Hope's Nose. The scenery is of that sheltered, well-wooded nature so characteristic of Torquay and of the North Devon coast near Clovelly.

It might be useful, here, to elaborate further our earlier remarks on cliff scenery in general. The grandeur is founded entirely on geology, that is, on the texture of the rock itself, and the position in which the old formative upheavals had placed it in relation to the sea. In Purbeck and Portland, for instance, the cliffs from Winspit to Durlston are in their correct plane and the erosion when it takes place at all is achieved in horizontally bedded shelves. At Hartland, on the other hand, the cliffs seem to be writhing in a Laocoön-like struggle with some unseen force. Erosion has taken place eccentrically, and everywhere extend jagged, shark-like teeth, picturesque but terrible. It may be taken as an axiom that when a hard rock meets a wild sea the cliff scene will be of the grandest. Exposure to the wintry gales, or the cold north-easters, will denude the surface of all trees, and leave either the living rock itself or oases of turf, enlivened in spring with the gay sea-pink. Again, where there is a mingling of soft and hard rocks, we shall find bold headlands and softly curved bays. The wind is possibly a greater force than the sea in moulding character, and immediately shelter has been provided from its devastating blasts, vegetation takes possession and flourishes. The bare limestone promontory of Berry Head has stood up against the Atlantic storms and allowed the tides to carve out of the softer sandstones the glorious sweep of

26

Tor Bay. On the north, Torquay itself lies buried in trees, protected from the north winds by Hope's Nose. On the south, Brixham Harbour nestles, with all its ancient seafaring smells, underneath the gallant limestone bluff.

Between Berry Head and the mouth of the Dart the coast, thanks to the resistant nature of the slates and grits and to exposure to the open Channel, is high and rugged, and most happily explored from the sea. It is here that the guillemot congregates so thickly in the nesting season. West of Froward Point shelter again takes the place of exposure and the clifflands are enriched by woods, which help, with the addition of two ruined castles, to provide a romantic approach to the ancient slopes of Dartmouth. In this part of Devon the whole landscape, both inland and on the coast, is hilly and exciting. The river mouth, the wooded banks of the harbour, the ships and sailing boats all combine to make a scene full of interest and charm. West of the Dart the picturesque cliffs of slate and grit continue to form bays and miniature coves, and the coastal road enables the less active visitor to catch glimpses of the cliffs and sea, through trees, or across green fields. The peaceful bay of Blackpool, so unlike its northern namesake, culminates in the higher land of Matthews Point; beyond this stretches another raised beach, which unlike the Chesil Beach in Dorset is entirely pleasing, carrying as it does the road which runs between the sands and the waters of Slapton Ley. Looking southwards from Torcross the coastal scene terminates most happily in Start Point, and includes the little fishing hamlets of Hallsands and Beesands. The cliffs north of Start Point are sloping and bare, and contrast strongly with the change in climate farther west.

The finest stretch of coastal scenery in South Devon begins immediately to the west of Start Point and continues to Bolt Tail. Here we are in the presence of some of the oldest and hardest rocks, entirely exposed to the fury of the elements, and the result is a series of magnificent cliffs and headlands, broken into by the estuary of Kingsbridge. The elemental grandeur of the scene is enhanced in the spring by a profusion of wild flowers, and it is still possible to find some of the rarer birds such as the raven and peregrine falcon, which have their homes in the inaccessible faces of the cliffs.

Start Point itself is one of those important angles of our coast where the land changes its direction and from which it is possible to obtain the most diverse views from different positions. Bolt Head and Prawle Point which form such grand sentinels at the entrance to the harbour, are composed of mica schist and hornblende schist, two highly resistant substances which have defied the action of tide and weather and face the sea with almost inaccessible cliffs. The high tableland which extends to Bolt Tail, itself a notable promontory of the same hard material, continues a landscape of masculine severity.

From Bolt Tail westwards there is an extensive view extending in clear weather beyond the red marl cliffs near the Avon mouth and the wide, sandy foreshore of Bigbury Bay as far as Rame Head in Cornwall. Erosion again is taking place in the soft sandstone below Bolt Tail, itself a perfect example of the effect of hard material on the coastal landscape. Beyond the red cliffs towards Ayrmer Cove and the mouth of the Erme there are high silver-toned cliffs of slate and shale with intricately folded strata. From Bigbury to Plymouth Sound the coast is almost entirely rural, though Plymouth is inclined to invade the district round Wembury and Bovisand. The two lovely wooded estuaries of the Erme and Yealm intersect a landscape of rich plough lands, and cliffs sloping to a rocky foreshore; a land where the difficulty of access and the lack of roads has prevented any serious spoliation of the rural aspect. Some of the finest views along the Cornish coast are obtained by following the private marine drive from Stoke round Gara Point, with Wembury Bay and the Great Mew Stone in the foreground. The cliffs are grey and slaty and little erosion has taken place. As a climax to the South Devon coast Plymouth Sound, in its superb setting of green-topped cliffs and rolling hills, leaves nothing to be desired. From Staddon Heights it is possible to enjoy the finest prospect of The Sound with Mount Edgecombe rising to the west above Cawsand Bay and carefully guarding the entrance to the Hamoaze.

We have returned once more to the rockbound coast of Cornwall. Here is a county with the sea on three sides and composed very largely of the hardest and most intractable materials. Clay slates are dominant, with numerous bands of greenstone, and the whole geological mass is contorted and penetrated by huge areas of granite. Land's End is entirely granite, a worthy toe to a great country. The Lizard is composed of serpentine which gives the rocks their highly coloured appearance. The whole county is almost a seascape, matched only by Pembroke in Wales. Except in the deep valleys of the south coast, it is impossible to forget the Atlantic gales, and the whole upland scene is wind-ridden and bleak.

To the west of Plymouth Sound stands Rame Head, with its jagged rocky foot, a promontory which forms a culminating feature of the Cornish coast looking eastwards. On the north coast, though in Devon, Hartland Point is the true end to that iron-bound shore. On the extreme south and west, Lizard Point and Land's End complete a noble quartet. Between them they enclose an entrancing coastline of promontory and bay, of sandy beach and rocky foreshore. The northern shore, as we have already to some extent noted, is almost without shelter, save in Padstow Bay and St. Ives Bay, and these are vulnerable in certain winds. The colour of the rocks

109 BOSCASTLE, CORNWALL

110 NEAR MEVAGISSEY, CORNWALL

III THE HELFORD ESTUARY NEAR PORTH NAVAS, CORNWALL

varies from grey to black with an occasional touch of
dusky violet or pink. The finest headland is possibly
Tintagel crowned by its ruined castle, but it is difficult
to particularise in a coast which consists entirely of headlands and perspectives of cliffs; Higher and Lower
Sharpnose, Pentire Point, Trevose Head, St. Agnes Head
and Navax Point, across the bay from St. Ives, are only
a few of the grander headlands which compose this
armoured shore.

Land's End itself is well approached from St. Ives along
that moorland road which gives the true flavour of the
Cornish scene. On the west is the Atlantic Ocean, with
an occasional glimpse of some cliff-top, or fisherman's
cottage; on the east the open moorland, dark with heather.
Every feature is subordinate to the vast expanse of water
running westwards for thousands of miles. The whole
coast from St. Ives to Mousehole consists of granite cliffs
with two little secluded valleys running inland at Treen
and Lamorna. East of Penzance the land rises again
above the wide, sandy Mounts Bay with its picturesque
island, till it reaches the grand rocky coastline which
extends from Lizard Point, past the Manacles, into the
entrance to the Helford River. It is impossible to favour
any stretch of this coast to the disadvantage of any other,
since all of it is glorious, and while one headland may be
higher and wilder, another is more highly coloured or of
a more intricate form. Nevertheless Falmouth Bay and
Carrack Roads with Pendennis Point, Nare Point and
Manacle Point when seen from the lighthouse at Zone
Point, with its landscape of shelving rocks, rivers, wooded
estuaries and sunny villages, is difficult to match in the
whole of the British Isles, for it traps the sun yet feels the
cool sea breezes and above all it contains the lovely name
of St. Anthony in Roseland. To the east of Zone Point
the coast is made up of a series of headlands and curving
bays, very similar in form and all bravely modelled.

Gerrans Bay is a place of the greatest charm with its wide, sandy beach, where waders feed and the curlew makes his mellow, liquid call, and where Nare Head raises his lofty heath-crowned top and provides a snug look-out to lie upon and watch the gulls on the little islets and isolated rocks. A feature of the coast is the warm brown colour of the ploughland which is taken right to the cliff-edge.

It only remains for us now to examine the North Devon coast between Bideford and Minehead and we shall have completed our survey of the English cliff scenery. Between Croyde and Coombe Martin the rocks are composed of a hard slate, strongly resistant to erosion, and the coast is worn into shallow bays and promontories. Great and Little Hangman are striking features of the region near Coombe Martin where the beach is composed of a grey sand. A feature, too, is the Heddon Valley which finds its way to the sea around the rocks at Heddons Mouth. The whole landscape has become increasingly interesting. The high moorlands of Exmoor run out to the sea in a series of rolling hills and valleys and the coast is alternately rocky and wooded, with magnificent views across the Bristol Channel to the Welsh coast. From Heddons Mouth right round to Porlock, past the superb height of Contisbury and the Foreland Point the coastal scenery is bold and beautiful. It has a less-exposed aspect than the Cornish coast, but where it loses in gaunt severity it gains in luxuriant colour and foliage. Near Porlock it is possible to walk between trees on the very edge of the cliff and watch the boats in the Channel below, which appear like toys. The finest cliff occurs in Somerset between Porlock and Minehead, where the large mass of North Hill forms an inaccessible climb for all but the rashest youths.

And so we end our survey of the English clifflands. It is far from complete and far from fairly balanced. Too much emphasis may have been given to some areas at the expense of others equally deserving of notice. It is impossible to avoid this, as personal preference and personal knowledge are bound to override impartial judgment. But the English coast does not consist entirely of cliff scenery, far from it, and some of the loveliest stretches of it all occur where those wide, flat, sandy estuaries extend for miles inland from the open sea. Here the beauty is achieved by long low horizons, with foregrounds of sand interwoven with winding muddy creeks, with groups of waders running across the wet sand or curlews flying shyly in large flocks; here the wind whistles mournfully through the sedgy banks and cattle browse on the salt marshes. There is no dramatic contrast between the rocky shore and the restless sea, only a coloured pattern of sand and water, and a sense of loneliness.

The greatest of these estuaries is to be found on the north-west coast of England, in Cheshire, Lancashire and Cumberland. The mouth of the River Dee, Morecambe Bay and Solway Firth all display the characteristics of extensive sand and winding channel, enjoyed at low tide by myriads of wading birds. All are entered by the tide at a surprisingly fast rate, and all provide excellent sport for the lovers of duck shooting. Moreover, each of them has a mountainous background. The Sands o' Dee, seen from the Wirral Peninsula form a splendid foil to the Welsh mountains which rise in their glory to the south and west: from Morecambe it is a delight to watch the highest lakeland hills light up in the evening sun and from Duddon Sands, a smaller estuary beyond the town of Barrow to the north, it is possible to see the bold rounded form of Black Combe thrusting out his fine escarpment almost to the Irish Sea. It must be said at once that the sandy estuary should be seen at low tide, as a full bay destroys all the charm of variety. Solway Firth extends, with an English shore of salt grassy marshes beloved of the curlew which appears there in great numbers, from Whitehaven to Carlisle. It is a curious experience to leave the great highway at Carlisle and follow the little road through Burgh on Sands to Bowness and onwards to Cardurnock near Morecambe Bay, for all touch with the noisy modern world seems to disappear and one is left with the flat marsh-like meadows, the birds and the sky, and miles of sandy flats. In the distance on a clear day the horizon is glorified by the Scottish moorlands or Galloway hills beyond Dumfries.

On the north-east coast in Northumberland there is a beautiful variation of the estuary landscape in the sands which join Holy Island at low tide to the mainland. Here the whole scene is more compact. In the foreground the yellow sands extend to the island, punctuated by tall posts driven into the sand to guide the driver who wishes to cross the sandy waste. After the tide has receded the colouring of the flats and shallow pools is incomparable. Blues of every shade, greens and pale yellows mingle in an endless variety. The island itself is low except where the outcropping basalt has formed a site for the Castle and shrine. A mile to the south a further lovely bay, known locally as "the Slakes," or more formally as Budle Bay, is a haunt of wild-fowl as well as a most beautiful example of the low-lying coastal landscape which we are studying. The spectacle at sunset, when the flaming sky is reflected in a million pools is unforgettable. The next estuary of importance is found at the mouth of the Tees. Here the approach is either from the Seaton Carew sands or from Redcar. In either case the long trudge is rewarded by the interesting spectacle of the main channel, denoted by posts with lights, each with a cormorant drying its wings. Here, as mentioned earlier, a new note is struck by the presence of the great steel works which appear so happily in the spacious setting. At Morecambe, of course, a feature of the landscape is the works at Millom which are sited on the very verge

112   BOSHAM HARBOUR ON ITS CREEK, SUSSEX

113　A LAKELAND RIVULET: STOCKLEY BECK, BORROWDALE

of the sea. The Humber with its dangerous shoals, and the Wash with its superlative sands, so haunted by the skilful fowler, continue the list of estuaries, which reach a high degree of beauty on the North Norfolk coast at Wells. Here a mingling of sand-dunes and marshes, of low headlands and muddy creeks, combine to form one of the most delightful stretches of the English coast. Beginning at Sandringham among the firs, where it is possible from some of the more open heathlands to gaze across the sandy wastes of the Wash to Lincolnshire, it continues by Brancaster Bay and Holkham Bay, to Blakeney, and includes the bird sanctuary of Scolt Head and the strange finger-like headland of The Marrams. In the evening sunshine, which suits this type of landscape better than the bright light of midday, the scene has a clearness and transparency of colour unsurpassed anywhere along the coast: the shapes of the low grey headlands add enormously to the beauty of the scene, which is further enriched by the black trees of Holkham Park.

A whole chapter could be devoted to the ramifications of the creeks which begin at Harwich and continue with the Blackwater and Crouch to the Thames estuary. They are a paradise for yachtsmen and are truly understood by sailors, amateur and professional, alone. Let it suffice here to say that a sense of Dutch flatness and loneliness pervades these tidal waters.

The coastline of Kent and Sussex has little to show in the way of estuaries until Chichester is reached. From Chichester, however, to Poole Harbour in Dorset, a distance of approximately fifty miles, the coast is indented by an intricate system of harbours, river mouths and straits, flat and muddy but of exquisite beauty. Here an entirely different coastal scene may be enjoyed from the lonely cliff landscape of Cornwall or the sandy wastes of Norfolk and the Wash. Here we find industry on a vast scale turning the reedy flats into trim but imposing harbours: here are yachtsmen in their polished boats taking the place of the more weatherbeaten fisherman or employing him as crew on some beautifully fitted vessel, or huge armoured warships riding at anchor and gigantic liners, with populations on board equal to an ancient town, gliding swiftly out to sea on a voyage to South Africa or New York. In the centre, at Southampton and Portsmouth, all is activity: at the extremities of our fifty-mile stretch, at Chichester and Poole, there is silence and loneliness once more, save at the height of the yachting season. Wide expanses of muddy flats, often fringed with sedge or grass occupy large areas: hundreds of birds feed at low tide or swim in flocks when the tide is in and the harbours are like inland lakes. In the background can be seen the soft outline of the chalk hills. At sunrise or sunset, or during the blessed days of spring or early summer, it is possible to explore the winding shore, to gaze from one promontory to the next, to sit quietly in the warm heath and listen to the wind rustling the branches of the gnarled oaks or lofty pines, and to see no other human being save a fisherman in his small boat or an outlying farmer with his horse and cart.

In South Devon we have already noted the beauty of Dartmouth. The mouth of the Exe forms a strong contrast, for instead of steep, rocky margins we find low, sandy banks. The Helford River in Cornwall brings us once again into touch with the world of yachting, and no more beautiful background could be found in the whole of England. It makes, with Carrack Roads, Falmouth, a superb picture of well-wooded banks and wide, though sheltered sheets of water. There is no pleasanter experience than to descend the hair-raising hill from Mawnan Smith and find the little inn, the beach and the muddy flats on the verge of Helford Passage, and then, after an appetising lunch, to cross to Helford itself by the ferry. After Helford there is no sheltered estuary till Bideford and Barnstaple are reached in North Devon. There, once more, we find ourselves in the presence of warm sand and turquoise-blue sea. Little boats, with red or white sails pass quietly to and fro, or show up surprisingly above the dunes of Braunton Burrows. The beach at Instow is a series of natural hollows and at high tide it is possible to lie in one of these and enjoy the feeling of being in a floating bath.

Another of our coastal types of scenery, the sand-dune, is well illustrated near Barnstaple. Blown by the wind and held in position by the roots of tough grasses, the sand has formed a range of miniature mountains, enriched by the blue of Viper's Buglos and the metallic silver of the Carline Thistle. It is a joy to wander in this desert-like world, where the waves of the sea seem to have been turned to sand. Sand-dunes occur at many points of our coast, but nowhere are they so entirely satisfactory, for at Southport, in Lancashire, they are spoilt by development, at Burnham in Somerset the coast is long and low, at Bamburgh in Northumberland and Seaton Carew in Durham they lack the colour and depth, and it is only on the North Norfolk coast that they display an equally wild and coloured aspect. To look their best they need a brilliant blue sea and sky, an evening sun which casts pale violet shadows across the flat plane of the shore, and a clearness of atmosphere to accentuate the perspective.

We have already mentioned the Chesil Beach in Dorset as a long pebble embankment washed up by the tide to form a natural bastion. As a landscape feature it is superb in the distant view, but dreary beyond words when it forms the near horizon. Nevertheless it is an exhilarating experience to stand on the Chesil Beach on a windy day and feel the shivering thud of the breakers as they hit the slope of shingle and tear with a grinding screech down its steep incline.

In Norfolk, between Yarmouth and Cromer, the low-lying hinterland is protected from the highest tides by a long sandy wall. The whole landscape is flat and marshy, and it is only when the summit of the sandbank is reached that the sea becomes visible stretching away to the north and south without any feature, save the sandy beach, relieved by patches of shingle. The bank itself needs constant supervision. It is reinforced with thorn bushes which help to collect and hold the blown sand. Only recently, at Horsey Gap, an exceptional wind-driven tide burst through a weak spot and flooded some miles of the lowlying farmland to the rear. To-day the gap is being reinforced but the old arable fields are foul with mud and the pasture soaked in salt water.

It is impossible in one short chapter to describe all the muddy inlets and sandy estuaries, for our coastline is richly endowed with inland waters. It is difficult, too, to decide which of the extremes of coastal scenery, the great cliff, or the horizontal sandy plane, with its soft bird music and its miles of opalescent mud, provides the finest landscape. The silent flats, however, are disturbed daily by the swift advent of high tide, which has only too often in the past overwhelmed some dilatory or negligent passenger crossing from shore to shore. The Severn bore, which sweeps with a roar up that long approach to Gloucester is a superb example of this.

Coves, cut by some freak of the tide, are a feature yet to be described. They thrill us by the unexpected abruptness of their appearance in some rockbound coast. The best-known cove in England is undoubtedly Lulworth Cove in Dorset. Here the sea has managed to burst through the outer bastion of Purbeck Rock and with a circular movement scoop this almost perfect circle out of the chalk rocks to the rear. It is a treacherous shelter for yachtsmen for the passage of the bar at its entrance in any but the finest weather is highly dangerous and winds spring up with a surprising suddenness on this temperamental coast. Mupe Bay, Worbarrow Bay, Kimmeridge Bay and Chapman's Pool are further examples in the same stretch of coast, of bays in process of formation. Sennon Cove in Cornwall, carved from the granite cliffs, is a good example of the commoner type of rocky cove found at a hundred points on all our rocky shores. A walk along the old coastguard track on any high cliff will give a series of wild pictures which will include promontories of more or less importance, and little shallow bays with, at times, a tiny unperceived harbour carved out of the living rock, where one or two fishing boats lie on a steep beach, to which a ladder or flight of steps gives precarious access. Such are the South and North Landings at Flamborough Head, Yorkshire, where steep steps lead down to restricted beaches. Here, in the softer chalk rocks, the sea has carved itself caves and pinnacles adding a fantastic touch to the whole scene.

Taken as a whole the English coastline is lonely and forlorn. In the past, before the speculative builder got to work with his bungalows and summer huts, it must have presented mile upon mile of sandy foreshore, peopled only by birds, and even to-day in the winter months it is possible to be alone for days on end on almost any stretch where the older settlements are absent. These, with a wise respect for the power of the winter gales, were sited either some little distance back from the sea, as at Lamorna in Cornwall, or Abbotsbury and Burton Bradstock in Dorset, or strategically placed on the margin of a sheltered harbour as at Whitby in Yorkshire, or St. Ives in Cornwall. They form some of the most interesting and beautiful incidents of coastal scenery. Employing the local materials, and through generations of experience, bowing to the same forces which carved out the harbours and moulded the cliffs, man has sited his houses in harmonious groups as near to the scene of his activities as discretion permitted. The cottages at St. Ives cluster in terraces round that beautiful harbour in a way beloved of the artist, who must have painted this scene till the houses almost blush at the publicity. Clovelly, in North Devon, is unique in England, and in spite of its almost universal fame, remains a gem of traditional architecture, set amidst romantically wooded cliffs. It is interesting, again, to study the regional flavour, a compound of race and site, which distinguishes Brixham in South Devon from Whitby in Yorkshire, or King's Lynn in Norfolk. Brixham, with a warm sturdiness, shelters behind Berry Head. Its menfolk are big-boned Devon men, quite unlike the smaller, quicker Cornishmen at St. Ives. At King's Lynn there is a Dutch stolidity about the whole scene, town, quay and inhabitants. Whitby is sturdily and wittily Yorkshire. There is a difference again in the touch of the sea on our cheeks. On the north Cornish coast there is a power behind the wind: the English Channel is soft and warm with an increasingly noticeable briskness as the Kentish corner is reached. The North Sea breezes are always salt-laden and biting and capable of making our cheeks burn and ache.

Of the old-fashioned seaside resorts Scarborough and Torquay share between them the honour of being the most beautiful. Both have superb sites on the lee side of a large bay. Scarborough nestles behind the Castle Hill, and Torquay lies buried in the wooded slopes near Hope's Nose. There is a Yorkshire freshness in the wide, sweeping sands, where the sea-birds feed in winter and the children play in summer. The scene is indeed complete for it contains the old quay and fishing harbour, the broad promenade backed by steep slopes and covered by stucco buildings, and the receding cliffs to the south. Torquay repeats the scene in a Devon setting. Where in Scarborough the prevailing shade is brown grey, in Torquay it is brilliant blue and red.

It is neither possible nor desirable to describe all the towns and fishing villages on the English coast: some like Folkestone, Brighton and Weymouth were planned in Georgian times with broad fronts parallel to the sea. Others like Lyme Regis and Whitby have developed from fishing towns or old-established harbours; while some, the least interesting, are modern and scattered. Bournemouth is an example of a town which is suffering from a scattered development. But a coastal scene at its finest, must be free from any but seafaring habitation. It must combine bold headland with sandy foreshore; windswept cliff with sheltered coves or long, low expanses of muddy flats, alive with waders and gulls. It must hold, unseen perhaps, but nevertheless sensed, some sign or threat of danger. It may be heard in the note of the waves as they lazily break with a crack on the coast; it may be found in the presence of the black-backed gull which is often a sign of heavy weather in the offing: it may be the boiling over of the waters of a race, such as that notorious death-trap off the end of Portland Beal: or it may be nothing more than the horrid promise of death, suggested by prongs of jagged rock jutting out wickedly under the sea.

It might be interesting to end with three pictures of the English coast which may be enjoyed by anyone to-day. Let us walk from the level-crossing at Beal in Northumberland to the edge of those fascinating sands which separate Holy Island from the main coast: from there let us proceed in a dog-cart to trot the track marked out by posts, between the shallow pools tinted every shade of blue and green. The whole sandy waste has become a magic world of sunlight and colour. As the island is approached it is possible to pick out the little pantiled houses, and, most blessed object, among them a small inn. The Castle rises farther to the east on a hard, black, basalt foundation. To the north Goswick Sands run out to meet the Snook: to the south Old Law, a second sandy point, projects almost into "The Harbour." If we order our fragrant ham and eggs and then walk on to the shelving foreshore we shall be able to look seawards to the archipelago of the Farne Islands where Grace Darling performed her feat of heroism. Bamburgh Castle stands up nobly on its tall headland and reminds us of the wild days when the border chiefs came riding across from beyond the Tweed and when we turn we are reminded by the ruins by the old Priory of St. Cuthbert of the early Northumbrian saints. It is impossible here to disentangle the sentimental from the aesthetic.

Let us leave Northumberland for our second picture and go to Somerset. Here we shall walk from Dunster across those flat, green, marshy meadows beyond the railway on to the golf links near Minehead. The coast is well protected by a stony embankment. On an autumn evening the air is still with a touch of frost to remind us that the year is ending. The wide, muddy beach is peopled by a mixed company of gulls and curlews and all those little, fast-moving, brown shore birds which are so hard for any but the practised bird-catcher to distinguish. Two great black-backed gulls stand aloof in majestic solitude. The distant noises of the town sound mysterious and the hoot of an owl or the bark of a dog can be heard from a great distance. As day melts into night the tremendous bluff of North Hill which dominates the town is gradually illuminated with a thousand little lights that mingle with the stars themselves to create a fairy-like world suspended above an almost silent sea.

Finally let us stand on the limestone heights above Weymouth and look out over that protected harbour to where the Citadel crowns the northern end of Portland. The stone breakwaters form a dark curved line in the sea. The sands and the front of Weymouth itself look like toys in a shop window. The sea is a rich blue with a touch of grey and white where the race boils and swirls in its ceaseless turbulent conflict. Suddenly in the distance appear the grey forms of the Fleet, returning from some practice cruise, and quickly the whole scene is changed from one of quiet natural tranquillity to one of grandeur and power. It is a most moving spectacle to watch the great English warships, heirs of generations of the gallant vessels which have gone forth to battle, and in their victory saved England herself from invasion. They express in their low menacing forms the sea-power of a country, bound in rock or sand or shingle, and whenever we stand on the edge of our island, we are bound to feel the thrill, so deeply engrafted in our people, of a freedom vouchsafed us by the sea.

INDEX

(The numerals in italic denote the *figure numbers* of illustrations)

244